MY SOULMATE

Me AND DANIEL

DIANAH DISANDRO

TABLE OF CONTENTS

Introduction   i
Acknowledgments   iii

Chapter One   Good Times?   1
Chapter Two   Oklahoma   50
Chapter Three   Daniel, An Immigrant's Son   82
Chapter Four   The DiSandro's In California 1943   92
Chapter Five   1954 Lousiana   109
Chapter Six   What To Do Now?   116
Chapter Seven   Dianah   130
Chapter Eight   Leaving Wisconsin   167
Chapter Nine   California Livin   190
Chapter Ten   Back to California   200
Chapter Eleven   What Now 1979   220
Chapter Twelve   1981 What's Next   265

INTRODUCTION

MEMORIES ARE JUST that—a story to be told from a unique perspective, the tales of history. The accounts given to you are in the mind's eye. This book, written by me and parts dictated by Daniel, is a recollection of happenings, people, and places, not necessarily chronological or accurate. The writing started approximately five years before completing the book, and when Daniel's health needed attention, I put it aside. We believed our life story to be out of the ordinary, certainly not dull. Many of the events told to friends and family are worth repeating, but some stories will be a first.

At the beginning of Daniel's history, he dictated his first 21 years, almost always over a strong cup of coffee with half and half. His coffee with stevia and I liked coarse ground granulated sugar. With very few exceptions, the morning began after a kiss and hug to start the day.

Health and desire did not allow Daniel to continue, so from the 21st year of his recollections forward, I filled in the blanks from our conversations over the years. The events, some of which I was part of, and others remembered from our hours of conversing. When Daniel stopped telling his life history, the book sat unfinished until four months after his death, when I began writing in earnest.

We were nearly as inseparable as life would allow over forty-four years of companionship. We didn't always agree. You will read about the understanding and caring nature of two individuals unique unto themselves that built a partnership and bond to last a lifetime. As I critique the events and the tears flow, the need to tell our story is ever-present.

All the events, emotions, and placement of importance remain at the story's heart, with the writer's description bringing the tales to life once again.

The accuracy of the writing is incidental to the story remembered.

After 1978, the datebooks helped. Though the books are helpful, they only provide a time and place; the emotion and the tale can only come from memories.

It has now been one year since Daniel's passing. I miss him at this time as much as the first day, and the book has only covered the first two to three years of our union; there's so much more. For that reason, I will continue to the next forty years in the forthcoming edition, with no less excitement.

Persons of importance in this book are held in the highest regard and brought forth as integral to our life story, be it mine or Daniels. The correctness of each experience is a vivid memory of the emotions connected to happenings and the time of events. The history of incidents, sad, happy, and angry, was a part of our life. Living doesn't happen without mistakes, no perfection on this side of the stream. The more experiences there are, the more decisions, and it stands to reason, the number of errors in judgment will increase. It's just the law of averages. In this book, I neither judge nor ask for opinions. Each episode was an education, and the writing and publishing of the book is a whole chapter unto itself.

I have faith you will enjoy reading these life events as much as I loved living them.

ACKNOWLEDGMENTS

I MUST THANK my sons, Toph and Tim, and their families for their support and encouragement. A thank you to CM and Kathy for their comfort in all the months of writing. My brother Frank for reminding me of events I forgot along this first journey. A thank you to friends The Ballards and the Roses for propping me up with confidence to keep going, and also my Florida friends Laura, Laura, and Laurie for encouragement to continue. Thank you to all who have been part of this story and the families of those who are no longer with us, for, without you, there would be missing memories.

Chapter One

GOOD TIMES?

THE YEAR IS 1976, April 24th. This month I have just made it to the ripe age of 31, a 5 ft. 4 inch brunette of 105 pounds, from the distant farmlands of central Wisconsin. I moved to California at age 18 without anyone's blessings. Now 13 years later, little did I realize my life was just beginning. How could I have known I was about to find an adventurer, a dreamer, someone who knew how to laugh, play, and enjoy life.

He knocks on the door. There are times when you know some things are more important than others. This was one of those memorable times. Am I ready for what life or fate is about to set forth?

"I don't know; what should I prepare for?"

Saying to myself, for peat sake, Dianah, just open the door; this isn't the first man to come into your life. As I open the door, my two boys, Toph, 11, and Tim, age 8, are staring at him with what appears to be sinister thoughts. Are kids sinister at this age? I only know they are quiet, that cannot be a good sign.

The boys and I are currently residing at the Executive Suites Motel, and it's a far cry from executive. It's an old cheaply built motel, probably

1950s era, two-story painted a nondescript tan and brown with poor lighting, a parking lot in front, with the oil-stained pavement.

I consider myself fortunate to get a downstairs unit; dragging everything upstairs is beyond my capabilities after a full day's work at the restaurant. Luckily, after too many calls, I found this unit with a kitchen and didn't need to sign a long-term lease; being close to work and school was heaven-sent. Renting by night hadn't been in the budget; the manager told me the payment was either daily or cheaper by the week. I only needed living quarters during this transition period for two to three weeks. Our accommodations are a little kitchenette, where the military stay when they can't find anything more suitable for the price in downtown Santa Ana, California.

The hour is about 8 PM, it's dark, noisy, and there's a smell of car fumes and smog in the air. It makes the whole place feel dirty. Is it safe? I don't know; it doesn't look safe and feels kind of creepy. I keep the door locked, and we do not venture outside for any reason. As I look out of the motel window, our car is still there. I don't worry too much about the car; it's not likely to be stolen, even I don't want it. No one has caused any problems, and if I can keep my imagination in check, we should be fine.

One of the many firsts is about to come my way. I'm newly divorced, making all my own choices, and praying that I don't screw up any more than I already have, and you ask, "How have you screwed up?" I don't know, but I must have done something wrong to end up here.

There's a knock on the door, I carefully open the motel door after peeking around the curtain, and as he is about to enter, there are two kids, a cat, ten houseplants, and as many suitcases as I could fit into the room. Everything is sitting in this little place, and one wide-eyed young woman is looking directly at him. Moments pass by as we analyze each other. She is telling herself, "Be calm and cool; all the stories say, 'Don't let them see you sweat.' Is this friend or foe? Apprehension sets in; how much do I know about this man? He is certainly no weakling, runs a company but doesn't dress in office attire. I want to be cautious; better stated, I need to be careful.

He looks in my eyes, "Can I come in"?

As Sergeant Joe Friday, from the 1950's Dragnet television series says, "This is my city, there are a million stories, and only the names have been changed to protect the innocent". I feel innocent, so why am I here? Aren't the innocent and truthful always protected? The difference is, this is not Hollywood; it's not the movies where everyone lives happily ever after. Like it or not, this is life.

We met in the coffee shop where I work, across the street from a large major shopping center. The restaurant food is ok; the decor is your standard 70's orange or reddish color, clean, and better than the average coffee shop. But it's just a place to derive income for food and shelter for the boys and me while we strive for better times.

He walks through the door. I close the motel door behind him, for we try to keep the cat in and the noise out. I quickly usher him into the kitchen—the bedroom is occupied by two beds, a disgruntled child in each, and a television. We have a newly acquired white family cat, actually Tim's cat, and we all do our best to help with its care. Well, the cat doesn't seem to be any happier about being here than the rest of us. No one would accept a dog when we moved from our home, and Tim loves his pets. I felt so bad; hence we have a cat.

I hand Toph the television remote control with instructions, "Watch whatever you want, but PLEASE keep it quiet, no teasing or horsing around." I get the look, an expression that doesn't require being an adult.

Standing in the dimly lit kitchen, leaning up against the counter, smiling, and relaxed as I enter the doorway, is this man wearing a striped T-shirt and faded blue jeans, clean and pressed. Standing at about 5 ft. 9 inches with an excellent muscular build, not strikingly handsome, but there's something about him I can't put my finger on.

I'm certainly intrigued. Not a man who sits at a desk all day. He's older than I am, which suits me just fine. The graying salt and pepper hair works well with the mustache. I've never been with a mustached man, something new. I have no interest in having conversations with someone searching for who they are or what they want to be in life. If you haven't already figured out who you are, best you leave. Maturity is a welcome commodity and so hard to find. I need to have some substance behind all the words that are thrown out there.

If what I'm doing is searching, then the saying, 'I say what I mean and mean what I say,' fits appropriately. Can men and women be just friends? A friend would be lovely to have right about now, someone to discuss the daily things in life coming my way. I need quality in life, no more lying, drinking, cheating. Been there, done that, it's time to move on.

His name is Daniel, Italian but doesn't look Italian, fair skin, graying hair, muscular. Maybe the nose is a giveaway. Then there are the baby blue enchanting eyes that can look into the deepest recesses of your soul; it's unnerving. Daniel and I had been on an outing a few days before. I wouldn't call it a date. He asked me several times about getting together. I kept putting him off; I wasn't ready to be dating, especially with someone who looked like a no-nonsense kind of person. He has this forceful way about him, and right now, I am in charge of my life, and the plan is to keep it that way. He didn't appear to be out for just a good time, which I thought was ok. But I have too many irons in the fire and didn't want one more. But he was persistent. Every few days, he would be at one of my tables. I couldn't just ignore him.

And Daniel is saying to himself, "She can't keep ignoring me. I'm not a bad guy, and besides that, I think I like her".

Daniel wasn't pushy but not shy.

I finally replied, "Okay, we can go out for coffee, and I'm bringing my two kids, thinking that will take care of this; he won't ask anymore."

He responds, "That sounds good. I'll bring my two youngest. See you Saturday at 1 o'clock at Winchell's, here's my phone number just in case".

" And your phone is?"

I was caught off guard, not knowing what to say. Am I so naive that I can't see these questions coming? The only thing I could think of; was the truth, oh boy, "I don't have a phone right now," and I couldn't tell if he believed me or not.

All he said was, "See you Saturday."

Saturday came, the kids and I arrived at Winchell's one o'clock on the dot, Daniel with son and daughter is already here. We walked in, and the kids were sizing each other up as we joined them at the table— Daniel and his two children on one side with me and the boys on the other side. At first, it was hard to tell if this was a friendly encounter, but Daniel had a way of smoothing things out; he has a gift of getting everyone to relax. The kids have ice cream; we drank coffee and made small talk—the kind of get-to-know-you small talk to determine if we want to do this again. Once the ice cream was gone, coffee time was over. There is only so much quiet four young people of the same age group will tolerate. I thanked him for the afternoon treat and got up to leave.

Rather than saying you're welcome, he said, "I would like to come over sometime in the evening. How about tomorrow"?

Before I could even think about what I was saying like I didn't have any control over my mind or speech, I don't know why I said yes; there is just something that draws me to him.

Then I had to explain about moving out of my house because it was not only being sold but had termites, the house had to be tented, or the buyers couldn't get their loan. The realtor told me I had to move right away or lose the sale; this being part of the divorce settlement, losing the deal would be unfathomable. The apartment I was going to rent wasn't ready yet, and my only alternative was the executive suite motel where the boys and I are currently living, which was taking a little effort on my part. I might say, more effort than I thought I was capable of.

Daniel offered help, but I said I had it all in hand. Taking care of everything on my own had always been my way of getting a job done, plus I just wasn't comfortable accepting his help. I didn't want him to know just how messy my life had become. Life was supposed to be orderly, at least in my book.

Having it all taken care of meant every morning, I would pack the car with everything possible. Then see the kids off to school, and unload this car after work. Then I hurried to pick up the boys from the neighbors, where they stayed until I could get to them. We would then eat something somewhere. Head to the motel to start it over the following day. There was one week to make this move complete and the house empty and ready for new buyers.

Unloading the car was at a friend of a friend's house in her garage that she was using for storage. The first order is to move her boxes and furniture in the garage, so there is room for our belongings. We convinced her boyfriend and his buddy to come with their truck to our house and load everything I couldn't get in the car on the last day. The guys were nice, but this is not what they wanted to do in their after-work time, nor did the friend of a friend want to give up her garage. There quite simply is nothing enjoyable about moving boxes, furniture, and bicycles. They were just hard-working people in a less-than-middle-class neighborhood trying to do the best they could and still help someone in need. Getting our belongings out of her garage was even more urgent than moving out of the house. I did not want to abuse her kindness, and when it came time to move into the apartment, I needed to coordinate the time with her boyfriend again.

I had never been a director; getting everyone to do what I needed them to seemed like an endless, no-reward feat of endurance. To make matters even more confusing for me, the realtor calls my ex-husband, who in turn calls me. Why the realtor didn't contact me directly, I have no clue. After all, I was the one in the house taking care of things. But I wasn't the man in charge. The ex never calls with good news. He says the sale is delayed. I don't have to move right now. I don't know whether to scream, cry, or try to be an adult about what I'm hearing. Managing a smidgeon of calmness, I say, "You know I have moved almost everything out. The boys and I are in a motel".

He always has to have the last word, "It's going to take a little longer, and you better hope it closes. I'm not paying for the motel because you screwed up".

Once again, I cannot believe what I hear; generosity is not his strong suit. I have got to get this man out of my life.

Here I am the following evening making coffee in this kitchenette; my mind is running in circles. I signed an apartment lease, and I'm paying the motel with restaurant tips. I can't afford the loan payment on the house; it's part of the divorce; what if the sale falls through. If my house doesn't sell, I'm up the creek without a paddle.

I look up, back to the moment at hand; yes, I'm still in the motel. Daniel is patiently at the table, one of those old chrome and Formica sets. It's unexpectedly warm for this time of year, and I attempt to open the window.

I tell him, "it's been painted shut too many times." Daniel brushes past my arm, I jump. I wasn't expecting him to be so close. Just a touch and the warmth of skin send a flurry of emotions in all directions. I'm trying not to be edgy, but I am stressed as tight as it gets. He opens the window, and, in comes the car fumes, the noise from the street, the sirens; we both decide the window would be better closed. I don't like this place. I didn't like it when I rented it, but I was out of options. Since there's no air conditioning, we'll deal with the heat, both room, and bodily emotions.

Daniel and I are having our coffee; we talk about the apartment that will become home and its location. It just so happens, it is right down the street and around the corner from where his kids live with their mother, so we are all in very close proximity. I'm beginning to relax a little. This apartment to become home was recommended by the friend of the friend where I'm moving the furniture; none of us know each other, and Daniel has never met any of them. There's a question sitting in the back of my mind? How do things just fall together sometimes and other times not? I don't believe coincidences are coincidental; there must be more to this picture than I know.

Daniel has four children, two boys and two girls, the two oldest, a boy and a girl, are teenagers busy doing what teenagers do. We talked about his work, construction, swimming pools, his partners, and about where I work. Then he reaches over, takes my hand, holds my hand up to his like he's just observing. Sparks are flying; at the same time, nerves are melting. Palm to palm, my fingertips don't even come up to the beginning of his fingers. I think this is a smooth way to hold someone's hand; I hadn't seen that one tried before, but I have no objections. My hands are moist and sweating, and his hands are smooth and dry, a few callouses from hard work but solid and kind to the touch. As he holds my hand, my heart is racing. I'm not thinking about anything else, just the touch, the sensuality of it all. I marvel; he notices my hands, my nervousness. He's not saying much and appears comfortable.

I take a deep breath; he's still holding my hand, only I forgot how to breathe. Finally, I exhaled. Daniel puts his hand gently on my face, draws me to him, and gives me the gentlest warm kiss. Slowly he pulls back, my eyes open. I look into his blue-searching eyes and wonder. What was I wondering? I stopped thinking. I am in the moment. There is nothing else, just his kiss, that's all; life is right here, right now. My inner body wants to jump into his arms, say to him, "Daniel hold me, protect me. I need a break from life."

Then the committee that's always telling me what I should be doing hits me square in the back of the head. What do you think you are doing? You don't know this man. You have two children to take care of, and after he's had what he wants, he'll be gone. You know what men are like; you know what they think. What's the matter with you?

Daniel's a decent sort, so the only thing saving me from myself at this point are two boys just in the other room watching TV.

Again with the committee in my mind telling me, "What would people think?" You know, no one in your family ever gets divorced. Here you are not only recently divorced but entertaining another man.

I'm telling the committee that sits in the subconscious that we are having a conversation, which is far from what you think of as entertaining.

I believe Daniel can read my thoughts. He's watching me, smiling, and takes a sip of coffee; he gets up from his chair, takes my hand, leads me to the corner like there's something over here we need to see. It's a blank wall and not too clean at that. He puts his arm around my waist and the other hand on the back of my neck. His arm could reach around me twice, and his gentle hands seemed to cover my back, holding me steady. Daniel leans in for the most beautiful kiss I can remember. All this is slow and soft, with no rush involved. I've heard the old-fashioned term swoon but never got the complete picture of the meaning. Now I know. However, other things are going on. There's a fire burning deep inside, a yearning, a need. Oh, Daniel.

Oh, I need help. Daniel's body is more than just strong; he is overpowering; I can feel the heat from his body. Every nerve in me is crying for release; I want to be held and loved, and then I push him away. You have got to leave, I plead. He says, "Ok," but doesn't move; I can't help myself, my hands are on his shoulders, I pull him to me, my body is saying, please don't leave. We kissed again; I couldn't possibly get any closer. I'm wrapped in all this manliness and hormones. I pushed him away again. I say, "it's too warm, you're too close," and still, I want more. He doesn't move; my arms wrap around his neck. Our bodies are so close we are one, I can feel his heartbeat, I'm drowning; my knees won't hold me. Again we kiss, hungry, urgent. I can't be doing this. My hands are on his shoulders; I want more. I know better. I give a soft nudge.

I was barely able to stand on my own two feet, out of breath. Daniel looks at me with a smile and those knowing blue eyes, "Dianah, you must make up your mind; under the circumstances, I don't think we can take this any farther tonight." Then common sense and dignity, or maybe it's the committee, again with the committee, back for more.

I emphatically state, " I have no intention of taking this, whatever this is, anywhere." I feel like Jekyll and Hyde, one minute, I can't get close enough, and the very next moment, I'm telling him to get lost. Daniel gave me a soft kiss goodnight with a smile, and even his eyes were smiling. I can just see him thinking, "She doesn't know what she wants."

Oh, she knows!

"I'll call you"; as he's walking out, closing the door, "Don't forget to lock the door," he says.

In a few minutes, I regained some composure, checked the boys; they were in bed for the night.

Toph says, "I can't sleep with Tim, he keeps kicking, and he's all over the bed."

I get Tim in my bed, trying to get him settled down. I know he's having a tough time, but how do I make it easier for him? It's also time for me to get some sleep before I start tomorrow all over again. While I'm brushing my teeth, I'm thinking, probably won't hear from Daniel again.

Daniel's thinking I can't get mixed up with a woman like this; she has kids; I'm concerned about my kids. She's got too much going on; it's just not a good idea.

As the following day continues its cycle, I wait for some indication, a flicker of hope that I will hear from him. I know he's not the only guy out there, and I tell myself there are probably better choices. I shouldn't even be thinking or looking. The facts were, I wasn't looking, I wasn't looking when we first met. And still, there's this longing, a need, a desire, and I wait.

The boxes are still getting loaded in the morning, the boys don't want to move, and then there's this white 1968 Buick which became the family car, bequeathed to me before the divorce by my ex-husband who said, "This is the kind of car you should have." He didn't ask, "Do you like the car, or what do you think?" As he explained to me, he had a new car that he needed to drive to work. I was also working; need I say more.

As you may have already surmised, this automobile has problems.

I'm loading the Buick with boxes, the boys need to get to school, I need to get to work, and it won't start. I know it's the carburetor; I've done all the right things they tell you to do. It still won't start. So ok, I'll do the inappropriate; I take some fuel from the lawnmower, take off the air cleaner, and pour just a little fuel in the carburetor, then turn the ignition. Nothing happens; get out of the car. I look at the engine, thinking, what did I miss? No clues, so I pour more fuel and try to start it again.

Toph is standing next to the Buick, yelling, "Mom, the car's on fire; it's really on fire." I could see the flames even with the hood blocking the view. I jumped out of the car, ran into the house to get some salt. You're thinking, why not a fire extinguisher. We couldn't possibly have a fire extinguisher, at least one not already packed. I can't find the salt; everything is boxed. I found the baking soda; the car is still flaming, burning the insulation on the hood. Frantically I tell the boys to get back away from the vehicle. It could blow; I tried sprinkling the baking soda, no luck. Hell, pour the baking soda. Now the carburetor is covered in white powder, but I can't have this car exploding; after all, what would the neighbors think?

There's that committee again. Oh, my gosh, this can't be happening. I have neither the time nor the money and am definitely out of energy to take care of one more emergency. Finally, the fire goes out; I take a deep breath, say a thank you, and turn the key. Unbelievably, Buick starts; I let it run while I finish loading a few odds and ends; it has to be packed as full as it can get; there's no time for more trips. Don't turn off the engine; who knows if it will start again. The boys leave for school, and I drive slower than usual to work. I guess I went slower just out of fear that something else was likely to happen, or I just hadn't recovered from the fire. I think I expected this car that didn't like me to all of a sudden and for no reason to just explode in my face. Now logic told me that wouldn't happen, but logic and the committee were doing battle right about now, and I was the victim.

No one knew about so many things that grew from day to day, and there was no one to confide in. Who would understand the full depth of my family events, which was just the boys and me? Is it complaining when you are stating the facts? Part of my mantra has always been not to complain; no one wants to hear it anyway.

When I tried to clean up the front yard of the house I was selling, this giant date palm needed trimming; it was hanging onto the place and had taken over the front yard. Well, it had more fortitude than I did. There are these long thorns on the palm fronds; for a full day, I cut and piled; needless to say, I came out bloody, and the tree didn't look any better than before I started. I detested that house and didn't like it from the beginning, and it was simply an unattractive structure, which became more detestable as time went on. I had worked on the house day and night to make sure it would show to new buyers as well as possible for what I would consider a reasonable sales price. I painted, cleaned, wallpapered, and tried to make it as cheery as possible without spending. There was this copper range and oven, excellent quality, but hadn't been cleaned in years. For weeks I scrubbed and polished; it was a nightmare, and my hands showed the battle scars. I didn't want it to look like the residents felt. I was determined to get as much as possible out of it, more than the amount the realtor or my ex said would happen. They told me it would never sell for what I insisted on. In one week, on the same day, three offers came in, one at full price.

The realtor explains the three contracts and says, "Sign here."

The ex-husband says, "I don't think I want to sell."

My turn! "You get to pay the realtor fee; he completed his part of the contract; can you do that?" The contract is then signed.

After the sale of the Huntington Beach property, now this was before the divorce and after the purchase of the house with the ugly Date Palm tree in the front yard. With minimal dollars left from the sale and purchase of homes, a small shopping list was scheduled. But we did need a sofa. So late in the evening, we went to a furniture store with friend Annabelle to buy a couch for the living room. They didn't choose the one I thought would be best; we were getting a different one. I thought, ok, the one they picked wasn't so bad, I won't make a fuss. Then it was over to the bar section. There's this black corner tuck and roll, dry bar with padded armrest, strictly for drinking. I could tell from the approach, the two of them had already been here and made decisions. When he pointed out this oversized man cave bar to put in the living room, I went into a rage; I begged, cried for him not to buy it. He bought it anyway. He was taking our savings to buy this monstrosity that I would have to look at and clean.

Most of the time, I was the only one home, anyway. When the divorce came, he wouldn't move it out of the house. It took up half the living room; there was no way you could hide it. Now it was my problem; I tried to leave it with the house sale. Emphatically, no one wanted it. The buyers were so adamant that they put it in the contract, remove the black bar from the house. I was going to get this house sold and would figure it out. I even thought about getting an ax and chopping it into pieces, which I might have done, but we didn't have an ax.

Amongst the many uncomplimentary to-do's, were taking the dog to the shelter. The dog's temperament was about as frazzled as the rest of us, a black and white mixed collie type dog; I couldn't find anyone who wanted our dog. The boys had tried to help and didn't want to see her go; we all knew the chances of someone taking her from the shelter. I couldn't just turn her out on the street. So that's when we got the cat. The only friend I had, Jayne that I didn't get to see very much, thought I was off my rocker, getting any kind of a pet.

She said, "Do you need more to do and another expense?" There was a need to do what little I could for the boys. We had moved to this house that I detested just a few months ago as a chance to make the marriage better, and it only made things worse. The boys were losing the family pet, changing schools again, and then there was the divorce. I was trying to hold us together while my ex-husband said I couldn't make it on my own, that he would take the children. I don't know; maybe his girlfriend left him by that point. I was long past the point of concern about what was going on in his life. It was time to move on; I had bounced back and forth for way too long.

I listen to myself, then think, don't become one of those bitter people. I am done with all the stuff that has been going on. There was a new life on the horizon, one with sunshine and smiles, relaxing and good times. I didn't know how it would happen, but I did know my life would get better. I would make sure life was worth living.

Then Daniel called at the motel, but we were both so busy, there was hardly time to breathe. As life would have it, I met a different sort of man. Studious, serious, somewhat shy, he asked the boys and me to join him at the park on a Sunday afternoon. He had an experimental miniature airplane. Tim was thrilled; Toph thought it was ok, and I honestly had not expected to watch a toy airplane for a whole afternoon on one of my only days off of work.

The weather was nice. I made a small picnic lunch; it would have been better if I had relaxed. Relaxing was not in the picture. Watching someone fly a model airplane was just not my thing. At the end of the afternoon, I thanked him, he was a friendly sort, and I was ready to leave.

We are now in the apartment, no more significant catastrophes, just a lot of hard work.

Daniel calls, "Would you like to go out to dinner."

I tell him, "I already have a date."

He says, "With who," like he doesn't believe me.

I say, "With an airline pilot," only I don't tell Daniel that it's the fellow with the model airplane. I thought telling Daniel I was dating a pilot was a good touch. I'm not sure what I was thinking; he needs to know he's not the only guy in town. Besides, maybe this fellow with the model plane has more going on than he's told me. He's a nice guy, and I probably didn't give him a fair chance. Just because he likes model planes doesn't mean that's all he does.

Daniel says, " I'll call you tomorrow," I respond, "Ok." And we said good night.

Dinner with the airplane fellow was so dull; we didn't have anything in common, there was no spark, and I found myself thinking about Daniel. When I was Daniel, I would linger and anticipate his every word. This evening I was cautious not to yawn. I couldn't wait to go home. Arriving home about 9 PM, we said our goodbyes; I gave him a quick kiss on the cheek good night and went inside. I changed clothes, paid the babysitter, and was about to rest for the evening when the phone rang.

Daniel said, "Did you have a nice dinner?"

I replied, "Yes, I had a lovely dinner. Have you been watching my apartment? I just came home."

"You know I would never do that," and then asks if he can come over.

"Daniel, that is not a good idea; I have work tomorrow; my day has been long enough; have a good night." I hung up the phone, thinking it would have been nice to see him, but no, I prompted myself not to call him back.

The next day was a holiday; I was at work, the boys were with their father, so I didn't feel quite so pressured; it didn't make any difference to me if I ate dinner. I walked into the apartment after work, and something didn't feel quite right. I glanced about, didn't see anything out of place, and went to change out of my uniform. Taking my sweet-natured time, I turned on some music; it was a beautiful sunny afternoon as usual. I was pleased with the way the apartment had turned out; it was soothing. Ferns were hanging in the front window; pictures were up, coordinated colors, greens, and tans with a bit of gold and orange. The desk was tidy, and it was quiet. Smiling to myself, I walked into the kitchen, and behold; there he sat.

Before he could say anything, I adamantly stated in a tone a little louder than my usual voice, "What are you doing here? How did you get in? Who said you could be here????" I was furious!

The next thing out of my mouth was, "Get out, Get out, and don't come back."

Daniel got up, walked into the living room, and sat back down. "Oh my God, that is not out; there's the door; it'll take you out just like you came in, and why haven't you told me how you got in to begin with?"

I was so mad I could have spit nails. Still, he didn't move. I went to the phone, "If you don't leave right now, I'm calling the police."

Daniel was up off the sofa but not too fast.

He said, " Yes, you can call the police, but I just wanted to see you."

I was so furious; it didn't make any difference what he said. He left, closed the door on his way out, didn't tell me how he came in; I know I locked the doors when I left this morning. I stomped around the apartment for at least half an hour before I calmed down to a roar. The frustration I was feeling was only enhanced by the calm coolness Daniel displayed. He didn't raise his voice or become agitated. All the while, I think this is my apartment, the invasion of my privacy; he can't do that; he so can't do that, realizing all the while he did just that. The next day the boys were back, we had dinner, the phone rang, and it was Daniel and never did tell me how he got in the apartment.

Years later, he said, "He just went in through the sliding glass door. It wasn't that difficult if you knew what you were doing".

But for tonight, Daniel apologized for upsetting me and was careful not to talk about the intrusion of privacy, for that steam wouldn't dissipate for a long while, years. We talked for hours.

Finally, Toph said, "Mom, are you going to watch television with us for a while. When Toph was about three years old, his speech was quite good; he would ask me if he could watch TV. I would explain to this dear child of mine; you must not be lazy. Using proper English and pronouncing your words is a sign of intelligence, so television is the correct name for that instrument. Not all instructions went that well, but that one stuck. I went in to watch television with the boys, dished them out some ice cream, and we relaxed for a short while before bed and prepared for the next day. Mornings started at 6:30 AM; if I didn't oversleep, we needed to be out the door by 7:30 AM for the 3 of us to be at our respective places by 8 am.

The Manager, Brian at the restaurant, is a young man in his 20's, took over for his father, and he's doing a decent job.

I had previously worked for his father and left on good terms when we moved from Huntington Beach to Tustin. The plan at the time was to move to Corona out by Riverside. It not only didn't happen but is a whole other story before the divorce.

Brian is a thoughtful, caring individual, not only about his job but the people he works with. When I applied for the job, I was undecided whether to divorce or give this life another chance. I asked Brian if I could just work weekends at the time of the job interview. Not a problem, he thought that was a great idea. My plan, if I were working weekends, I wouldn't have to be around when my husband was home, and during the week, he would be gone. Maybe it would be like a separation, and he generally wasn't around in the evenings anyway. Things did not improve after 2 to 3 months; the downhill slide moved faster than ever.

I went in to talk with Brian again, explaining that I'm going to get a divorce, have two young boys, won't be able to afford a babysitter, and these are the hours they will be in school. "Do you think there's any kind of schedule you can come up with that can work around all of my requirements? I know it's asking a lot, but you know I'll do my very best."

Brian shakes his head, "It wasn't that long ago you just wanted weekends. Now, no weekends and only during school hours, no one has that kind of schedule".

There was nothing I could say; I knew he was right. There was silence, and he had people coming and going out of his office.

Brian stood up, said, "Give me a couple of days; I'll look at the schedule. Call me on Thursday; I should know by then."

I thanked him ever so much. Brian was probably wondering if I was worth all the trouble, and what else was she going to ask?

On Thursday, I called.

When Brian came to the phone, he said, "I have your new schedule, Monday thru Friday, 8 AM to 3 PM, and you need to work this weekend". There won't be any overtime pay even though you're working seven days straight through this week; we'll work that out over the next two weeks".

Once again, I thanked him, step one accomplished. I'm aware of how difficult it can be to work full time and take care of children. But the ball is now rolling; take a deep breath and muster up some strength because it will get rougher before things smooth out.

After I had worked that shift for about a month, I noticed Brian always working on the station rotations. I asked him if he had ever considered the girls being in a continuous working area, so they didn't have to change the tables they worked. It would be easier, faster, and smoother if you didn't have to rethink each movement. I volunteered to be his trial run, taking the worst station in the restaurant to see if my plan would work. The worst station to the back of the restaurant had the most tables. If I played my cards right, the station would fill up, and I would have my self-imposed raise. Plan number 2 is underway. I didn't make any enemies doing it. That station had more clean-up, farther from the kitchen, so more running, so none of the girls wanted it anyway. I was there for one reason only, enough income for the boys and me to make it on our own.

Daniel would come to the restaurant frequently for a late lunch. He generally ordered a chef salad with extra dressing, enjoying the whole salad, which was not small. Daniel took his time, and we would have a few minutes for conversation. One of those days, he commented, "You look a little tired." I had to admit it was a lot of walking for 7 hours almost nonstop; figure 8 hours by the time you cleaned up. I knew this was not a long-term solution to life and one that I couldn't continue. I needed to look for an alternative with more money and stability. As I was standing at his table, coffee pot in hand, resting it on the tabletop, Daniel briefly touched my hand. The mind kicks into gear and the nervous system into high alert, and then there's that damn committee that sits in the back of my mind, always telling me what to do. This man that I adore is trying to give me some sound advice; I must pay attention. Put the hormones back in the box.

I hear, "Have you considered real estate? You would be a great real estate agent".

"Oh no, I say, the numbers are too big. I'm used to $10's and $20's, besides I don't know how to sell".

Daniel could look directly into your eyes and know he had your full attention, "Dianah, it's only numbers; the 10's and '20s are still the same, just a few more zeros. Give it some thought, check it out, all you have to do is take a test; there are people to help you with the rest".

I didn't give him an answer, but I thought he had a point.

Daniel would stop by in the evening whenever there was time, one of those times, as we were talking, he said, "That airplane pilot you went out with, that was a model airplane, yes?" Once again, he didn't tell me how he found out. It was another one of those easy moments; we both let it slide. Besides, a kiss and a hold were ever so much better than talking about model airplanes.

One evening as we have an especially nice dinner, the phone rings, and it's for Daniel. As he's listening to the conversation, I can tell it must be important.

He sits back down and says, "The apartment house is on fire; the phone call was Jose, the manager. He called the fire department, and they are in the process of putting it out."

"Don't you have to be there, see what's happening?"

"No, we are having a special dinner you prepared, no one is hurt, the fire department doesn't need me to put out the fire. After dinner, I will go over, check it out, and call the insurance company. Let's finish dinner."

Directly after dinner, Daniel is on his way to the apartments. Around 8 PM, he came back and gave me the lowdown. One of his tenants fell asleep with a lit cigarette burning in the ashtray, and with combustible items in the ashtray, it didn't take much to get to a blaze. The tenant is ok, and the insurance company is notified. Daniel's manager has everything in control.

Easter is just around the corner; it's the end of May. I can hardly believe that so much has happened in only a month. Daniel has invited me to dinner, and the problem is finding a babysitter. There's a girl in the apartment complex who has stayed with the boys previously. The apartments feel safe, and I don't worry about the neighbors. The units have patios, covered parking, two bed, two bath, trees, lawn, pool, and clean, single-story, well managed. I feel pretty good about the people I'm surrounded by. The girl for babysitting is 15, almost 16. I've talked with her mother, and she is a little young for watching over the boys. It's all ok except Toph says she doesn't know what she's doing, and he and she are having a conflict. One evening I came home to find Ketchup spilled on the table and the wall, but nobody knew what happened. Toph was always tall for his age and would like to take charge but wasn't quite ready; Tim was playing the innocent bystander. Babysitting was the wrong term; neither of them were babies anymore and faced with enough of life's realities to have thoughts of their own.

Toph was mature for his age and quick to temper right now. He also had too much going on in his life that was beyond his control and beyond me to help him. He didn't like his teacher, all she talked about was her latest operation, so I had to wonder just what he was getting out of class. Then I was sent a note from the school to meet with the principal. Toph took a little boy scout knife to school; I had difficulty comprehending what had happened. Then I find out there's another boy involved; he has a switchblade, parents from Mexico and the two boys don't like each other. There had been fights, one I knew about and thought it would blow over. There was detention, and I don't believe that ever solved anything, but everyone was aware of the situation.

I never found out if this had to do with kids calling Tim names because he was wearing glasses at the time. Tim's teacher said she moved him from the back of the classroom to the front because he was too quiet, and she didn't think he could see well. So Tim and I go to the optometrist; Doc says Tim needs glasses, and what do I know? I started wearing glasses for headaches right after the divorce. Did it help? Maybe yes, maybe no. We got Tim glasses, he would leave for school with glasses on, and once around the corner, they would be off. I can't blame him, first of all I don't know if they helped; secondly, kids can be so cruel to one another, calling him names, tormenting him because he wore glasses. I tried to tell Tim; those kids didn't know what they were saying; he needed to be strong and above their ignorance. I couldn't take him to school; that would be too early, which could make matters worse. It's so hard for a youngster to be an outsider. There is nothing new about bullies; we just lived through it because we are supposed to be tough. One way or another, you lose a certain amount of innocence, toughen up and hopefully move on. If all goes well, you find the middle of the road.

Life keeps going; I'm working, paying the bills, and the kids are not wandering the street. When I went to turn on the electricity for the apartment, the gal taking the order said, "You will have to give a $120.00 deposit", my retort is, "Why?" She says, "Because you don't have an account with us." I explained where our last service was; our account was paid in full and always on time.

Once again, she says, "But it wasn't in your name," Oh, the injustice of life!

I explained to her who I was, that I had just divorced, and that the account was in good standing because I wrote the checks. Fortunately, I had someone who not only understood but cared, and so the account was opened in my name even if she had to fudge some paperwork. Yes, women were in the workplace, but for most of the country, we still belonged to someone else, belonging being the optimum word, either a father or a husband, and they were the ones in charge, the ones who made the decisions, the only one to receive the credit.

I have a date with Daniel, dinner on the eve of Easter; I explained the babysitter situation, Daniel said we'll only be gone a couple of hours, three at the most. If the boys have any real big problems, my kids and ex-wife are right around the corner. So don't worry, Toph is a responsible young man, he will have all kinds of phone numbers. And it's only for two or three hours. Okay, we will go to dinner, no babysitter. I talk with boys, make sure they have phone numbers, talk with them about getting along with each other, Tim about minding his brother, "Your brother is in charge, no teasing." The evening arrives, and then I find out we are flying to Palm Springs for dinner.

Daniel says, "We are only about an hour away and will be home before you know it."

I talk to the boys again, feeling apprehensive, but there are people close at hand, and I have called the mother of the 15-year-old babysitter just in case, in case of what I wouldn't know.

We are on our way to the Long Beach airport to meet Ken, Daniel's friend and partner in what will be their new company. As we travel, I thought the boys will be OK; they spend about an hour alone between school and me getting home from work. So three hours should not be that big of a deal, right? My parents left me with tiny babies when I was eight years old; there were no catastrophes.

We get to the airport, into the four-seater plane. I have never been in a small plane before, so many first times with Daniel, some more challenging than others. Ken is the pilot; Daniel knows how to fly and previously had his pilot's license. He explained, he was formerly a fair-weather pilot with too many irons in the fire to keep up with a pilot's license requirements. He let his license lapse. Daniel said it's a great hobby if you have time. Ken's girlfriend and I get into the back of the plane; I find Ken's date to be a no-nonsense business person, friendly and reserved, not flashy. Different from the type of girl Ken usually dated. He liked southern blondes, most didn't generally have too much ambition, so I am told. Ken was originally from Oklahoma, football in high school and college. Tall, red hair, freckles, and always drank his coffee so hot, and so fast, we were amazed he didn't burn himself.

We take off, arrive in Palm Springs in no time; a little bit of turbulence comes in, but all is well. We get a taxi to the restaurant; I find a public phone and call the kids. They say everything is OK, I talk with Tim, make sure he's not tormenting his brother, and the four of us go to dinner. Dinner was fine; it's night time so you really can't see anything of Palm Springs. All seems well; Daniel and Ken have been true gentlemen throughout dinner. It's time to leave for the airport. We get to the airport; there's wind turbulence, too much to let us fly out. We wait; it's now 11 PM; Daniel and Ken have called the tower every half hour with no forward movement. The weather is not in our favor. I call the boys before we leave the airport to tell them that we can't fly out and won't be home until tomorrow morning. I tell Toph the Easter Bunny is in the car's trunk, and the car keys are in the jewelry box. Don't go out there until morning, don't make yourself sick; I will be home just as soon as possible. You have all kinds of phone numbers if you need anything at all.

We are now driving around Palm Springs looking for a motel to sleep in for the evening. It's Easter weekend, spring break, and we finally find something at about 2 AM on the outskirts of town; not great. The room was dark and didn't smell clean. I checked the bathroom and the bed, didn't see anything crawling, so we'll make do. It's a bed and a shower. Everyone has somewhere to be the following day. Ken's girlfriend is supposed to be with family; Ken is supposed to be seeing his other girlfriend. Daniel is supposed to be picking up his two youngest kids, and everyone knows where I'm supposed to be. We are all on edge, however I am not the least concerned about their affairs. I have two children and would never intentionally do this, my heart is breaking. When we got to the motel, I called Toph again. I know he should be sleeping, but I just have to check.

Morning has arrived, 6 AM everyone is up and ready to leave. We find a quick bite of breakfast and coffee, and the four of us head to the airport. First thing in the airport, I called the boys, it's now about 8 AM. They have had some cereal, found the candy, and are watching television. Nothing disastrous has happened, but I need to get home.

Ken is checking with the flight controller, and he's telling us it is still too windy. You'll have to wait. And so we wait. Daniel and I walk outside for some fresh air. The sun is shining, the sky is clear, you can see the Palm Springs hills in the background. What a beautiful day, if only there weren't so many other things going on. None of us are talking much; we all have something else on our minds. Daniel points to a commercial airliner that's coming into land. One of those that seats about 120 passengers. There's a number of us outside standing and watching. When out of nowhere comes this two-seater plane directly into the flight path of the airliner. The pilot already has the landing gear down of this long multi seated commercial airliner. The tower is screaming Abort, Abort, Abort. The little plane doesn't seem to have a clue. I grab Daniels's arm for support. I feel weak. The commercial pilots are doing all they can. The landing gears go up the plane heaves you can hear the creaking of the aircraft as it works to abort the landing, trying to get back into the sky. My heart is in my throat. I'm about to see a catastrophe? It's right there, so close to the runway as it's trying to head for the sky, the sound is unbelievable. You can hear the metal, with sounds like it's buckling, too much pressure, it couldn't flex, and yet it needed to get back in the air. There are two mountains. The pilots can't just take their time maneuvering. It's too close to the ground. The plane is groaning. The rivets are shaking. The engine is roaring. We can see the pilots. Oh dear God, don't let this happen. The airliner, directly in front of us, struggles back into the air space, so close to no return.

The tower finally gets the attention of the small plane and sends him five miles out. We watch the airliner come in and land. My appreciation for those pilots goes beyond words. They should be given accommodations at least. I'm sure what they received was another day's work.

Time has passed, it's about 11 AM, I have made another call from the public phone on Daniel's phone bill, nothing is free in this time of life. The tower has given us the ok to fly.

Noon and we are in the air, there's huge billowy clouds, layer upon layer. We take a higher elevation, up above the clouds. Since we are fair-weather flyers, not instrument rated, our elevation is supposed to be regulated at a lower altitude. But one does not want to encounter another aircraft in the clouds. We've been in the air a short while, it's a little bumpy, and then before anyone can say hold on, we hit an air pocket, we drop down about 300 feet in seconds, Ken's girlfriend and I hit our heads on the ceiling like you wouldn't believe, yes, we had our seat belts on. With aching heads, we snug up the seat belts, the guys ask us if we're okay. "Do you need an aspirin?" We both took two.

A few more minutes out Daniel, says to Ken, "Think we should dip down and see where we are? I think we have been heading in this direction long enough."

Kens is not sure, it's not legal to fly too low and he doesn't want to go back into the clouds, but we need to go below the clouds so we can see, it's our only choice. We go down to visible territory, which seems like a long distance, trying to determine our location.

I look down, hay Guys, "I don't swim."

We are out over the Pacific by about 20 minutes and need to fly back now another 20 minutes plus find the Long Beach airport, and we don't know where we are over the Pacific, hoping we have not drifted too far off course. Thankfully there's plenty of fuel, but there's been a shortage of comfort in this trip. Within 30 minutes, we land in Long Beach, illegally under the cloud cover, with no tower or flight plan. The plane gets checked out, we shakily make it to the parking lot to head in our separate directions. Daniel and I walk to the car, as we look at each other, there is nothing to say. Our auto has a totally flat tire. He is about as deflated as I am, which has nothing over on the tire. Another walk back into the airport to call for assistance, I call the boys again and wait another 45 minutes for the tire to be replaced.

It must have been at least 3 o'clock before we got back to the apartment, no one was happy, everyone was making do with unplanned events. It was not one of our finer moments. Daniel apologized, said he was heading to his kid's house and I was going to try to make the boys a decent meal and see if there was anything I could do to salvage Easter Day. Monday morning would come soon enough.

Later that same Sunday evening Daniel was back on the phone

asking how everyone was and if there was anything he could do. I let him know I was tired as I was sure he was just as tired, the boys weren't happy but we couldn't do anything about it. The next couple of weeks were a blur, work, and school, a few phone calls, and recoup from an evening of more events than anyone wanted.

Daniel and Ken are putting a new business plan together, they've rented a shop, put the legalese in order, obtained office furniture and supplies. The next big thing is equipment. Next door to their shop is an auto mechanic, Aki Yonahara, not only was he an exceptional mechanic but he was a really nice man. We became good friends. Aki explained one day, the family tradition he came from, the oldest son always inherited the family estate, and the oldest son always married first. Consequently, Aki, who was now in his early 50's, never married. He had set up living quarters in his auto shop and he was always alone. He was our go-to guy for auto repair until it was no longer practical.

Daniel and I went to a dinner show in Newport starring Morey Amsterdam, who in his day was fairly famous, such as on the cast of the Dick Van Dyke show. We were in California and it was so easy to do all these great things if you only took the time. I had come from a place where we did very little but work, I found this lifestyle amazing.

Daniel would come for dinner, and generally be late, but would call to let me know. When he arrived, he'd sit on the sofa and instantly fall asleep. I have this lamp with a black shade. I would turn it on to keep him awake. The light would shine in his eyes, which he didn't like. He wouldn't turn it off, he was in my house, and it didn't keep him awake.

One evening Toph said, "Mom, Daniel is going to disturb the neighbors he's snoring so loud."

I was always on the boys, not to be noisy, we needed to be considerate of the neighbors, we did not want them complaining to the manager. I was forever on guard about offending someone or causing a problem that I might not know how to fix. There's the committee again; I must get them out of my head.

Daniel was coming to dinner; it was a memorable evening. I made a huge salad, wine, and candlelight, for the 4 of us just because we needed to be special. Daniel had a plan. He thanked me many times at dinner and told us he was taking the crew out on a fishing trip. The ship was about 120 feet long, and they were going 70 miles into the Pacific Ocean. Toph is invited for the fishing trip, and Daniel's youngest son CM would be joining them. Daniel explained to Tim that he wasn't quite old enough; the construction crews on the ship weren't the kind to look out for younger kids.

Daniel repeated, "Tim, next time, I will do my best to do something special for you."

So they were going out on a 3-day fishing trip; it was summer, and school was out. I had the kids lined up for summer school to keep things in line with my work schedule. I didn't believe in summer school. But having them sit in the apartment while I was working and with a babysitter that I couldn't find wasn't the answer either.

Daniel was taking the two Christophers, his son CM was Christopher Mark. Toph was short for Christopher. Nicknames were a must, otherwise it was way to confusing.

I asked Toph if he would like to go on that kind of fishing trip and of course, it was a resounding yes. So Daniel, CM, Toph, and his construction crews were on their way.

At the same time my Aunt Agnes, my favorite aunt, and her new husband Burt with my sister Linda were planning their trip to California. Agnes was now the designated white glove lady of the family, in her mind, there are always proper ways to do things. She always said what was on her mind, straight out, no soft shoeing. Agnes had a few skeletons in her closet, just like most folk, but that never slowed her down.

As I was growing up, Agnes was my idol. She dressed right, made her own stylish clothing, decorated her home with all the latest. Her hair and nails were always done. Agnes may have been from the farm, but you would never know it.

There was a family story about Agnes when she was about to get a divorce from her first husband, Cecil. Cecil didn't seem to be a bad sort, good to the kids, loved baseball and new cars. Bought a new Ford every year. Told a few not so true stories, which the adults didn't appreciate but seemed ok otherwise. Then I heard the story, Cecile had girlfriends, many girl friends. Agnes pleaded, to go to counseling, make a clean start, he wouldn't change his ways.

One evening he was on his way out and Agnes knew it was to see one of his girls. She tried to stop him. She pulled on his arm as he went out the door, he threw her back. She got up, ran out to him, he was in the car and starting to leave. She threw herself on the hood of this new red and white Ford, thinking he would stop. He turned the car, she rolled off and he drove away. Agnes got a couple of scratches and a few bruises, which couldn't come close to the emotional hurt and humiliation she had to put behind her. Now a few years later here we are, new husband, new life. She looks happy, she looks like the Agnes I know, a little older and more conservative. The new husband was no frills kind of guy.

Linda, my sister was 10 years younger than me, we didn't have much in common other than I was her sister and caretaker as we were growing up. Linda is staying with me and Tim, while Agnes and Burt got a motel and did some sightseeing. I worked during the day, but everything was managing to fit in for their vacation.

Meanwhile, the guys are out at sea, with more turbulence than I knew about. There were no fish, the construction crews made themselves happy with liquor, the seas were wild. Waves washed over the ship as it would dip 30 feet out of the water and crash back down. Both the Christophers wanted to go out on the deck, so Daniel lashed them to the deck, so they wouldn't wash into the sea, I guess that was fun or so I heard. It's a good thing I wasn't there, and I can say that now that they are all back safe and sound. The galley ran out of food because there was so much drinking and no fishing. I listened to the story of some of the guys rolling out of the three-story bunks, crashing to the floor, as the ship rolled and dipped in the ocean. I can not fathom this as a good time, but then no one asked.

Aunt Agnes, her new husband Burt, and sister Linda arrive. It's a Sunday afternoon, Tim and I are at home. Everyone is seated in the living room, even Tim. It's almost too proper; this is, after all, California, not known for Emily Post Etiquette. Friendly, maybe, but adhering to what is considered the appropriate behavior, that would be a midwest thing.

We are having a family reacquainting when there's a knock on the door. It's the guys back from their fishing expedition. Before I even let them inside, I can tell where they've been. The odor is unmistakable. They enter; I leave the door open for fresh air and needed ventilation. They may not have caught any fish, but you would never guess that from this fishy odor that came with them through the door. Introductions are made, brief salutations, a short description of the trip, and Daniel departs with one Christopher, the other Christopher, Toph heads for the shower. Shortly after that, Agnes and Burt depart; I show Linda to my bedroom to put her things away, and I try to get ready for the next day.

The following day, Burt and Agnes come by, and we have dinner at a nearby restaurant; and they want to tour Disneyland tomorrow. Disneyland is an all-day affair, the boys and Linda do the rides. Good time, one could say; I might have been a little on edge. Entertaining my relatives is something I haven't done before. The boys knew without me telling them to be on their best behavior. After Disneyland, we went to Knottsberry Farms; we covered as much ground as possible with work in between. On the day of departure, Daniel took everyone to breakfast, and then to the airport. I think they had a good time, no one said, and I didn't ask, but they were smiling. One should be thankful for small favors.

Around 4 PM midweek, Daniel came by the apartment; my schedule was pretty standard at this time. Everyone counted on me being home by 3:30 PM; I was surprised to see him at what we considered mid-day. We were standing in the living room; he looked directly into my eyes to make sure he had my undivided attention and said: "I have something important to tell you."

Immediately my mind conjures all kinds of possibilities of things I don't want to hear. Daniel, are you leaving? You don't want to see me anymore, maybe he's sick, but before I can say anything, and glad I didn't.

"I've been offered a new job, a new position."

"Oh." I am so relieved; I can handle that. Daniel then tells me it's a substantial promotion. It would mean more time at work, more responsibility, different types of contacts, and different social groups; everything would change. The new position would mean a six-figure income, not starting with one.

This was vocabulary I wasn't familiar with, and how could he possibly put in more time, as I'm trying to assimilate just what that meant. The boys and I were currently living on $1,000 a month, doing okay as long as there were no significant problems, so my world in dollar figures revolved around $12K a year. I could not truly comprehend just what six figures would mean to us, and I was guessing $200K annual was what he was talking about, maybe more. I'm standing, pondering, saying nothing with all this running through my mind; and before I could ask any questions, Daniel was giving me answers that I still didn't understand.

" I don't believe this is what I want to do," as he's watching for my reaction.

I said, "Daniel, if this is such a great opportunity with so much money, what is it that you don't want or that's not good?"

He took me in his arms, held me ever so close, and softly whispered in my ear as though it were a secret, "Do not worry, I am here for you; you will never have to do without." I will make sure you are always cared for. I must make some changes; more money will not make our life better.

He said," You see these hands, I will wash dishes if necessary." We will always have a roof over our heads and food on the table. I will be here for you. I didn't understand, but I knew being held in arms like this meant more to me than any bank account ever could.

It was not my decision on what his life work should be. Daniel is 12 years older than I; and to me, he may be a man of the world, a world I'm not familiar with. Between street smarts and exceptional common sense, Daniel had an answer for most things. He didn't ask me for advice or to make a choice; he was confiding, putting forth a trust, a trust I cherished more than words could express. During this brief period, we have built a friendship that is beyond romance and physical heat. We didn't know each other's deepest secrets; we only knew there was a closeness that may only happen once in a lifetime, with a hold that continues to strengthen as each day comes forth.

There was no more talk about a new job. We would have our Sunday morning coffee at Winchell's Donut Shop; the four kids would have hot chocolate and donuts. Daniel and I would go through the Sunday paper while the kids terrorized the parking lot. I don't think they did anything wrong; they just had lots of energy and needed to explore. We let them run, have some fun, and counted on the fact that they were good kids.

During one of the Sunday paper reads, Daniel said, "Would you like to go to the theatre?" I thought he meant a movie and turned my nose up at the thought.

He explained, "Zero Mostel is playing at the Dorothy Chandler Pavilion in Los Angeles; it's a formal affair. I know the Chandlers and can get some good seats. Fiddler on the Roof is the performance and sure to be sold out in no time if it isn't already. With a little friendly persuasion, I don't believe we'll have any problem getting good seats."

Having never been to the theatre, I was thrilled. Zero Mostel in Fiddler on the Roof, I would love to go. Daniel is at the door the evening of the play, dressed in a suit and tie, looking very debonair, very handsome indeed. We needed to hurry, and didn't want to be late for the start of the performance. I was concerned that I didn't have an evening dress; but with the once-over look of approval, he said I looked fetching and would be the prettiest girl there. Even though I knew it was a familiar line, it still made me smile. The boys with baby-sitter and treats were settled.

It's a 45-minute drive, and I was still apprehensive about fitting in. I thought if I didn't fit in, not only would he not attend this type of function, but I wouldn't fit in Daniel's world. I didn't know. Daniel kept assuring me I would be just fine, and with the size of the crowd, it was just a matter of getting to our seats. We pulled up in front, it was crowded; Daniel gave the keys to the attendant. Another first for me, I had never thought about someone parking your car for you. As we walked up the stairs through the massive glass doors, into the main hall with the huge staircases, towering chandeliers, women in their evening gowns and jewels and furs, men in their tuxedos, throngs of theatre-goers, I was enthralled. Daniel ordered cocktails as we waited for the doors to open, the ushers would guide us to our seats. The end of the aisle and easy to see. Once again, I felt the farm girl in a world I knew nothing about. The performance was outstanding, the orchestra was flawless, I knew this was a highlight worth remembering for a lifetime. At intermission, Daniel leads me to the Ladies' room; I was forever getting lost. Most people have an inborn compass; I do not; if there are two choices, I will almost always choose the wrong direction. The usher guided us back to our seats; the second half was equally as excellent. The performance was over, the actors received their accolades, and made their multiple bows to the audience. It was a standing ovation with several curtain calls.

We made our way through the crowd; everyone was deciding where to have dinner after the theatre. The valet brought our car as we proceeded to drive past several restaurants that serve theatre patrons, and they were not only packed but with significant waiting lines. Agreeing, dinner was not necessary. Neither of us wanted to wait in line, and the day had been long enough. Decision made, we started for home, we were both tired. I wasn't the least disappointed at not having dinner; the evening had been fabulous.

Unlocking the apartment door, paying the babysitter, I checked on the boys; they were asleep. Daniel wrapped me in his arms, warm, safe, and loving. I could stay this way forever. A tender, lingering good night kiss; I'll see you tomorrow. I felt 16 all over again; I'm in love. What a perfect night, ecstasy was here; if tomorrow never came, I had an evening that could carry me through a lifetime.

My life became a circle of activity centered around the boys and Daniel. When he wasn't working, which was most of the time, he was at the apartment. We had multiple conversations about food and recipes, the children, his and mine, but mostly about business and travel. I was always intrigued.

There were all the daily chores of life; the white cat got an infection in its paw, I took it to the vet, who prescribed antibiotics that had to be put in the wound three times a day. We managed to get it healed, and shortly after that, the cat went outside, took off; we never saw it again.

The kids said someone probably found it and took it for themselves. They were justifiably correct, I was sure. Tim probably missed the cat, but it was not a loving creature, and I wasn't ready to replace it.

Daniel and I would take a drive whenever the boys were with their father. We are about to turn on to the freeway; and Daniel says, "See that guy on the side of the road."

I said, "yes."

Daniel said, "He's an old pool builder, and he was an executive not that long ago, you can tell by the cut of his pants".

The pants were up above his ankles, he was hitchhiking, and it looked like he lived on the street, which he probably did. This was not the first time Daniel had mentioned seeing an old pool builder under similar circumstances.

I was amazed, I said, "There were a lot more guys in the pool business than I would have thought, and it doesn't appear that they fared too well".

Daniel had the biggest, silliest grin on his face as he chuckled, and then laughed, and finally, I got the picture. It had been a joke that took me forever, weeks to catch on to the story. I think he's still laughing.

Another time, again, we are driving in his Ford pickup, bench seat, and he says, "Dianah, you know Ford made bench seats for a reason."

I say, "yes?"

Daniel said, "And they didn't move the steering wheel."

I said, "OK."

Once again, he said, "You know the steering wheel doesn't move."

I said, "Yes, I know."

He said, "They made a solid seat all the way across so the whole seat could be used."

I didn't know where this conversation was going. Finally, Daniel said, "Dianah, my love, come over and sit next to me on this side of the truck."

I said, "Oh, well, why didn't you just say so." I thought to myself sometimes men are so hard to understand. Daniel just shook his head, put his arm around me, we snuggled; he was happy, and even though I thought it was the one of the silliest stories, I couldn't have felt better next to this warm caring man and the gentle squeeze of the strong arm and the hand on my shoulder. Little else mattered.

It's Saturday, bright and sunny, pleasantly warm; Daniels at the apartment and says one of the company Trucks needs picking up in San Diego. I need to get the truck, would you like to come along. I didn't comprehend the full scope; he said, "We'll drive down in the car, the four kids will come with us, and the company truck will pull the car back. Just take a couple of hours, no big deal, what do you think?"

I said, "Ok." Sunday morning, "Kids, let's get ready to go." We all get in the car, three boys in the back, Daniels' daughter Lisa in front with us, and we go to San Diego. It's a nice sunny day, not too much traffic and everyone is pretty chipper.

We do the two hour drive to San Diego, there's the truck. A big truck, three axles on the back, dump bed, ten-speed, I am feeling apprehensive; I volunteered to drive the car back behind him. Daniel said, Oh no, then you can't ride with me.

"Okay?"

He hooks up the car to the back of the truck; all the kids get in the dump bed, they can barely see over the edge and me upfront. We start home, well the truck is not running too smoothly. From San Diego to Anaheim on the freeway, we crawl along at 30 to 20 miles per hour with lots of traffic. It's midday; all the Sunday drivers are out, the sun is now much warmer than it was on the way down. Daniel has the emergency flashers running most of the way. There was a reason why the employee left the truck in San Diego; he didn't want to limp back or possibly break down on the highway, which was where we were. Generally, sunshine and cool ocean breezes are a pleasant afternoon, but not when you're on the freeway with car fumes in bumper-to-bumper traffic. It was no picnic for the kids; every bump and shift was a jolt, and sitting in the sun all afternoon would not soon be forgotten. It was too long of a ride for everyone, including Daniel. He had to keep shifting, and had three shifting rods, which I never did figure out, evidently had to do with a 10 speed transmission that wasn't in the best of conditions. We were all tired by the evening; and stopped for hamburgers and fries and called it a day. But as I said, life was never boring with Daniel.

Early one morning, Toph came to me, he obviously had a problem.

"Mom, I broke the watch band, and I don't know how to fix it." This was a watch he had received from his father.

So we took a look at it. The pin that held the band to the watch was simply gone. I looked to see if there was anything I had that would do the repair. No such luck. I didn't know you could get a pin from most anywhere that sold watches, never having done a repair before. I think there were quite a few things I didn't know about. A couple of hours later Daniel was over, and I presented him with the problem.

He said, "Toph, don't worry. It's an easy fix, I have to leave on business and as soon as I return I'll have the part, we'll put it back together. Two days passed, and Daniel always called at least once a day. He was due back and I let Toph and Tim know.

Toph said, "He'll probably forget about the watch pin."

I said, "Well, you know he's very busy with a lot of things on his mind, but just wait till he gets here, ok."

Daniel arrived later that day, walked into the apartment, put down his briefcase, and as always, I received a loving hug and sweet kiss. He greets each one of the boys with a shoulder pat or hair tousle and asks if there's coffee. After giving Daniel a few minutes to settle in, both the boys are waiting to see if he remembered the watch pin. It wasn't so much the pin, it was if he remembered to complete a request for a boy who had been let down too many times.

As Daniel came back into the room, sat at the table with his coffee, he said, "Toph, bring me your watch."

He took out his wallet, and retrieved the pin, and in 5 minutes repair was complete with a thank you and a happy young man. If only the rest of life could be that easy.

I've only been divorced for a few months, still have my ex-husband's credit cards, just in case of emergencies for the boys. All the credit cards were in his name, I didn't have any with my name on them and after the divorce I never used his cards, they didn't belong to me, and I didn't want them.

During our marriage I handled all the household expenses. One time when the property tax bill came, I went into a panic. Here was this large bill that I didn't have the funds for. One of the few times, I called him at work and explained the bill. He wasn't concerned, he just said, I'll put some more money in the account so you can write the check. I didn't know there was more money, another undisclosed secret. Well I guess if I think about it, if it were disclosed, then it wouldn't be a secret anymore. Trying to keep a sense of humor is my only salvation.

I go to work, there's a new waitress today, doesn't seem like a bad sort. We all go about doing our job. Before the day was over she had cleaned out everybody's locker. Took their cash, credit cards, and whatever else she thought was useful. I had about $50 in my wallet, that was a good day's tip but not the end of the world. She took everyone's credit cards, and we reported our losses to the police. That evening I called my ex, explained what had happened, and told him I was calling all the credit card companies and reporting the cards stolen.

I said, "Get yourself some new cards."

It shouldn't have mattered to me, they weren't my cards. I didn't have any credit. Nothing I did would make any difference, but I called all the companies. It was the responsible thing to do. I had always taken care of these things and it didn't occur to me that I didn't have to do that any longer.

A few months later the boys are spending a holiday with their father, and when they return home, I hear an interesting story. Their father had been shopping at one of these posh department stores for his girlfriend, and went to use his credit card. The clerk swiped the card and immediately called security. They handcuffed him, took him away, fingerprinted, the whole nine yards, because once again what I told him was of no importance. I shouldn't have been happy but there was a moment of satisfaction that justice was being served in its own time.

I'm at work, Daniel stops by for lunch, tells me he just saw a nice car, clean, not too many miles, talked to the owner and it sounds like a good buy.

I'm apprehensive, "What kind of car, a Buick you know is out of the question".

"No, it's a Mercury Monterey".

"It doesn't sound like a smaller car, but I'll look, and what am I going to do with the Buick?"

Daniel said, "Don't worry we'll sell it".

"Really? Someone will buy it?"

He said, "It doesn't look bad, at the right price it will sell." We look at the Merc, yes it's clean. No dents, no scratches, good tires, about 60K miles, and drives very smooth. Again another big car, but I need to replace the Buick before it just stops and leaves us stranded. It's one thing for me, but not with 2 children.

Daniel says, I need to finance the car. No, No, No. I don't want to give the bank interest, why should they make money on me? I've worked too hard for my income and I don't want a car payment.

Daniel took my hand, calmly, he says, "If you want to be independent, you need to establish credit. To establish credit, and get a credit card you need a credit rating and to get that you need a loan. Now you have some money in the bank, so we go to the bank, you ask for a loan against the savings you have. You are receiving 6% interest and they will charge you 8% interest, it's only costing you 2% and you still have your savings. You pay on the loan for about 6 months, get a credit card in the process and at the end of 6 months you pay it off. You still have most of your savings, you have credit and a better car, and we will sell the Buick to help pay for the Merc."

Daniel reminds me about trying to turn on the utilities and everything was in my ex-husbands' name, I had nothing.

" Trust me," Daniel says.

Well, that was the wrong thing to say, I was immediately doubtful, anytime someone says, Trust me, the red lights flash before my eyes and the lack of trust is first in my mind.

Daniel said, "Let me help you, I'll go to the bank with you, the car will be in your name. At the end of six months, you'll be a financially independent woman and on your way to financial freedom".

I didn't like the plan, but I couldn't disagree, it made sense. We went to the bank. I bought the car. A pretty nice car, it didn't give near the headaches of the Buick. Much to my surprise, I sold the Buick with a sign in the window. I thought Daniel would take care of the sale for me, but no, this is your car and you'll do just fine. Talk to the guys, and let them take it for a drive. They came back, gave me cash and I gave them what work had been done on the car. I signed it over, and received their information all within about 45 minutes. Was I surprised.

Now this car of mine that I bought, with Daniel's help, and rather proud of, is mint green, with a dark green vinyl top, still the new car fragrance inside, the best car I have had. I feel progress is being made, I'm not quite a second rate citizen anymore.

It's 7:45 AM, I'm pulling into the parking lot at the restaurant, going to park in the back row where no one generally parks, thinking if no one will be here the car won't get dinged. As I'm turning into the stall, I get a jolt in the rear right fender, how can this be? I am stunned. There's no one else in this part of the parking lot. Looking in the rear-view mirror, sure enough, there's a car with a man sitting in it directly behind me. I get out of the car to see what damage has been done, this middle-aged over weight male, with an attitude, approaches me and says you stupid woman why don't you watch where you're going. I cannot believe what I'm hearing, do I look stupid? He was behind me, I was parking in the very last row, there were no other cars around, there were acres of space and he couldn't see me. He couldn't stop, how fast was he going when he ran into me? How can this be my fault and why is he shouting at me? He dented the side of what was a pristine car and told me it was my fault. I have to go to work and I cannot for the life of me comprehend how this is happening. Was I not supposed to have a decent car?

" For peat sake man get off my back, you ran into me"! We exchange information, and I go to work in a state of anxiety. The insurance company says it's a no-fault because we both have the same insurance company. Give me a break, once again, he ran into me.

I tell Daniel about it, he says "Dianah, let it go". It may not be right but it's not a battle worth fighting. I work at swallowing my pride and the injustice of the whole thing and try to move on, with now less than a pristine car that I had just purchased less than a week ago. Getting the fender repaired wouldn't work, because my insurance didn't provide for a loaner car, and I had $1000 deductible, so I will do my best to ignore it.

Sunday morning coffee and donuts at Winchell's, and it's decided by all that we should take a drive out to the desert, away from the city. We take the new car, the kids can't all fit in Daniels truck. The boys sit in the back, Lisa is upfront with Daniel and me. We pack up some snacks and liquid and we're off. We get to an area, where there aren't very many cars, country-type roads, definitely desert.

Daniel says, "This looks like a good place to get off the road".

I said, "What do you mean"?

He says, "We'll just drive back into the hills".

My first statement is, "Not with this car".

He says, "It'll be fine, see it's nice and level", as we go bouncing across the rocks, ruts, sagebrush, and cactus.

Daniel says, "I've done this lots of times". We are on our way to the hill, so everyone can get out to stretch their legs, do a walkabout. About halfway to the hill, we go over a rock, which results in an enormous amount of noise from the car. Daniel stops, everyone gets out of the car, we all assess the damage. Sure enough, the muffler is off, we need a good size piece of wire and there's none in the trunk.

Daniel snickered, "Okay guys, go find us a piece of wire",

I reply, "There's not going to be any wire out here, there's no road, no buildings, won't happen".

I am not in the best frame of mind, I might as well have the Buick if this is what is going to transpire. Couldn't have been 10 minutes and the boys were back with wire. They wired the muffler to the car, we turned around, headed for home. We stopped for burgers, and fries, along the way and when we got in the car I looked at Daniel, he knew what was on my mind.

"Don't worry about the muffler, it's an easy fix, I'll take care of it. You'll be fine for a few days until I have time to get to it." Getting to it was no small matter. But that's another story.

It's midweek, I have been busy preparing dinner and now dinner is ready, the boys are ready. Daniel said he would be here for dinner. Where is he? It's not all that unusual for him to be late, he'll come rushing in with a perfectly logical reason why he's late and what can you say? About a half hour goes by and here is Daniel. I start to reheat dinner, and I hear the reason for the tardiness. He was in downtown Los Angeles, he could have stopped the explanation right there and I would have bought the story.

But he continued on, "At the corner of Main and 9th at the stop light was this stunning brunette woman in a sheik green dress, not too tight or too loose, but just right. She was something. When the light changed I drove around the block so I could get another look. By the time I was back at the corner, she was gone, I wasted my time and that's why I'm late for dinner."

Daniel said, "I didn't have to tell you this, but I want you to know that I will always look, not touch, and here is where I want to be."

Being too practical, I said, " You were being overly foolish thinking you would get around the block in rush hour traffic and she would still be there. The only reason to continue to be there is if she was guardian of the corner or rented it by the hour."

Needless to say, the explanation was not what I wanted to hear, nor was I happy about it, but what was there left for me to say. I could have said you're being too honest, and no I just came from that type of relationship with no honesty. After dinner we watched a movie with the boys and once they were in bed, Daniel took me in his arms.

He said, "I know you didn't like my reason for being late, but I will never lie to you. You are the one I want to be with. Let me show you."

I didn't forget his story, but he was here with me and there was nothing wrong with being in his arms, held ever so tight and kissed sweetly into the night.

Daniel was managing swimming pool construction crews. Most of the guys were a reasonable sort, but others were your typical macho, God's gift to women type. Seems they all had something to prove to the world and any woman that would give them the time of day. Ten to fifteen of the guys would lumber into the restaurant where I worked, and order their coffee. They were supposed to be on a coffee break of about 10 to 15 minutes, the trucks would be left running in the parking lot, they would check out all the waitresses, the uniform skirts were short and the guys would slide down in their seats on the chance they might see underwear while the waitress was cleaning a table. Really? They hadn't seen a woman's undies before. Give me a break. They would tell their stories and then would leave. Now 10 to15 minutes generally turned into 30 or more.

On this particular day, I hear one of them say, "Look out, here comes God".

All look to the parking lot as this pristine yellow Ford LTD pulls in front of the restaurant and out steps Daniel. I did my best to keep the smile off my face. Daniel was not a happy camper, he knew how long the trucks had been sitting there running, how many guys were getting paid by the hour to sit and drink coffee, and the fact that the scheduled jobs weren't getting done. He came in, sat at the table with the foreman, I poured coffee all around, and shortly thereafter the crews left. No harsh words, but there would be repercussions.

I asked Daniel if he would like breakfast.

He replied rather sternly, "Just toast this morning, Thanks".

I told him about God pulling into the parking lot in his yellow Ford LTD.

He smiled, "That will be taken care of also, don't you worry."

A few days later after dinner, Daniel says, "I need to take a ride tonight a little after 9 PM, would you like to ride along? We won't be gone long."

I told the boys we were going to take a ride later, they could stay up. A little after 9 PM we drive over to the construction yard, but before we arrive Daniel turns off the car lights. He parks close to the building, gets out his binoculars and we watch. There are men on the other side of the construction yard that was gated and locked. They were pulling 20 ft lengths of construction rebar for concrete work through the chain link fence one piece at a time. They would steal it from one company and sell it to the competitor. I asked Daniel what he was going to do.

He said, "I'll take care of it tomorrow."

"Do you know who they are?"

"Oh yes, it's one of the crews, but we're not doing anything tonight." He took down the license plate numbers of the other two cars parked in the street and knew the truck that was being loaded was one of the company trucks. We quietly backed out with no one seeing us and drove home. Another first for me, so much in life going on that I didn't see and never even thought about.

The boys and I had been out to dinner with Daniel when he stated he needed to stop by his apartment to pick up some paperwork. To this point I had not been to his apartment. He showed us the apartment, sparse, the decorator had not been here and it appeared Daniel didn't spend much time there either. Smaller than ours, but then it was furnished for one person, just the basics. He had a picnic table, a pull-out sofa bed, bedroom had a bed, nightstand, and small dresser. Now I was impressed with the closet, the clothes were categorized, color-coordinated and each hanger a certain distance from the other. Shoes were lined up, also by category and color. This closet was right out of the magazine. If I had any doubts about him being a neat nick, my questions were answered here and now.

There was only one habit I had a problem with, he would line up the condiments on the table so they were precisely at right angles from each other and equal distance apart. If he was on the phone, the condiments were rearranged again with too much precision.

I said, "Daniel, do you believe the salt and pepper tastes better if it's properly placed?"

I did not receive an answer, but to watch this at every meal was a bit unnerving; however, with a little time, we would work through it.

If you haven't guessed it by now, Daniel and I spent every moment we could with each other, and there wasn't a time when one of us said, give me some space. We not only liked being together, but it was also a desire, a need. Walking down the street, he would put his arm around my waist and hold me so close I could barely walk, and it felt good. His love could portray a possessive quality, but I didn't object. There were times I thought he wanted everyone to know I was his, I belonged to only him. I would suppose, an old-fashioned Italian trait. He was, after all, from Providence, Rhode Island, an Italian district in the Federal Hill area. The family immigrated from Italy in 1919.

If it was Daniel's intention to make a point, there was no objection from me. I was overjoyed with having a man who was intelligent, strong, hard-working, funny at times, and wanted to spend all the time he could with me. There was no greater compliment he could give me.

Daniel's oldest daughter was a very active typical teenager with teen friends. Her home is close to Daniel's apartment, making it easy for him whenever his kids needed anything. He could be available, even though he and his ex-wife couldn't get along. He and one of his sub-contractor friends were putting a roof on the kids house, a new refrigerator, and a stove in the kitchen. He even bought her a Mercury Grand Marquis, which she got in an accident with and they sued Daniel because it was still in his name.

His apartment had a nice pool and his kids did not. So the eldest daughter and friends decided to make themselves at home. They had a boisterous time in the pool more than once, without Daniel's knowledge. The second time according to the manager, they took it too far, too much noise, diving, not allowed and of course, Daniel not being home. When Daniel arrived home, he had an eviction notice waiting for him. He tried talking with the manager, explaining he didn't know the girls had been there and it wouldn't happen again. Unfortunately, the manager was not to be dissuaded, Daniel had two weeks to move. In between working, he would be looking for an apartment.

Finally, I said, "Daniel, you are probably here at my apartment more than yours anyway, would you like to move in."

He didn't believe it was the best option for everyone concerned and said he was going to keep looking. I was always insisting he leave before the boys got up, carry his shoes out and park out in the street, not in the carport area. Since he only had two weeks, his time for apartment looking was short-lived. I explained to the boys that this was going to be Daniels home now too. I hadn't even thought about what someone might think, how the boys would address it to friends and other families. As far as I was concerned, we were better to each other than most married couples. We cared about each other, we didn't cheat or tell lies, we didn't try to take advantage of each other's finances. Daniel

ME AND DANIEL

would help me wash dishes, do clothes, whatever needed doing, there was no man's work or woman's work. I had been a teen of the '60s, anti-establishment. My point of view, if I'm not asking for a handout, I'm not taking from someone or hurting anyone, then whatever I do is my business and no one else's concern. Some didn't see it that way, but our life was full, there was no time for what others may or may not think or say.

This was the era of what they designated as the sexual revolution. In my elders' world, no man spent a night with an unmarried woman, it just wasn't the respectable thing to do. Divorces were still taboo, and the establishment was, as always, in full force. Yes, women could vote, but a good percentage of them were told by their husbands how and who they should be voting for. My way of thinking didn't fall in that category and Daniel had no problem with my independence.

While Daniel was going through all his company upheaval, I had decided to study and get my real estate license. It took more study than I wanted to do. It had been several years since school and having to concentrate, memorize, and remember all the things that would be needed to pass a test, plus work was a bit daunting. Daniel would sit with the boys when he was home so I could concentrate and complete all the California requirements to qualify for the test. There were 9 courses, each with its manual of three to 500 pages. I had never been afraid of school, however, it turned out to be a larger project than I was envisioning and might take longer than anticipated. I was told once the test was passed, there was very little that would apply to the actual selling real estate.

Daniel said, "Just start in the beginning, one course at a time, I know you'll do just fine."

I knew that going to work, keeping up with boys, and having any kind of love life was going to be a superb challenge on top of starting a new career. I certainly hope I'm up to it. But I made what I considered an investment in books, fees, and application costs. I am not in the habit of throwing money at a project with the thought, it might not work. I must go into this with the attitude that I will complete this successfully on time. There could be no questions in my mind.

The problems with Daniel's partners at the current company where he was spending so much time were mounting daily. Each day brought a new series of events, between the partners wanting him to do more, the partners spending more, and the habitual problems with the employees, it was wearing him down. There were a total of 4 partners, Daniel was the only one with hands-on experience in the construction industry. Jake had a background in the Marines, was a good friend, and was good with finances. Neil had been with several different companies and to describe him as a bull in a china shop is an understatement. Then there was Doug from a large corporation that always had expendable cash. This was a new company, in the black financially but any large mistakes or new projects could deplete any headway in a hurry. There was no way to keep Doug and Neil from making unnecessary purchases. Daniel made his decision. He was leaving the company, what the partners didn't know, he would be starting his own company.

Daniel came home on Wednesday at 3:30 PM. When he walked in the door, to my look of surprise and with a question in my voice.

"Your home early"?

He said, "I quit!"

A little confused, I asked," For the day?"

"No".

"For the week?"

He took me in his arms, "I have quit the company, they will get the company car back when I am ready. Don't you worry, everything will be just fine."

With some trepidation, I accepted his choice of what needed to be and somehow knew we would work through this too.

We had been together for such a short time and had already developed a trust in each other that takes many people a lifetime. That evening we had dinner, watched a little television with the boys. I didn't ask Daniel what his plans were, for I knew he had a plan. If there was one thing I found out early on, he was always thinking and there was always another plan. If plan A didn't work, then go to plan B.

Days go by, I'm working, Daniel has closed his position with his former partners and is in the process of starting his own gunite company. Ken from the Easter airplane ride, is the new investor partner. Ken is a paleontologist, employed with Union 76. He has written papers about oil diggings, been to Egypt to explore drilling sites. He's a very learned man, a little quirky at times but dependable. Ken is not familiar with construction, but a quick study and this is just an investment for him that he will help out with as time allows. Daniel's time is consumed with putting the equipment together, they already have an office with space for equipment. The largest of which is the gunite rig which Daniel is working on customizing to his specs. I wasn't aware of the amount of fabrication that went into customization of construction equipment. I soon became educated. Within a couple of weeks, they have the company and the equipment put together and the jobs lined up. He has hired a crew of about six guys from Mexico, who know what they're doing, work hard and show up on time. They are a little temperamental on occasion but always do a good job. So Daniel now has a new corporation, running a new company. I watched it all come together, another part of the world I had never been exposed to.

Late evening, we are asleep, a light shines in my eyes. I look up, here are two very large men in uniform standing over the bed.

The tallest one says, "Mam, are you ok?"

"I think so?"

"We'll step out in the other room, while you get a robe. We need to ask you some questions."

I look at Daniel, "He says this is your apartment, you better take care of it."

I hurry out to the living room, the two police officers are standing there. Their presence takes up the whole room. They tower over me, I didn't know whether to be afraid or annoyed that they just walked in.

I ask, "Why are you here?"

The other one tells me, "A neighbor called, said someone was trying to break into their place when they heard him, he ran off, going through your patio. We checked your door, it wasn't locked. Can we check the other rooms to make sure no one came in?"

I said, "ok, but let me check on the boys, I would rather not wake them up".

The two officers checked the patio and the rest of the apartment and said if I heard anything to call and please make sure to lock all doors.

Some lessons are really hard to learn. Daniel was none too happy, an unlocked door? I hadn't lived the farm life for a good long while, but as growing up, we didn't have a key to any door. There was always someone home and as far as doors went, it was either don't let the flies in or in the winter the cold air. We didn't have keys or phones, maybe a tad too simple. I promised to be more diligent. I would check and lock all doors. I heard no more about break ins or theft.

We are all as busy as ever, Daniel with the new company. On weekends his youngest son, CM would stay with us and he and Toph would help Daniel at the shop service the trucks and other equipment. I think sometimes they had more grease on them than the trucks did. But they had a good time. Daniel would be smiling, enjoying the boys. Tim and I would do groceries, we would have dinner on the patio, and watch the fireworks from Disneyland.

On occasion, a Sunday brunch buffet would be a specialty at one of the hotel restaurants, the Disneyland Hotel was a favorite.

Ken would join us sometimes with a girlfriend. We would revel in all the scrumptious foods from around the world, just about anything you could think of would be there for your treat. Mimosas came with brunch, and all would eat way too much, and go home exhausted. But I wouldn't have missed it for anything.

Life is so good with more love than I knew two people could have!

I have completed the required real estate courses, and made the appointment to take the test? Everyone has told me about all the things to concentrate on while taking the test. Like go with your first answer, don't change it. Don't skip around questions. And everyone said, the hardest test of all 50 states is California. Where am I? I'm thinking to myself, "Do I always do things the hard way"?

The test is set for 10 days from now in Los Angeles, I have never driven to Los Angeles myself.

"Daniel, I'm sure to get lost, you know I always do."

"Sweetpea, I will drive you to the test. I will wait for you, for however long it takes. All you need to do is calm yourself, take the test, I know you will ace it. You're smart, it's not that hard and afterward, we can go have some pie and coffee, then come home."

"Sounds like a plan?"

Test day arrives, nice dry sunny day. Daniel drives to the test site, no problems. I have my needed paperwork and identification, plus the butterflies in my stomach. I give Daniel a kiss and a hug. He says, "Go get 'em, tiger!"

I walk to the building, through the doors. There are a lot of people taking this test, it's a huge room. Someone said 137 people are testing here, just today, and they say that only about 50% will pass. "Well, that makes me feel good?" It's a 3-hour test with one 15 minute break halfway.

Two and half hours later, I'm out the door. Simply don't want to think anymore.

I get to the car, "Daniel, I am so ready to get out of here".

"How do you think it went?"

"I don't know, but I have to wait until they send the results in the mail, which they say, takes about a week."

Chapter Two

———— ∽ ————

OKLAHOMA

IT'S MID-JULY, ONLY about two and half months since Daniel and I became a team. The day is California warm. The coastal weather generally has a slight ocean breeze, very little humidity, and just the right amount of warmth with soothing, relaxing sunshine. Go to the beach, sit by the pool, play in the yard, the first thing that comes to your mind after a hard day at work.

I've just arrived home from the restaurant and can't wait to get out of this uniform, put on a swimsuit for a half hour or so, and go by the pool. I've worked up a perfect tan, the best tan I've ever had without getting burned. Just about to take off my shoes when the phone rings.

"Hello,"

" Dianah,"

"Yes, Daniel."

"I have something important to tell you."

"I'm listening."

"We are moving the company to Oklahoma."

Silence.

Then I say, "Oklahoma?" My mind is racing, trying to picture it on the map.

You're serious; nobody moves to Oklahoma." "Tell me why Oklahoma?" My mind is racing; I know where Oklahoma is on the map. I can't think of a reason why one would want to go there.

"Daniel, Oklahoma?"

"Dianah, I'm taking the company and the crews to Tulsa, Oklahoma, partnering with another company there. There's a ton of business that no one is taking care of; it'll be good for the company."

I'm still thinking to myself, Tulsa, who in their right mind moves to the middle of the country, especially Oklahoma; besides that, we haven't even talked about this. There's been no mention of moving the company anywhere.

And then I hear, " You can come if you want,"

" Excuse me! I can come if I want?"

" Well, of course, I want you to come, but I'm not going to talk you into it. I do need to go check it out."

" You do that. Will I see you this evening?"

"Of course, I haven't left yet. I may be late for dinner, though."

"I'll be here when you get home."

There goes my restful half-hour by the pool. Our conversation was a little terse, but really, leave California to go to Oklahoma. The only thing I remember hearing of Oklahoma is Okies, Bible Belt, and bad weather. If I could shut off the last 5-minute conversation, I would. Who in heaven's name moves to Oklahoma? I just can't wrap my mind around what I just heard. It makes absolutely no sense; I don't care how much money is involved. What on earth is he thinking? "Are we talking weeks, months, not years?" "Oh no!" And, I can come if I want, does he even care?

I don't want to be here without him, but why would you leave California and go to Oklahoma? I know I'm repeating myself. I just can't get beyond that point. I'll start dinner, and maybe I'll think better; I need to check on the boys. This isn't good; I know it.

Daniel and I had a lovely morning, a little love, a little coffee, another kiss. I rustled his hair, and he patted my tush. Daniel sprinkled water on me to get me out of bed; I poured a glass of water on him. He grabbed my hand, we rumbled in the bed, and nine hours later, life has flipped upside down. Come on, Daniel, I was just getting used to this. You give me morning kisses, hold me tight, we laugh and talk. I don't want to give that up; besides that, I even like you. I need to know, 'What is going on?" Do I need to go there to stay in love? Or because of love?

Daniel's back; it's dinner time. As he comes into the kitchen, I'm at the kitchen sink; he kisses me on the neck, a hug around the waist, and what's for dinner? One of his favorites is pasta and salad; I want this evening off to a good start.

Once we are all seated at dinner, He says, "What are you thinking?"

I can tell he is already on the go. The planning is in progress.

"Daniel, tell us what your plan is; I don't know what to think?"

He says, "I have to make a phone call."

In the middle of dinner, both boys look at me. I can see the questions coming forth.

"Boys, I need to hear what Daniel has to say before I can tell you anything. Right now, I'm not sure I know any more than you do."

In five minutes, Daniel is back at the table. We are waiting breathlessly to hear anything he has to say.

"Please, tell us what is going on."

He says, "I'm flying out on Wednesday, tomorrow. I'll meet with the partners, assess the business, and be back on Friday. If all goes well, the trucks, the equipment, and the crews will drive there the following week. If you decide to come along, you can fly with me tomorrow to check it out. Then if it's a go, we will all drive there in the next couple of weeks. What do you think?"

I'm in shock; I look at the boys. The boys are both staring at me. Tim says, "Do we have to go to school tomorrow?"

I say to Daniel, "Tomorrow! You're flying out tomorrow?"

"The boys can stay with my kids; it's only three days. Dianah, when we come back, we'll know what the plan is".

Daniel, "I have work."

"Call them tonight. You have a family emergency".

"Yes, Tim, you both go to school tomorrow."

I look at the boys; they look excited. If I'm even going to believe this far-fetched plan, and I have never been to Oklahoma, never considered it, what's more, it doesn't sound like where I would want to be.

" I will fly to Oklahoma tomorrow, Daniel, but I think this is crazy."

We finished dinner; I hardly remember eating or clearing the table. I must call work to let the manager know my father is very ill and I expect to be gone for three days. I'll get the suitcase ready for the boys, pack a bag for me; I must be forgetting something-

"Daniel, what's the weather like there?"

"Hot"!

"Thanks."

Daniel arranged for the boys to stay at his ex's house and called the airlines for my ticket. Morning comes before I can blink. I need to get the boys over to his kid's house first thing. Come back, pick up our bags, make sure the apartment is secure, jump in the car, and off to the airport. Must I be losing my mind? Does this make any sense?

We get on the plane, and off we go to Tulsa, Oklahoma. I feel as though I'm dreaming; it might be a nightmare. We landed in Tulsa, an easy flight, and it's now about 8 p.m, dark and busy. Into the airport we go, bright lights and everyone is rushing. We get our bags, and a couple of tall rugged-looking guys are waiting to take us to the motel; they don't smile. All these men walk faster than I do; I work to keep up; come on, guys, a little common courtesy. The flight was long, and I was struggling not to admit to myself how tired I was. I know I'm not part of the construction crew, but where are your manners? The sliding doors open from the airport lobby; I feel I have just run into a wall. The air is so hot, so humid; I'm not sure I can breathe.

We hike to their truck and are literally dropped off at the motel.

Someone will pick us up in the morning. At the moment, I have the impression of not being any more important than one of those suitcases.

Daniel says, "You don't have to go to the meeting in the morning, take your time, have some breakfast, and I'll be back after the meeting." He is operating in high gear; nothing is moving at a moderate speed or smooth. Everything is too fast; I feel misplaced; maybe I shouldn't have come.

Morning arrives, Daniel tells me he's sorry, but he needs to get going. There's a brief hug and a kiss, and he's out the door. I know he needs to focus; if only I could get my own direction, I need to get a feel for this place. I walk Daniel out to the truck, where the Oklahoma boys are waiting for him.

"Ok," I say, "I'll be here when you get back."

Daniel says, " After the meeting and contracts, we can do some of the searching, see the city. I'll let you know what went on, and you won't have to worry."

It won't make any difference if I go to the meeting. No one needs to hear my opinion. How can I give any input, I don't know what they're doing. I'll stay at the motel, talk to the staff, and find out what people think of their town.

As I walk outside, it's hot, too hot, and oh, so humid, and there are bugs. Giant bugs are crawling, and flying. I hate bugs. Appropriately called insects; that's too sophisticated for what I see. These creatures are just plain ugly and scary, there are roaches, and scorpions, and monster spiders, a few I don't know what they are. And, why am I thinking of moving here? I must be out of my mind; I believe I said that yesterday when this first came up. And still, here we are.

The men have their meeting, and it's now mid-afternoon. Daniel comes back and says, "They are working out the details."

We go to lunch and usually have a multitude of things to discuss, but not today. We are both absorbed in our thoughts.

I ask him, "How do you think it's going?"

Daniel replies It's difficult to tell at this point, but I think we'll come to a meeting of the minds. " Dianah, I know this is trying for you, but it could be so beneficial for the company."

The drive around town isn't bad but not enlightening. It's like any other city, with traffic, highways, and a lot of nondescript buildings. We see Oral Roberts University, it's a spacious campus, again everything is the same color and 1960's design, it leaves me with no opinion one way or another. An evening snack is ordered and back to the motel. There will be more meetings in the morning.

I met two families involved in this venture who are also from California, mid aged with older children and everyone is so busy we don't have time to become acquainted. If I view this as an adventure, it would mean the "ad" in adventure is for better things to come. I don't believe this qualifies. It appears the California groups are Tulsa bound.

One more meeting in the morning, we hop on the plane, and back to Orange County Airport.

We arrive back late afternoon, pick up the boys, go to the apartment, and now the plans begin to take action.

I retrieve the mail. I have passed the real estate test. I know I must place the license with a broker to make it active. If I do nothing, it will lapse into an inactive and non-usable category. And here I am moving to another state where I can't use the license and will have to start all over again.

Daniel says, "The broker at Century 21 just around the corner is flexible; having your license there part-time shouldn't be a problem."

The following day I visited the broker. I signed up as a part-time agent and ordered my business cards. I know this is a temporary solution to an unknown future. I suppose everything in life is temporary. I'll just do what I need to do right now and when tomorrow comes, take care of it then. This whole thing of getting my license and placing it with a broker, having a new career, would be a huge deal, except moving to Oklahoma sounds like it's an even bigger episode.

George, the Century 21 Broker, is a gray-haired six-foot, pleasant enough fellow, but he never did know my name; to him, I was

"Dinah," and I didn't appreciate his lack of awareness. But after the first time of correcting him, it was a moot point; let it go. I am working primarily from home and one or two days in the office. I have given a 2-week notice at the restaurant, and after the first week, the manager told me, you can leave because we have the shift covered. I shouldn't have been surprised; I thought I might have some unique friendships, we worked as a team. The manager had done all those great things for me, or was I just another tool getting his job done? It's a jab at one's ego to acknowledge that you're not that special. It all has to do with dollars, and I was leaving. I needed to accept it for what it was and move on to future times and places. Inexperience and pride have an odd hold on a person, and it takes effort to keep both in their proper perspective. With final paycheck, a smile and farewell, knowing most of whom I considered friends will never be seen again.

In about four weeks, the move to Oklahoma will be in progress. We'll get there in time for the boys to start school at the beginning of the school year and it will give me a couple of weeks to pack for the move.

Daniel said we'll take all 4 of the kids because it's still summer; and the trip out can give him some time with his two children also. He will drive the moving truck, and I will follow in the car, piece of cake? I've never taken a trip like this before, so my education continues. Once we arrive, all we have to do is find a place to live or, better stated; I need to find a home because Daniel, my dear man, will be working at his new partnership and construction company.

Oh yes, he forgot to tell me there's another flight scheduled before we drive to Tulsa.

Daniel says, "I will need to leave it up to you to get the crew's families on the plane; they don't speak English. I am getting all the equipment together to drive out there. Then I'll fly back, and we can drive all our household to Tulsa. It's all planned, don't worry about it, Dianah. I know it seems like a big project to you, but I have everything in order."

Daniel may have it all under control; But what do I have under control? My state of mind is getting through the day because tomorrow, there'll be a whole new horizon. I am closing up the apartment, semi-working at the real estate office, and asked the broker if, at a specific date, I could put my license on hold until I got back. I didn't know if I was coming back.

He said, "No problem," and I don't think he cared. My cozy little world was in turmoil, but no one else was bothered or seemed to know.

My ex was saying, "You can't take the boys out of state."

While I was exclaiming," It was alright for you to move to Utah with no notification, and if you had been somewhere else in the country, you didn't bother to tell me. So I'm on my way."

Meanwhile, I say, "Daniel, did it occur to you that I don't speak Spanish."

Daniel says, "Dianah, don't worry, everything is taken care of; you need to be there, just in case one of the families needs you."

"Just in case of what?"

I met the families, wives, girlfriends, and children at the bus depot, and they did not speak any English whatsoever, but those women still knew more about traveling than I did. They were just fine; I don't think I was of any help at all. I said "Hello" to the bus driver who was taking us to the airport; I did tell him they were all with me. He gave the nod, and we were on our way.

At the airport, we all lined up; and they knew what seats to take as we boarded the plane. Why they needed me, I still hadn't figured out. When we arrived, their husbands and boyfriends were there to pick them up and get wives, children, and girlfriends on their way. Daniel's crew is now taken care of; I am flagged down by a real estate agent, who whisks me away to see as many houses as possible before I get back on the plane tomorrow.

I saw so many houses; there was no way to keep neighborhoods and places in any assemblance of comprehension.

One of the Oklahoma boys took me back to the airport the following day, barely speaking a word.

Daniel was at the Orange County airport when I arrived. He had delivered his trucks and flew back on a different flight. Exhaustion is just a breath away for both of us.

We had lunch; I talked about houses, he talked about the move and work that was already in progress in Tulsa. I hadn't known that work had already begun. Previously pools had been started by contractors who didn't know how to build in the Tulsa soils. The Tulsa contractors weren't capable of finishing the pool construction and landscaping jobs. Daniels' crews were now there, they were more experienced, and his equipment was much better. The workers knew what was needed, and within the week, they were on the job, starting the cleanup process from the previous builders. The plan is for the clean-up to be completed when Daniel arrives, and the new construction can begin.

"Daniel, have you had a chance to think about where we will be living with four youngsters while I'm choosing and closing on a house."

"We'll just stay at a motel; it shouldn't take too long. Meanwhile, Daniel is telling me there are a whole group of vacant properties. I'm sure you'll find one that works."

Daniel, " We haven't discussed what price range you want to buy, and what kind of property you have in mind? Has anyone you know suggested certain neighborhoods in Tulsa?"

"Pick a small town outside of Tulsa; I've talked to the agent about the price and the loan amount; I have it all prearranged with the bank. As far as the house is concerned, I won't have time for repairs, so something in good condition with as large of a lot as possible, preferably acreage."

"Do you know where the other people from California are moving to?"

"I think they are planning to get something in Broken Arrow. We have a map, you can take a look, and you can see what's available in about 5 to 15 miles of Tulsa."

"Daniel, you'll need to take a look at the property before you buy?"

"Once you find the one you like, we'll drive by it and around the neighborhood in the evening. I trust your judgment once I see the house exterior, neighborhood, and lot size. I know you are not going to buy a dump." If you're happy with the inside, I will be too."

I'm overwhelmed. Can I live up to the expectations? I not only don't want to disappoint Daniel, but I also don't want to disappoint Dianah. Knowing I am capable is a small part; being afraid of making mistakes is the more significant part of the equation. I had yet to understand; most errors can be corrected. That knowledge, however, is years down the road.

The evening came to us faster than we were prepared. I'd say good night to the boys; I would tuck them in. Not because it was cold, the straightening of the blankets and pillows and a good night kiss was for love. I always felt I was falling short in that category but had never developed a plan to compensate.

The time has come to pack the truck, load the car and start the journey. Things are happening that I didn't expect. Cleaning the apartment was hard work, and then the manager said I would not get back the cleaning deposit because they had to paint. I thought the painting was the standard operating procedure. Evidently, the normal process was not to refund deposits. There's no time to argue a probable no-win, so I let it go.

My ex said, "His attorney would file an injunction against me for leaving the state. I told him his attorney could talk to my attorney. I didn't have an attorney, but I didn't think he did either. That was another wasted conversation. Just another moment of the nerves tugging, and the stomach was doing an upside-down again.

I'm working on the real estate sale that I'll give to another agent; it won't close before moving, so I have the hope of receiving 50% of the commission check after the broker takes his cut.

Daniel has a multitude of events on his list of to-dos. The crews in Tulsa were having trouble with the equipment. They hadn't cleaned the spray nozzle of the gunite hose properly for the next day's use. The nozzles were clogged with dry cement, and Daniel is giving them instructions on how to remedy the problem, but without being there, you're never sure how the job will get done. His ex-wife was making demands that were going nowhere but with a lot of shouting, but I soon found out that was normal for them.

Meanwhile, he was setting up his partner Ken on the California side to take care of business here. Ken would pick up the apartment rents from Daniel's manager, but we would pick up the one due now.

We arrive at the eight-unit apartment building with the plan of a quick in and out of picking up the rent. However, there are four not-so-friendly fellows standing in the front stoop. Maybe not as quick of an in and out as we thought. Daniel says, lock the door and don't come out no matter what. He walks over and says I understand one of you seems to be having a difficult time with this month's rent. The shorter Spanish guy gets real close and says he's not paying it, too much. Daniel steps in, now they are almost nose to nose, and Daniel says, you will pay, or you're out right now. Two of the other guys start to move closer, and Daniel says, "I wouldn't if I were you."

Everyone decided to pay their rent. Daniel backed away, came over to the truck. I unlocked the door, he climbed inside, and we were off. I said, "Daniel, really?" He told me, you just have to prove who's in charge. I don't ever try to get physical, my nose will break just like anyone else, and that is not what I want to do.

We are almost ready to go. Daniel gave his ugly brown Plymouth station wagon to his daughter, who now has a serious boyfriend. CM and Lisa are taking the long drive with us and will stay for about a month in our new house that we haven't found.

Tomorrow morning is a moving day. Daniel's driving the Ryder Moving Van, I am driving my Mercury, and the muffler is still being held by rusty desert wire. One of the four kids rides with Daniel, and the other three ride with me. Lisa spent the most time with Daniel; she wasn't keen on riding with the boys. The weather is hot, air conditioning helps, but is not always as capable as we think it should be. Someplace through New Mexico, the boys open the windows, take off their shoes and put their feet out the window. They were joking and laughing about how bad their feet smelled. Once they took off their shoes, I was breathless. I suggested they throw the socks away.

We stopped in the evening for dinner and a motel: Daniel and the boys in one room with Lisa and me in the other room. Daniel and I share a hug and a sweet kiss each evening and the following day before getting back on the road. For a brief second, there's the gaze into each other's eyes to stay closer, to embrace just a few more moments. But not now; we must get to Tulsa. After three days of hard driving, we have arrived without an incident.

There are now three boys, one girl, ages 8 to 12, in a motel with nothing to do. After a few short days, the kids are beyond bored. No amount of going to eat and watching TV in the motel will satisfy the hours. So Daniel takes all four with him to the jobs, so I can go with the real estate agent to find a house.

House hunting seems like finding a deer in the forest. The type of property Daniel would like to have is not coming forth at the right price. On the third day out to start looking again, one of the men on Daniel's crew told him about a house for sale by the owner.

When I met with the agent, I mentioned the property and suggested we drive by. She reluctantly did the drive-by at the end of the tour. I then asked her to contact the owner and work it out with him; however, she needed to, so she could potentially write the contract. The kids are still at the motel, climbing the walls, and no one wants to stay in any longer.

Daniel and I drove by the owner's home, planning to buy even before seeing the inside. A basic white three-bedroom, two-bath, two-story 1960's farmhouse on 4 acres at the right price. Country property with minimal road front appeal, just your plain Jane house in need of landscaping and paint. The owner and the realtor had made contact; the seller decided he could do better by himself. Daniel made arrangements for the contract and a loan through the company bank. We were in the farmhouse within a week. It wasn't bad, keeping in mind, it was a 1960's do-it-yourself property. The acreage backed up to the school, and the town was about 800 people. The land had not been taken care of, and there were two trees, one in front and one in back. The insurance man lived across the street, and his father, a minister with four hound dogs, lived next door.

One of the first things Daniel did was to hire a bush hog to cut the field; he felt it could be a fire hazard. I was busy setting up housekeeping and making plans for paint and shrubbery.

As we were settling in, the Baptist Minister from down the road came to visit and said he wanted to welcome us to the neighborhood. He told us that he had to buy some property next to his place to protect himself from undesirable circumstances. The Minister couldn't have just anybody moving in next door. As he said, this was only concerning someone not up to his standards.

The insurance man across the street came over once to make sure we had insurance, and his fathers' dogs barked all night long, almost every night. But this was no surprise, and Daniel said, for now, we will leave it alone. He understood better than I the attitude of our neighbors.

My real estate license was now suitable but not for Oklahoma; I needed to put my fingerprints on file if I wanted to work. The licensing bureau said fingerprinting is by the courthouse in Tulsa at the county jail. The fee is $15.00. When the process is completed, they will send it to the licensing department, which will forward it to the real estate department, and you may proceed with getting your real estate license. I will never forget going into that jail, an institution I knew nothing about in any state. I walked in the front door, went to the counter, and explained why I was there.

The uniformed policeman said, "Someone will come to lead the way and show you to the correct office." I followed another uniformed man, with each barred door slamming harder than the last as we went along the corridor. The metal of the old iron bars echoing and bouncing off the green concrete walls. I didn't see dirt on the iron bars, needing more green paint, but nothing felt clean. After about four doors, I thought I might never get out of here. The fingerprinting was easy compared to the green mile walk. Afterward, I was lead back to the counter to pay for my torture.

Dianah Oklahoma

At our home, we became acquainted with the owl who came every night for dinner; he would sit on the tree by the kitchen window and hoot until dinner was served. His favorite was hot dogs. On occasion, the Barn owl even stopped by for breakfast. The bugs here were bigger than at the airport, giant bugs. The kids had a BB Gun and a slingshot which they would use to kill spiders and scorpions outside. One morning as I looked out the front window, the entire front porch was covered with one giant spider web from side to side. I made sure everyone knew it was not my job to remove this animal's night of work. If you want out the front door, best take a broom and make sure the spider is far away.

We are almost settled in the house, but summer is just about over. The master bedroom is upstairs with a king-size window viewing the Tulsa skyline. Daniel and I could lie in bed, look out at the harvest moon as it would shine in the window, and cast the shadows of two lovers wrapped in each other's arms, forgetting about the rest of the world.

It's time for CM and Lisa to return to California and time for Tim and Toph to start school. Daniel has been working nonstop, and other than one or two drives, we haven't had much time to enjoy the countryside. The school was going better for the boys, and Toph decided to try playing the clarinet. He likes his teacher more than any other instructors I've heard him talk about. Tim is struggling with class work, and I try to help. It's difficult for a parent to watch a child struggle; you want to whisk them away and say, it doesn't matter; everything will work out eventually. So you continue with words of encouragement, hoping the little things help. If there's more I can do to help, no one told me.

Daniel is starting to tell me about things that are not kosher with the work environment. The Oklahoma partners want to seize the California partners' new cement trucks. So far, they haven't said anything about Daniel's equipment, but we think it's just a matter of time. Carey, his wife, and his son have moved everything here to Tulsa just like we did, and things are getting tense. Every evening trucks are driving down our street, and we live on a quiet dead-end road. The trucks have gun racks, and I can see rifles in them. There always seem to be two guys in any of the vehicles that go by.

Daniel had been leaving his gunite rig in the yard for the morning crews, but not now. Theft is wide open, with nothing we can do about it. Every night, he's been parking both trucks at home. The vehicles are behind the house, with the truck's side tight against the wall. Daniel then climbs out the passenger door. Each rig is under the bedroom window for watching intruders and causing difficulty for anyone to open the door and take off. The parade of pick-up truck traffic coming and doing the turn around at the street end continues all hours of the night.

I ask Daniel, "What's going on?"

He tells me, "They want to steal all the equipment." They have already taken Careys' trucks, put them in a yard with barbed wire chain link fencing, locked gates, and guard dogs.

"Daniel, this is no small thing; what are we gonna do?"

"Carey is filing a petition with the judge to get his trucks back. The trucks are registered under Carey's name, and he has the registration. There's a loan against the trucks that Carey has been paying on. The insurance is in Carey's name, and everything is up to date. We need to wait for the court date next week."

In the meantime, since I don't have any income and have always been self-sufficient, I feel I need a job. There's been no indication of what time frame we are looking at to get things settled. Daniel has been covering expenses, but I need my own paycheck. I feel naked without having any daily expenses covered. I got a job a couple of miles down the road at the Village Inn Restaurant. The kids are in school, and I'll get home right after they do.

The court date has arrived for Carey's trucks to be released to him. Carey, his son, and Daniel are there at the courthouse, and Carey presents his case. The Judge says, "The trucks are in the construction yard, under lock and key, and it looks like possession is nine-tenths of the law."

Carey says, "But I have all the proof, insurance, registration, loan payments."

Judge says, "Case closed," he slams the gavel down. "Next case."

Tempers are escalating. Daniel and Carey decide they will file liens on all the properties they worked on that are still under construction and haven't been paid, but not before they have collected monies owed from the Tulsa company for the work completed.

It was questionable whether they would be able to collect any money, mainly what was due. But the guy's both come home after cashing their checks at the bank, a sizable amount. Now that the money is collected, the traffic down our street is triple-fold. It's now time to get Carey's trucks back, that are still behind locked gates. Once the trucks are out of the construction yard, it's out of Oklahoma, or kiss the equipment goodbye. The Oklahoma boys tell the crews from California; we'll pay you more money than you're currently getting; by just working directly for us. You don't need to go through Daniel or Carey. Daniel informed the crews, you do what you want, but they are not trustworthy. You need to decide what team you're on. Some of the workers and their families made preparations to head back to

California, while others stayed.

The night came to get Carey's trucks; we are talking about millions of dollars worth of equipment; it's not something you can just leave. And Carey is still on the hook for huge loans against the trucks. Just because someone steals your vehicle doesn't mean the bank will overlook it. Forced to get Oklahoma insurance, it's hard telling what the insurance company is doing.

Daniel said, "Once we have Carey's trucks, I'll be right back to get our trucks; I will be leaving at whatever time it is and driving back to California. Keep the doors locked, don't let anyone in. I will call you when I get there. That evening we slept fitfully; the following day went much as usual until evening.

Daniel, Carey, and his son meet at Carey's house; they would need three drivers. The steaks laced with sleeping powder and heavy-duty bolt cutters are ready to go. The three are now proceeding to the yard where Carey's trucks have been taken hostage. It's about midnight. They throw the steaks in the yard, which the dogs eat, fierce-looking Rottweilers and German Shepherds, and within half an hour, the dogs are sleeping. Daniel and Carey cut a hole in the fence, climbed through and ran for the trucks. Carey has his extra set of keys for both the trucks and all his paperwork with him. The trucks start, the engines roar, and there's no waiting for the trucks to warm up. They have to get out of there right now. It may be their trucks, but they are breaking Oklahoma law in Oklahoma. All three of them know by now, if you are from anywhere else, you better be ready to move and not come back; with the might and size of the trucks, they drive as fast as they can get the Freightliners started, smashing through the gates. The gates fly open, tearing the hinges off the posts. Carey and his son are on their way to California. Daniel gets back in his truck, high tails it back to our house, hooks up the smaller truck to the gunite rig; as I watch the street for anyone coming. He gives me a hug and a kiss. Says, "Wish me well," and heads down the road as I watch him go to cross the state line.

I don't know when I'll see him again or what will happen as they cross the country in what could be a hot pursuit. The closest state line is Kansas; once out of Oklahoma, the local authorities don't have jurisdiction in the next state, and then drive non-stop to California. It takes Daniel a full day of driving to catch up with Carey. Carey made a wrong turn somewhere along the way and ended up behind Daniel. Midway they come across the crews that have decided to leave. They are now all caravaning on their way back.

Meanwhile, I'm still working at the restaurant, and the trucks are surveying our street; the kids are still in school. Carey's wife is at their house, and Carey and Daniel are driving nonstop. I haven't heard from them yet, so I have to pray everything is alright. Once he arrived and called, he said it was one of the most arduous drives he has ever made. Daniel said, "I'm going to shower, fall into bed, and sleep. I'll call again later."

Now I have to find a real estate agent to sell the house. Carey's wife is coming over every evening to see if I know any more than she knows. Which I don't think I do, but even if I did, I couldn't tell her. She was drinking way too much; even Toph, my 11-year-old son, is saying, "Tell her to bring her own beer."

It's the end of October; it's Tim's birthday. We invited some school friends and had a fun birthday party for Tim. There are only 4 or 5 kids, but I think they had a good time.

Daniel calls and says, "It's time for you to leave."

"What do you want me to do?"

"You close everything up as tight as you can, give the real estate agent the key, pack the car with as much as you can get in it, and drive to Wichita, Kansas."

"I don't know how to get there; I don't have a map. What road do I get on? What day do I leave?"

Daniel replies, "I will be arriving at the Wichita airport at 7:30 AM on Tuesday. If you leave the house at about 3 or 4 AM, you will be there in plenty of time". Drive into Tulsa; you should be able to get a map at any one of the gas stations".

"Oh Daniel, I've never driven across the country by myself and in the middle of the night".

"You will be ok, believe me. I will call you until the phones are disconnected, have everything turned off and locked up, and trust that it will all work."

I scurried about like there was no tomorrow. I couldn't let anyone know what I was doing. So I just quit my job and started closing things up.

I put nails in the garage doors, and it should be burglar-proof. I cleaned out all the food I could, had all the utilities set to turn off. I couldn't tell the boys what was going on; they might mention that they were leaving and who knows what would happen if word got back to the wrong people. I had cut ties with Carey's wife by this point, but I couldn't find a map. I went to grocery stores, gas stations, 7-11s. Nobody in Tulsa had a map of Oklahoma.

I told one person at a convenience store, "Don't you folks ever go anywhere?"

He said, "We mostly have always lived here and know where we're going."

But he said, "If you want to go to Wichita, just get on this highway, and it will take you straight to the airport. Now it's a toll road, so take some money with you and make sure you have gas because there's no place to stop along the way." He was just a nice ole country boy; I thanked him and went on my way.

My stomach hurts, and I have a headache; this cloak and dagger are not my modus operandi.

The night we are to leave, I tell the boys what we are about to do when they come home from school. They don't understand why they can't say goodbye to their friends. I have to tell them no one must know, if the wrong people find out it could cause many problems for all of us. Both the boys look at me with sorrow and say, but we wouldn't tell anyone. I wanted to cry, but I needed to be the strong one. I try to explain that it is dangerous, we don't know what could happen.

ME AND DANIEL

"Boys, we must leave."

Somehow all the things that haven't been packed will get back to us in California. Daniel will try to find us a place in Tustin in the same school district for the boys to go to school where they know the kids. Right now, we are packing up the car with everything we can.

Toph has a clarinet that needs to go back to the school here in the Tulsa area. I didn't want to send the clarinet back for fear they would know where we were. Later, Daniel explained to me it didn't matter anymore, that part of the puzzle was behind us. The boys and I will try to get some sleep and then leave early in the morning before the sun comes up to meet Daniel at the Wichita airport.

"I'm sorry, guys, but there's no other way."

At 2 AM, I am up, doing the very last-minute things, putting lunch and snacks in the car. Pillows and blankets, it's cold out. The trunk is overloaded, the Merc looks like a lowrider. I get the kids up, tell them it's time. There's stuff to eat in the car, and you can go back to sleep. I want you both to sit in the back seat and try to sleep.

I get on the highway and pray to God I'm headed in the right direction; it's pitch black out, no stars. We're in the country, with no lights and very few signs of any kind. And so I drive, the farther I drive the more I worry, and see nothing but the white line on the road.

After a while, Toph says," Mom, do you think we are going the right way."

I tell him, "I certainly hope so."

It's now about 5 AM, still dark. We've crossed the Kansas state line; I stop for the toll booth, pay, and then miss my exit. Fortunately, I did have the presence of mind to drive until I could turn and get back going north. I get to the toll booth again; the same guy is there to retake more money again.

It's now just after 5 AM. He says, "Mam, are you lost?"

I said, "OH no, I just like touring toll roads in the wee hours of the morning."

Then remembering my manners, and it's not his fault I don't know where I'm going, I tell him I need to go to the airport.

"The airport, Mam, is only about 5 miles away, just straight down this road, you can't miss it".

He doesn't know how easily I can get lost. We will be there early if his directions are accurate. I don't know how big the airport is or how much traffic there could be.

We get to the Wichita airport; I think it's the airport. As far as I know there is only one airport in Wichita; I had never considered there might be more than one. It doesn't look like any airport I've ever seen. There's just one little building; the parking lot is small. There is no activity, and the building is closed; two cars are in the parking lot.

"What the hell is this!" Frustration is at an all-time high. It's cold; I'm tired, the kids are hungry. Give me a break. Oh Daniel, how could you do this to me? I'm too tired to drive around, and I don't know where I am. I must be at the airport; otherwise, I don't know what I'm going to do.

About 10 minutes later, I see a janitor open the door. Alright, at least I can get the kids inside out of the cold. The boys and I walk to the building. I look for a reader board outside, none, and there's no board inside to tell you what flights are coming or going. There's no attendant, just the janitor. I try to find anyone who might know something. Finally, I asked the janitor about flights while he started sweeping the floor.

"Do you have any idea when a flight will arrive?"

He says, "Oh yeah, there are generally flights that start coming in around seven or 7:30; they'll be along shortly, you'll see". He says, "While you're waiting, there is a coffee machine and hot chocolate around the corner ." "You just relax. The planes will get here sooner or later".

We waited a few minutes; Daniel was supposed to arrive at 7 AM, no Daniel. It's now about 7:30, one plane arrives, no Daniel. The boys and I decide we'll get something hot to drink. It's getting close to 8:30.

Toph says, "Daniel's not coming" Tim just looks sad.

I may be a tad bit concerned, I think it's a long drive back, but I can't stay in Wichita. A few minutes later, a plane arrives, people are getting off and coming through the lobby. I don't see Daniel. My heart does a leap; there he is. Oh my gosh, I shouldn't have doubted him. We all hurry to him, lots of hugs, oh but he feels good.

I ask, "Do you want coffee; it's awful.

Daniel apologizes for being so late, he had a touchdown in Denver, and it started snowing, which delayed the plane from taking off. They had to de-ice the runway and the airplane. He had no way of calling, no phones on the plane, and at that time, Witchata was closed. He was waiting in Denver, and we were waiting in Wichita with no way to let each other know. I think about the people who waited for each other, sometimes years with no way of knowing. But we're together now, and new adventures are on the horizon.

Daniel says, "I will tell you everything as we drive, but first, we all need breakfast."

We jump in the car, and Daniel drives; I'm so glad he's driving; I was so frazzled if he hadn't made it to the airport when he did; I don't honestly know how strong I could have been to drive the boys and me anywhere?

Breakfast was a welcome relief; whether it was good or not, we relaxed for a bit, fueled the car, and the drive continued.

I asked, "Where are we going? I know that California is west, and we are driving north, the sign said so".

"You haven't seen your parents in a long time, and I've never met them. It's just a short ride up the road."

Now I know what a short ride up the road is, driving from Wichita to central Wisconsin is not a mere jaunt up the road. However, Daniel has a plan and a reason. As we drove to Wisconsin, Daniel brought cassette tapes, Carley Simone and Charlie Rich, for the trip. Just two tapes, which we listened to over and over. Toph told me later; he didn't want to hear that music ever again. Along the way, we taught the boys how to read maps, road signs and appreciate the countryside in the cold of winter.

Daniel's been doing all the driving, "He says we need to call your folks and let them know we are stopping by."

While I say, "I think it's best just to let it be a surprise; my mother will get all flustered and want to bake and cook and expect us to stay a long time. If we just knock on the door, say we are going to be here for just a couple of days, it will be easier."

I can tell Daniel doesn't think that's the best plan, but it's my folks, so he goes along with it. The farther north we go, the colder it gets. The snow is getting higher, and we are all feeling a little weary at this point. From Kansas to Central Wisconsin, there isn't much to see, especially in the winter. It just looks cold.

We finally arrived at my parents' house, and they hadn't seen the boys for a long time.

We climb out of the car, stretch a bit; I knock on the door. My brother Frank comes to the door; at first, he doesn't recognize me until I say, "Hi Frank, is everyone home?"

"Oh, Yeah! Dianah, come on in."

We all entered the house. I introduce Daniel, of course, everyone is surprised to see us. They had no idea what we had been doing or that we had ventured in their direction. We stayed for a couple of hours, and Mom had to make dinner because this is what my mother does.

Then we said, "We have got to get a room for the night, and we needed to go to the next town because there was no place in Omro". Driving the highway to Oshkosh was a familiar feeling; it was cold and wet, the motel was frosty. I had always wondered why people choose to live in this part of the world. We were tired and slept through the night. The following day we spent at my parent's house, talking and thanked Mom for more food. When Dad came home from work, dinner was ready, and I told everybody we would be leaving mid-day tomorrow. They all said, you can't go already, but we just had to let them know that the need to return was imminent. The boys needed to get back to school, so it went well though it was a short visit. As could be expected, Mom was sad we were leaving so soon, but Daniel assured her the next time would be longer. We said our goodbyes to Dad that night. He left early in the morning for work and said our farewells to the rest of the family after breakfast the following day.

My mother and dad never did have a handle on what I was doing, whether it was today or ten years ago. They would just shake their heads with some sorrow and say, "GoodBye."

We are back on the road. It's November, lots of snow as we drive through the wide-open plains. Thankfully, Daniel was driving at one point in Minnesota; we followed the snow plow on this main highway for miles. The snow banks were up above the car; all you could see was white. The road was icy, and the plow moved slowly. It was a long afternoon with only the white flurry of the snow flying through the air from the truck in front of us and the gray sky. We finally made it into California on Thanksgiving Day. The plan is to have a nice Thanksgiving Dinner, but one must find a serving restaurant. Most of the commercial businesses are closed, including restaurants. We all dress a little special; Daniel even puts on a suit.

Now, remember, we are driving the Merc that made the fateful trip out to the desert over the rocks. The muffler fell off in the desert, and with luck, it was wired in place and would be taken care of later. Later is on the way to Thanksgiving Dinner, we are leaving the motel, driving down the street, and there's scraping on the roadway.

I worriedly said, "Daniel, we have lost part of the car."

Daniel pulled over under a gas station canopy and had to get under the car in his suit. Fortunately, we had a blanket in the trunk for the dirty pavement; he wired the muffler back up one more time. Only his hands were dirty when he had finished. The muffler would be okay once again. The four of us have Thanksgiving Dinner at the only place we can find in this town in Northern California. It isn't anything to write home about, but it filled the void.

We ate, left, and drove until we found another motel for the evening. At least we were heading south; I was looking forward to getting out of the cold. The following day we are south of San Francisco on a country tree-lined road with small farms and hills when the muffler comes loose again. He pulled over on the side of the road, and Daniel is looking for something to fix or repair until we get home. There's still nothing in the car that will do the trick. I was looking around when I spotted the farmer's mailbox, wired to a post.

I told Daniel, "I'll go get that wire."

Daniel said, "No, that's how he holds up his mailbox."

"Daniel, farmers always have lots of wire and leftover stuff, he may not be happy, but right now, we need it more than he does, and anyway, he's not home. After all, we're not destroying his mailbox or stealing it, just borrowing a piece of wire". So I went and got the wire and he fixed the muffler one more time.

Daniel had rented us a condo; I previously told him I wanted a place in Tustin. Then boys could go back to the same school they had when I sold the house in Tustin. I know he did his best. He rented a nice condo in Tustin, but he just couldn't get it in the same school district. I tried to fudge the system and drive the boys to school, but it was a no-go. They would have to start at another school.

We are now into December; we have the condo and the belongings that were in the car. Two Pillows, two blankets, two sleeping bags, a 13 inch TV, our clothes, and toiletries. The new place has no furniture, not even a refrigerator. We bought an ice chest and would stand at the counter or sit on the floor to eat meals. Daniel and I shared a pillow and a sleeping bag, while the boys did likewise.

Daniel had made a deal with the Oklahoma boys to pick up our furniture, load it in the truck and drive it to California. It would be a vacation for them; they only have to pay for their room and board along the way.

All I have to do is fly back to Tulsa, pack up the furniture, and get it in the truck. The plans are made. The boys are in school, Daniel will watch over them, and I will be gone for about five days. I get tired just thinking about it, not on my wish list of to-dos. Daniel can't go back

74   ME AND DANIEL

because the Oklahoma Partners might be looking for him. So Tulsa, here I come one more time.

Once again, I am off to the airport. Beforehand, I talk with Tim and Toph about minding Daniel; whatever he says goes. Okay! I will be back in 5 days; then we can have beds and television, your bikes, and all your stuff.

Daniel gives me a long kiss and a tight hug; he says, be careful. The guys will pick you up at the airport and get you whatever you need.

The flight is not any shorter than it was before, and why would it be. Daniel has told me about the two guys that will drive me to the airport and as I arrive at the airport; I don't trust them, but I have no choice. They drive me to the house; I tell them I am going to need some boxes. I get the yea, ok, and they are gone. I go into the house; it's dark, it's spooky.

Our bedroom is upstairs, no I don't want to sleep up there. If someone is going to come walking in; I want to know it right now. I walk through all the rooms making a mental note of what must be packed and ensuring no unwanted surprises. Oh yes, the garage; I walk out into the garage, turn on the light. Something doesn't look right. Then I see it. All the tools, except the old stuff, are gone. The kids' new bikes and the tennis rackets, half the garden tools. The only things left are the old items that are not of much use. I can see the door I nailed shut, not good enough; even though I bolted it, I just didn't fix it strong enough.

I better go back through the house again; I need to make sure everything in the place is still there. Thinking to myself, there are four hound dogs next door, our insurance agent across the street, and no one heard anything? I'll have to take care of it tomorrow. I started packing dresser drawers, filling the washing machine and dryer with items. By 10 PM, I am out of steam; I get a pillow and blanket to sleep on the couch. The following day, 5 AM, I'm up; there's no coffee and not much food, just some canned things. By 7 AM, there should be a convenience store open; it's about six blocks; I'll get some coffee and a bite of something. I need to find out where the police station is. The guy at the 7-11 tells me the Police Station is just about five blocks over that way, and there should be someone there by 8 o'clock. I drink my coffee; it's hot; that's about all I can say for it. I buy some food for the rest of the day and ask him if he has any spare boxes I could use for moving. He gets me a couple, an okay guy, just not too personable. I thank him, take my food, put it in the boxes, and hike over to the sheriffs' office. It's frosty and cold outside, no sidewalks and I'm carrying moving boxes. So by the time I get to the sheriff's office, I am not in the best frame of mind.

The County sheriff says, "Don't know how that could have happened, Mam, we hardly have any crime in this town. Might've been kids since your property backs up to the school."

I said, "I need to file a report."

"You sure?"

"Yes, I'm sure. How else will I file a claim with my insurance company?"

"Yes, Mam, here's the form. I'll make a burglary report, and you can pick it up tomorrow."

"Aren't you going to come out to the house?"

"No, Mam, I know where your house is."

"Do you have a phone I can use?"

He says, "Will it be long-distance?"

I try to stifle my sarcasm as I say, "Yes, I'll make it a collect call."

I call Daniel, tell him the story, and that the guys need to bring me some boxes.

"Babe, I'm sorry for all this." " Are you okay?"

"I'm okay, I love you, and I'm looking forward to coming home. I'll call you again tomorrow unless something else comes up. I'll be fine".

Walking back to the house, I notice the frost is melting, and there aren't any other stores. So unless the boys show up with the boxes, I will have to be very creative in my packing maneuvers. After I've been packing most of the day, I decided it was time for a break. The insurance

ME AND DANIEL

agent is across the street, and I haven't talked with him yet. So I'll do that.

He told me he hadn't heard anything and was very surprised. But as soon as I got the police report, he would file the claim.

" Okay, I tell him I don't have a phone, so he'll need to come across the street if anything is needed."

He's a neighbor and our insurance agent, but doesn't volunteer the use of his phone. So I simply walk back to the house.

Do more packing and organizing? Finally, at about 6 PM, the Oklahoma boys show up with half a dozen boxes. I wonder, have these guys never moved?

I tell them I will need more boxes.

The reply is, "This is all we could find."

I say to myself; I will just have to work this out, somehow.

Morning comes, I'll walk back to the 7-11, get some coffee, and over to the sheriff's office. He has the report; I ask him if there's anything else I need to do? Or that he needs to know?

" Nope, that's about all we can do and the likelihood of finding any of your missing items is very unlikely."

I didn't expect much, but he was going to do as little as he possibly could. I asked myself if the local sheriff knew the partnership breakup between the California guys and the Tulsa guys. I'll never know.

Back to the house, and more packing. It's about 10:30 AM, and the sky is getting dark, not like rain or snow. The sky looks brown, and it doesn't feel right outside. I don't have a radio, but I can tell there's some kind of storm brewing. Within an hour, there's a wind starting to blow; I don't know if it's a tornado or a sand storm, but it's not pretty. I haven't seen any of the neighbors; generally, neighbors check on each other in times of need. They know more about the weather here, so it's not a big deal. Either way, I remembered we have a storm shelter with this property. It is over on the side of the property out by the field, and the opening is like an old cellar door; you pull it open from just above the ground. The entry is cumbersome, and the door is heavy. It wants to stick; fortunately, it wasn't locked. I was almost afraid to open it, not knowing what I might find. I give a heave with all the strength I had; it slams open to the other side. The wind is blowing harder, almost blowing the door off its hinges. I look down on the steps; it's dark, I don't have a flashlight and it's hard to see. Then oh my gosh, I understand why I can't see anything. It's covered, every square inch, with crickets, black crawling hundreds and hundreds of them. We all know how I feel about creepy crawlers. It is just disgusting. The storm can come and take me; there is no way I'm going down there.

I get the door, slam it shut, and run back to the house. Now, the wind is howling, tree branches are coming down, the sky is black, and the sand is blowing. I lock everything up in the house; the electricity is out. I shove towels under the door and on the window sills. Thinking to myself, I have one day left to pack, which is a moot point if the storm blows me away. But if it doesn't, everything still needs to be done. Everything that I can do regarding the storm is complete. So I go back to packing; if the windows blow out or the roof comes off, I guess I'll address it at that time.

By about 4 PM, the storm had died down, but now it's cold. The house has one of those old oil furnaces in the floor with an iron grate. I'm trying to light it, which I've never done before. After about a half-hour of struggling with it, I give up. But it is freezing.

Telling myself, "Keep packing, stay busy; you won't be so cold." It is now 10 PM. The cookstove is gas; I light the oven, leave the door open, get a pillow and as many blankets that I haven't packed, set myself up on the floor in front of the oven, and say a prayer. I'm well aware of all of the dangers of a gas oven and not to use the oven for heat, but I'm tired, I'm cold, I'm hungry, so I'll just lay down and sleep for a while.

I woke up about 4 AM; surprised; I'm still alive. I guess that means I need to finish the packing job. Daniel has been able to call the real estate agent who must come by and get the keys. He doesn't spend much time; I talk to him about a lockbox and sign in front and he leaves.

Daniel called a neighbor down the street; how he found her number

I don't know. I didn't ask, but she came over and said he was on the phone and needed to talk with me.

I rushed over to her house, "Daniel, Hi,"

"Babe, are you okay? I've been so worried."

"I'm okay, the storm has blown over, and the packing will be complete when they get here."

Daniel says, "The guys will be there today with a Ryder Truck; they'll load everything you tell them to take. Then you can close the house, and they will take you to the airport."

"I'll get it all done; I miss you. Are the kids okay?

"The boys are fine and miss you.

"I'll see you at the airport tonight, Daniel; I love you."

The Oklahoma boys show up with the truck; within 3 hours, they have everything loaded and ready to go to California. I convince them to take the big black bar that I'm still dragging around, and with some hesitation, they agree. They tell me they can't get the bar or the picnic bench in the truck. If they had packed better, it would have easily fit, but today I didn't care. I found out later Daniel wanted the picnic table. I tell them they can come back later and get what's left; there's nothing left in the house to take.

One of them takes the Ryder truck; I get in the pickup truck with the other guy. Now I'm off to the airport, probably the only time I haven't had a shower, and I didn't care what my hair looked like; all I know is I'm going home to collapse.

Once I arrive, Daniels is waiting at the airport, and I think I fall into his arms, he kisses me, I tell him I'm a mess, and he hugs me so tight, he almost carries me to the car. We get to the condo; there's still no furniture; everything is in the truck. I hug the boys, take a quick shower and curl up with a pillow. My day is done. Our refrigerator is still an ice chest, a styrofoam ice chest and every day Daniel goes out and buys ice. The boys are so bored after school, they've taken to walking on top of the concrete block wall fence; it's about a 5 to a 6-foot high wall; I don't know how they got up there, but the neighbors aren't happy about it. I'm sure the neighbors wonder about all the ice Daniel was coming home with daily and no furniture delivery. We always have the windows covered, so we could keep roving eyes from seeing that we had no furniture.

We are waiting patiently for the Ryder truck to arrive; there's no way to contact them because they are on the road. The boys are going to school; Daniels is selling his gunite truck to a fellow he used to work with at the old California company.

Trevor, originally from England, liked to eat raw onions, like the rest of us would eat apples. The tears would stream down his face, but he thought it was great. Trevor and Daniel had been friends, so selling the equipment to him was more straightforward than an unknown company.

I've been working at the real estate office for about two months now, with no furniture, not even a refrigerator. We have been living like gypsies. I say to myself; it could be worse. Yes, it could be worse, but then, on the other hand, it could be better. And so, it is what is, and life will go on.

I think we almost got used to sleeping on the floor. It took the guys with our furniture six weeks to arrive. They decided to take their girl-friends and vacation along the way. I guess I was just happy they finally showed up at all. Daniel set the record straight; the Tulsa boys wanted more money because it took them longer to deliver the furniture; that was not going to happen. The truck was costing us more because they took their sweet-natured time. It has never ceased to amaze me how some people will always ask for more even when it's evident that what-ever they are asking for is not due to them. Once the furniture is un-loaded, Daniel gives them the amount of pay they are due, says thank you and have a safe drive back.

We are all trying to catch our breath from the Oklahoma roller coaster. The house back there hasn't sold yet, so my first commission check makes the mortgage payment.

Daniels, battling with the finance company that has the gunite rig loan, he sold to Trevor. They say Trevor can't assume the loan, and Daniel tells them they have already accepted payment without recourse written on the checks.

Daniel says, "Have your attorney call me. Once payment is taken three times, a precedent is set."

The attorney does call, and after a short explanation, the company will send documentation declaring Trevor as the new owner. Trevor already registered the truck in his name anyway. Daniel won that battle.

Finally, the house in Oklahoma sold, we didn't make any money on it, but we didn't lose. The paint chipped on the house, and I thought we would be there for a while at one point. So I scraped the paint, getting it ready for a fresh, colorful coat of paint, which didn't happen. I only made the house appear in worse disrepair than before the purchase. The broken garage door was never repaired, the inside needed to be in better condition, but there was no preparation for a sale that could happen. All in all, we did pretty well, considering the circumstances.

The boys were sad about their new bikes; I said we would get new ones soon to replace the stolen ones. Daniel was missing tools, and he had wanted his picnic bench. These were replaceable items, and we were out of the turmoil. Communication from Oklahoma was now totally silent.

The condo was nice enough, better than an apartment, but not our kind of place. It was sterile. Everything is the same color, painted tan, inside and out. It's basic living, there is not an ounce of creativity in the entire complex, and it's not a place to provide for two growing boys. We are all aware this will be short-lived.

Chapter Three

DANIEL, AN IMMIGRANT'S SON

THE YEAR WAS 1933, the depression was still ongoing, and World War II was getting into full swing. Daniel Fileteo Anthony DiSandro was born in Providence, Rhode Island. His father, Daniel Anthony DiSandro, an Italian immigrant, and young Daniels's Mother is Anna Gretchner, of Lithuanian heritage.

The family line from Daniel's paternal Grandmother has an aristocratic background, believing the ancestral tree dates back to the painting of the Sistine Chapel.

Daniel's life starts in a small two-story house of genuine wood construction with wooden pegs and miter joints, no nails or screws. In the basement is where Granddad keeps all the provolone, prosciutto, pepperoni, and garlic hanging from the rafters. Grapes for crushing, and the bottling of wine, and once a year at harvest time, the wine-making begins. Grandad even has the equipment and the vat where we stomped the grapes and then pressed for the barrels. Depending on how many neighbors came to visit, the plan was to always have enough wine for the year. The next-door neighbor

Neighbor and Grandparents, where should the fence line be

constantly argues whether the fence line is one or two inches too far over; no one ever determined which direction the fence should go. But when they forgot about the property line, a glass of wine would make the day go smoother. And then, every so often, someone starts the discussion all over again.

It's an Italian neighborhood, and Daniels' family is from Naples, Italy, and Nice, France, where his father spent part of his childhood.

1933 is the beginning of World War II in Europe, and still, the depression is lingering. Most of us think of the depression as a one-year event happening in 1929. The residual effects of this catastrophic era lasted much longer than a year. The sacrifices were numerous, and the burdens were never-ending. If one is going to relate to another person, history is essential. Whether we think so or not, world events play a large part in developing our lives.

The highlights during the year 1933 included:
President Franklin Rosevelt announced leaving the Gold Standard,
Heinrich Himmler becomes Police Commander of Germany,
Nazi Germany begins persecuting the Jews,
The first airplane flight over Mt Everest;
The Us Dirigible Akron crashes off the coast of NJ, 73 die
Prohibition ends,
The University Bridge in Seattle opens for traffic.
One of the top songs was the Easter Parade by Irving Berlin.
The hot new toys for 1933 were the erector set, Radio Flyer wagon, the "Liberty Coaster,"
Crayola Crayons, Raggedy Ann, and Chinese Checkers,

Bread was $.07
Milk was $.41/gal
Eggs were $.52/doz.
Car was $550.
Gas was $.18/gal
House was $5,759
Stamps $.03/ea
Avg income$1,409/yr
Dow avg 100

Daniel's maternal Grandfather, Grandmother, four aunts, and uncles lived on the third floor in a multi-story tenement with a dumb waiter. He was a roofer for the tall buildings in Providence. Grandpa was always happy to see Daniel; they would go to the Jewish bakery and get fresh bread with the burnt cinders on the bottom.

Grandpa would say, "Sonny, be careful. You don't want to break a tooth on the cinders."

Daniel and his cousin Raymond visited the park with their mothers and climbed on the statue of a horse as though it were a real thing. They could then stop at the ice cream store for a colossal nickel cone of genuine ice cream.

A large percentage of multi-generational families lived together in modest households. The DiSandro's were no exception, Grandparents, parents, and babies surrounded by aunts, uncles, and cousins. Like most Italian families, they loved good food, good company; and the door was always open for the neighbors or anyone passing by. All the family listened to Italian opera on the radio and spent much of their time in the kitchen. The women made pasta dishes of every shape and size; there would be loaves of garlic bread, sausages, cheeses, olives, salads, and wine. Whatever the DiSandro's had available was there for sharing. And then there were times of only olive oil, wine vinegar, and bread, which would be the only meal for the day.

Daniel's life began in Providence down the street from Federal Hill, the Italian district. Businesses paid for protection to keep their families and stores safe; it's just the way it was.

His father worked for the famous Biltmore Hotel as one of the Master Chefs. The Biltmore was world-famous and constructed in 1922; the banquet room could seat 1000 patrons. There were 20 chefs with high hats, white gloves, an unsurpassed opulence in its day.

As a chef, his father was well-liked and could use the golf course, go on extravagant hunts with the members of the Agawam Hunt club, where he also worked. He could bring home the extra food from the large parties, like demitasse sandwiches and beautiful desserts. Daniel's father was able to associate with the area's upper crust and partake in the elite world. During the depression, the wealthy were still very rich, and only the poor became poorer.

There was a rumor that Daniels' Dad carried a violin case when the need arose. It was a time when protection became a part of life. A lot depended on who your associates were. Because his dad was connected to the right people, he had expensive camera equipment with his private darkroom. He had golf clubs and riding clothes for the hunt, yet the depression was still here, and at times food in the home was still scarce.

When Franklin Roosevelt's son married, the reception was at the Biltmore, and Daniel's father was one of the honored chefs for the myriad of festivities. The kitchen had a chef for every item: soup, horderves, salad, pastry, not to mention the main courses. It was one of the most prestigious affairs of its time.

When Daniel was five, he was crossing the street and hit by a car. The driver stopped to help, but Daniel was so scared he ran around the corner and up the staircase onto the roof. His parents are frantically calling for him, searching the neighborhood. They finally found him on the roof-top, wrapped him in a blanket, and rushed to the hospital. He had a few scratches and bumps, but he would be okay. For Daniel, being frightened of the trouble he could be in, is worse than being hit by a car. Daniel's discipline and punishment were to kneel on sprinkled rice on the floor facing the corner, sometimes for hours. He often said that if you think as a punishment, it doesn't sound all that bad; give it a try without moving because if you shift, the time frame will start all over again.

Times were harsh, and the disciplines were strict. As a family, they had love, but the need for strength to fight all odds was above and beyond. To have that strength, you had to be stubborn, and sometimes people were illogical in family behaviors. It was a time of war, poverty, and crime. Mother Nature also put her two cents in, and it was when a hurricane of massive proportions swept the fishing vessels and some of the cargo ships into downtown Boston and Providence. Many homes had the first floor underwater; you could still find the water lines decades later on many homes. In the winter, snowbanks were up to the second floor; and most neighbors worked to rescue each other out of the winter cold.

Daniel watched as one fellow shot another as he was on his way to school. The guy with the gun just walked away like nothing happened.

The only person he felt he could tell was his Grandfather, who said, "Sony, I'm glad you came to me. What you saw is something we

Providence RI
Winter 1938

will keep between the two of us." "Nobody else needs to know, and we don't want to cause any trouble, Ok."

It was never to be mentioned again.

Grandpa and Sony were the best of friends, and joining Grandpa in the basement is the ultimate for Daniel. The senior DiSandro had the grapes shipped in so he could make the wine. Soaking his cigars in the wine was one of the Grandpas' favorites. He and Sony would be down there, and he would say, "Sony want some provolone or salami, and Grandpa would cut off a hunk. They would sit together in the basement and have a treat while no one was looking.

At this age, Daniel was the spittin image of Denis, the menace. He was small in stature, had wispy light blonde hair, and was always mischievous. If there were a pie in the window, this young lad would help himself. He loved butter; a quarter pound of stick butter separately wrapped in waxed paper is like candy to the young lad. He would take one from the icebox, run to the back yard, climb the grapevine trellis and sit up there enjoying the butter.

The Sunday meal is an all-day affair starting precisely at noon after Mass. All the families attend the five to seven-course individual servings accompanied by wine and demitasse coffees for all. Daniel and his cousin Raymond are under the table during one of the Sunday meals, tickling the lady's ankles. When Daniels' Dad chased them from under the table, they headed to the basement and thought they would try one of Grandpa's stogies, the wine-soaked cigars. The boys poured a little wine from the barrel like

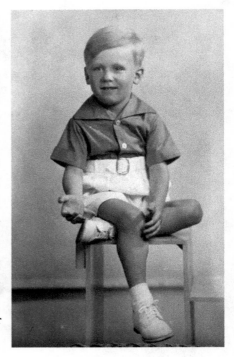

Daniel or Denis the menace

Grandpa would do and acted out the scene of being the men of the household. When the family found them, it was off to the doctor. Between the stogies and the wine, they were as sick as they could be.

For most second-generation Italian and American children who grew up in the late '30s and '40s, there was a definite distinction between them and us. We were Italians and everybody else, the Irish, Polish, Germans, they were Americans. Americans ate peanut butter on mushy bread. We knew the milkman, egg man, bread man, the fresh veggies purchased daily, the butcher, and all the Americans went to the A&P. We were different.

Our family life was different; everyone in our household had wine with dinner, listened to opera on the radio, and thanked God for what we had.

At age 7, his greatest desire was a bicycle. The family found a bike that required numerous repairs, but when Dad and Grandpa had finished, the wheels were straight new spokes, the handlebars were usable, a new seat, and little paint, they even found a horn to put on the handlebars. Daniel was in heaven and ready to ride. He didn't have the bike very long when he rode too far into the Irish neighborhood, only 6 or 7 blocks. The fellows there saw him coming; they were bigger and older. They also

Daniels first bike

liked this spiffy bike. Hey, kid, let us take a ride. Daniel said "no way" and tried to ride away. But they were faster, stronger, and mean. Just taking the bike wasn't enough; a beating went with it. When he got home, they rushed him to the hospital, where he stayed for 2 or 3 days. After coming home, the cousins that lived behind him came over.

They said, "Can you go outside now?"

The Parents are working, and the Grandparents are home, but boys can always find a way to do what's on their minds. Daniel and his cousins went back to the neighborhood, found the bike and the other kids. Now the bike was back, and the cousins evened the score. But Daniel didn't ride back into that neighborhood again.

The Catholic school days were not rewarding; the Irish Nuns had their way of instructing. Many days he would come home with bruised, scraped knuckles. Being left-handed was not acceptable; the hardwood ruler wood came crashing down until the right hand would be used. Having to stay after school because the penmanship was illegible, and I frequently disrupted the class by using my left hand. The family said, "Pay attention to the teacher, stay out of trouble, the teachers know best.

Rena, Dad's sister, John Massaro, and Grandma DiSandro made uniforms for the marines in their tailor shop. The FBI came to visit John and Rena, telling them there is no threat, but they were under surveillance during that time. As Italian immigrants, they couldn't be out after 10 PM. John and Rena weren't citizens yet but were working for the US government. The FBI never investigated father because he worked in the shipyards for the military and was a citizen. The army draft cards had arrived. Dad wanted to remain a chef, and the military gave him a choice, build ships here in Providence or go active in the army.

I would look out the window from the second floor of our home. I saw the neighborhood store opened with a new family from Naples; they looked like friendly people. The family had visitors from the Hill; this big black car drove up in front of their store, and men in suits went into the store. Unfortunately, they had decided not to pay for protection. About a week later, the store exploded and burned; the living quarters were upstairs, the family had been sleeping, there was no escape. Police said it must have been a gas line. Daniel heard his Dad and Grandad talking; Grandad said, "This was not an accident." That's when Dad said it's time to move.

Times were not getting any easier; now, into World War II, there's gas rationing and required stamps to purchase staples, like sugar, tires; many of the daily items taken for granted were no longer readily available. It was 1942. The family pooled all their resources. There wasn't much money, but the family accumulated stamps and whatever they could sell. Dad managed to get extra gas vouchers from some of the people he worked with, calling in all favors owed. They were making preparations to make the big move. The family includes Grandparents, Daniel's parents, his Aunt, and Uncle with two cousins. They needed something large enough for everyone to cross the country. Dad found a hearse, a 1937 Plymouth. More favors called in made it possible to get a couple of extra tires roped on the top of the hearse along with suitcases and boxes of only the needed items. There was no room for a bicycle or golf clubs or camera equipment. The sewing machine was loaded for income once they arrived in California, the place of promise, where the sun always shines, and everyone has a life of plenty. Each of the adults had a place to sit in the hearse. Daniel got the jump seat for the extra passenger; he weighed the least, and it was the only spot left in the auto. The men loaded the back of the hearse with belongings from the three families, roping items to the top and the trunk.

Selling the houses was not easy, and much of the furnishings were given away; very few people had money, most were barely getting by. It is April 1, 1943. The family is ready to leave on the long 3500 mile trip along route 66. As they traveled, there were still signs of the dust storm of 1935 that had never recovered. The road was rough, and with the car being so loaded and nine passengers, it was slow going. We had a flat tire along the way, didn't stop at restaurants, but had to continuously check the load, plus let everyone get a needed stretch from their cramped quarters. Twenty-four days later, on Easter Sunday, April 25, Daniel's birthday, we arrived in California.

Chapter Four

———∞———

THE DISANDRO'S IN
CALIFORNIA 1943

NINE OF US arrive in San Gabriel, California, in our 1937 Plymouth hearse with all our worldly possessions either packed inside or roped on top of the car. The first place we stopped was the Rio Hondo Motel on the river. It's Easter Sunday, my 10th birthday. A new life begins.

Relatives who lived in Paramount City; were the first ones we wanted to visit and ask for a bit of assistance; they had orange groves and a fancy lifestyle that didn't include us.

After a couple of weeks in a motel, we found a house in Monterey Park and houses almost next door for the family. I have enrolled in Catholic school once again, and Dad went to work at the Biltmore Hotel in Los Angeles.

By age 14, I was driving Dad's pride and joy, the LaSalle. Dad's pristine Lasalle was a classic auto, long and sleek with all the latest refinements of its time. I found it necessary to sit on a phone book to see over the dashboard. We lived next to the police station, and parking was right next to it. It was a bright sunny California day; I was parking the LaSalle, my foot slipped off the brake and hit the foot feed. Before I knew what happened, I was through the wall and in the police station; I had even moved the Chief's desk to the far wall. I was stunned and did the first thing that came to mind. I leaped from the car; now, I was in real trouble. Hurrying behind the police station to the next store, I climbed the roof, and there I hid all day. I could hear them calling me. No way was I going to face this disaster. Late that evening, I gave in and came down. The police chief wasn't mad, and all my Dad said, you know what's needed now.

We had to rebuild the wall, everyone knew it was an accident, but it seemed I was always in hot water for something. I polished the scratches out of Dad's car the best I could.

When it was time for high school, I told my parents no more catholic school. They weren't pleased, but I made it pretty clear I would not go there again. Public school was where I spent the next three and half years. I had completed all the necessary mandatory classes in three years, but the school insisted I take some electives. So I signed up for study hall, photography, and gym. Once again, Dad wasn't pleased, but that didn't seem to be anything new.

I had a great coach in gym class, Coach Howard Hunt. He wasn't easy on us; he was fair, liked us, and did his job. I could do the iron cross in gym class and climb the rope 20 feet in the allotted few seconds given. A fun class until I slipped. Fell on my back and was out of the course for the season. The friendships made in high school became my lifelong buddies. We worked, played, and fought; we were always there for each other. Bud, my best friend, and I got into a tiff; we were rolling around in the grass, got ourselves a little bloody, and then Coach Hunt saw us. He had us running five laps around the track, and then we had to go to the principal's office.

Principle Vincent Peale and I were on a first-name basis. I said, "Hi, Vince." Well, he was still Mr. Peale to me, but he knew my first name.

One of the instructors had a small car, like a Citroen. It wasn't too heavy. The guys and I picked it up and put it in between two trees, touching the trees. We didn't damage the car, but you couldn't drive it out of there. It took them two days to get it moved. No one said who the credit belonged to for the location of the car.

I rode my motorcycle through the school hall, down the steps, and out the door while my buddies held the doors open. I never hurt anyone or caused any real damage; it's just that school was boring.

Age 14 was a significant year for me. I was in high school, started driving, and worked for my Dad. Dad had me making umbrella poles. I convinced my friends to work too. We called it weenie wiping; the rods were dipped in enlarged vats of green stain and wiped dry. No aprons or rubber gloves, you were always green by the end of the day, and it didn't wash off. The poles had brass brackets and end caps; each had to be drilled and screwed for the rod and the spines to attach to the umbrella. Everything was by hand. We made seats and backs for lawn swings with springs and wood slats to take to the distributor for cushions. All this was for Sears and Roebuck. Our main products were swimming pool filters, ladders, lights, and I helped design many of these items to sell to pool builders and manufacturers. We also made diving boards of kiln-dried vertical-grain douglas fir with applied casein glue, nailed and clamped, which took about 36 hours to dry. Our plainer Charlie Alker, a stout Frenchman, a true craftsman, tapered the board, giving it a specific spring. Charlie built church altars and pews as his mainstay; his work was beautiful. Charlie had a classic Auburn car parked in his garage, we would get to see it sometimes, but we never did convince him to take us for a ride.

After Charlie finished with the board, it would come back to us to be routed, sanded, coated with three coats of spar varnish, then covered with a cocoa mat or white sicsele. Our pool boards and equipment were in such demand that we were constantly busy and almost always behind.

All this was being done after school, me and two friends. We were paid the gross sum of 75 cents per hour each. After several months I told Dad we needed more money or we would quit. That created a volcanic eruption in the DiSandro household. Dad said either I had to do the work or get out. My answer, OK! I told Dad we wanted $7.50 a board each; we knew how long it would take us to make each board. I said, "You can find someone else to do the work if you don't like it." There were several cold nights in the DiSandro household. And now I was paying $14.50 a week to live at home.

My first introduction into the business world, state your terms and conditions within reason and stand your ground. I won, depending on how you look at it. Our business was a new industry; you had to know how to build these quality products. My Dad and his partner were still busy, and everyone worked more hours than they cared to. Plus all these products had to be delivered. From there, I started building sand filters. The sand filters were heavy. Dad had a 2 ton Army REO truck. Reo was an auto and truck company created by the founder of Oldsmobile back in 1915. At age 15, Bud, my best friend, and I delivered filters all over Los Angeles, San Fernando, and Orange County. We saw some sights we would never mention to anyone.

I am now earning enough money to buy my first car and still go to school. Let me tell you about going to school. Being first-generation Italian, education was paramount throughout the families. Mandatory, I had to take all college prep required classes. They all needed me to study and know; therefore, I accumulated enough credits to graduate in three and half years—no such thing as advanced schooling that's available now.

During this part of life, we decided to build a cabana for the Sunday family dinners. The families were the DiSandro's, The Amodies, the Massaro's, and Grandma DiSandro was the matriarch. Every Sunday at noon after Mass, we are served an inside sit-down dinner, at least 5 to 6 courses of home-cooked gourmet Italian delicacies, and loud family conversation with hand gestures and laughing. It is, after all, an Italian household. Fitting into the California lifestyle, we decided after the cabana; there was a need for a barbeque. It could not be just any barbeque. The brick and mortar and design were befitting of the family heritage.

The Barbeque had to be gas and wood-fired, including running water and a prep area covered by a 6x6 structure with a picnic table. The family built it like the Romans erected it to last more than a lifetime. During the building of this masterpiece, we had the cement mixer powered by an electric motor with a crank handle. The handle flew off. I was the recipient of the handle at the bridge of my nose. Lots of blood, but Dad decided that I didn't need to do anything about it. Put some ice on it, and in about half an hour, it stopped bleeding, now back to work. Just get the job done.

Years later, I had my nose re-broken and a submucous resection, with internal packing, black eyes, and looking like the other guy won. The doctor for that operation and I became good friends. I happened to stop by one day on my way to a job, and his wife was on the floor with internal bleeding; I couldn't get a hold of Ed, so I rushed her to the hospital. The Doc on call said, "I saved his wife's life." I was the Godfather to their children and built them a splendid unique pool.

Back to the first car I owned, the 1937 Plymouth, not the hearse, four-door, sh..t rental brown, and as life goes, you'll discover this scenario was doomed to be repeated.

This truly amazing automobile came with specific requirements. The battery is tired, but we live at the top of the hill. Problem solved, coast down the hill, pop it in second gear, let the clutch out, and that baby would start. Off to school, the parking lot is flat, and it pays to have friends. Every evening my friends and I would jump-start this car, and I could make it home. After about three weeks, there was enough money to buy a battery. I always had big choices, make do with the battery, put gas in the car, or take out the latest love of my life.

Everyone has the tale of their first four wheels on the road. I am on my way on a bright sunny, wonderful weekend day. The radio is working, but I can't find the station I like. Like all bright 16-year-olds playing with the radio, it's a straight road; there's no traffic, and all of a sudden, I redesign my car's passenger side and the drivers' side of two parked vehicles. Fortunately for me and anyone else, no one was there, and no one got hurt. I left my name and address on both cars; we didn't have a phone at that time. Things became more exciting than usual at the DiSandro household, and we had a few visitors. The two owners of the vehicles came, no police. I made amends and paid for any damages to their cars. My mandatory savings of 20% of earnings will pay for my negligence. My car is now a little less than the original.

A spur-of-the-moment trip with Bud and cousin Ray in my 1937 Plymouth 6 cylinder, three-speed on the floor, I am proud of this car. We are going out to the desert for Easter week. We hunted cottontail rabbits in Morongo Valley by my Dad's cabin, which he placed on a homesteaded 5-acre land tract. We built the cabin because you could get 5 acres by homesteading the land and having housing within five years, no dollars involved.

While out hunting, we came across prospector's claims with rocks piled on their claims. When we took the rockpile apart, some of the written claims went back 100 years. We always put everything back and continued. Hiking through the mountains, we met with several rattlesnakes and had to shoot one coiled and ready to strike. One of us had brought along a six-pack of beer, and it took us all week to finish it. Drinking was just not our thing.

Tired of hunting, and it was still Easter week, so time to move on. Many of the kids were vacationing at the beach, which sounded adventurous. Leaving Marungo Valley, we pass by Palm Springs, go up over the ridge, pass by Lake Elsinore, and end up in the San Juan Capistrano area, then continue to Laguna Beach. We had been up early; it was a long day, everyone was tired. I did all the driving. So I pulled off the roadside, Andy and Ray crashed in the back seat, and I in the front. We locked the doors; the windows were up.

Then a car full of guys drove up, and one tried to open our door. He yelled, "What the F.. are you doing in there?" Bud rolled down the window, stuck the gun out, and more or less told them to get lost. They were gone before you could blink. We settled back down and slept until sunrise. Back on the road, and we were starving, we found a little place to eat and continued driving north while still in Laguna Beach. Cousin Ray sat in the back, looking over the front seat; we were all laughing and talking. The gun we had been hunting with was propped up with the butt end by the shift and the barrel leaning against the front seat's back with the barrel up. The car went over a bump in the road, everything jumped, and the gun went off. I was driving, Bud was sitting in the front in the passenger seat, and Ray was still in the back. When the gun went off, I looked at Bud, and nobody said anything. I was so scared. Both Bud and I thought Ray'd been shot. We thought we killed Ray. Ray was as white as a ghost when we looked in the back, but only the car's roof had any damage. Somebody up there loves me and was indeed looking after Ray. We continued through Laguna Beach, didn't see any of our friends, and decided to go home.

Driving to pick up my girl for mass on a school morning, I gazed at the sunrise at about 6 AM and said a prayer when the truck stopped in front of me. At 60 MPH, I hit the truck in front of me, and my chest crushed the steering wheel, throwing my body back against the driver's door. The door flew open, throwing me from the car into the oncoming lane; fortunately, there was no oncoming traffic. My car was totaled, the steering column was bent by the thrust to my chest, now black and blue, and they carted me away in the ambulance. My girlfriend's mother was unhappy because I didn't show up but cooled down when she found out I was in the hospital. Again, somebody likes me; I came away with a bruised chest, no broken bones, and alive. My Dad could not have been more displeased because of the healing time; it kept me from work.

As time passed, I bought a 1934 Ford Phaeton. It's a four-door convertible with no glass in the windows. A classic, there are steel rods that you put plexiglass in for all four of the windows. The driver and passenger doors were suicide doors opening from the front to back. I painted the car black with multi coats of hand-rubbed lacquer, the

Daniel and one of the many autos

spoked wheels were painted red, and the spare tire on the back was a white boot cover. There was no doubt about this car and the owner. Everything on this auto that could be chrome was when you opened the hood; it sparkled, even the dashboard. I had a friend in the chroming business and got all the parts chromed at cost.

I was driving down Garvey Avenue in Monterey Park when I saw this girl. She caught my eye; I flipped a Huey and drove down her street, pulled alongside the walk on the wrong side of the road, and I asked her if she would like to go out. She said she would think about it. Later I learned from my friend Gene that two brothers wanted to date her. The competition was on. She and I started dating, and for about four months, things were going well; then, to my surprise, she told me her parents were moving to Laguna Beach, which was a bit of a drive. I drove to Laguna Beach for about two months, roughly 60 miles along the coast.

Around this same time, my household was not running smoothly. I found a job in Laguna Beach as a pearl diver (dishwasher) for a couple of german gals who owned the restaurant. They taught me how to make pies and how to stay in line. They were not an easy-going pair. But I was living at the beach in a garage apartment, had a pretty girl-friend, and for the summer, it was fun. I'd take my girl to the beach, show off by walking down the beach on my hands. Life was as good as I had known. One late afternoon as the sun was setting, a sailboat passed by; I was with my girl as the sun shone into the red sail; the radio played Red Sails in the Sunset. It was postcard perfect.

She lived on a small knoll called Wards Terrace about a block from the beach. Her Dad was a salesman and spent a lot of time on the road. The German ladies at the coffee haus made the best pies around. I thought life was moving forward and in a direction that didn't feel too bad.

We were hitting it off, and then she decided to start dating a guy named Dave. I continued to live in the apartment and work at the restaurant; my cousin Andy would come on weekends, and we went diving for abalone, not legal, but we sold it to the restaurants on the QT. While I was working one day at the restaurant, one of the guys who also rented a room from my girlfriends' mother came in asking if he could take my 1934 Ford for a drive; this is the car I spent so much time on, three coats of hand-rubbed lacquer, red spoked wheels, and all the chrome.

I told him he was out of his mind. But after talking for a while and I was a trusting soul, I said he could drive it home but no farther. He was supposed to pick me up after work, and he didn't show. As I un-happily walked home and rounded the corner to the apartment, I no-ticed my classic Ford had a whole new design to the front end. He was standing by the front door and started to run. I was screaming at him as I chased him down. His Dad, Rick, came running out of the house and stood in front of him. I told him to get his dead ass out here, and we'll take care of this now. After a much-heated discussion, Rick said he and his son would make sure that he would pay for all the damages so I could repair my car as it was. He asked how much; I said I would get an estimate, and it would probably be around $700 to a thousand.

The following day there was no one around; they moved out during the night with no word to anyone. Andy came and towed me back, sixty miles to my parent's house. The amount of time I spent in my Dad's garage did not make him happy. I always had everything laid out in the order, better pity the poor soul who put anything out of place. Dad had a 220 electric outlet put in above the workbench, but he didn't label which outlet had changed. I was using his power drill; that baby took off like there was no tomorrow, and then it sparked, smoked, and fried. Dad was not a mild-mannered soul, I said, you should have marked it. If I said nothing, I would have fared better.

I now repair all the runnable parts on my classic, damaged auto, with the body parts put back in prime only. It took me about two months to get it to that point. I had put so much work into it; I just didn't feel good about it anymore. I put it up for sale. Several buyers already knew about the car, so it wouldn't be hard to sell. A fellow named Shorty Jendian made an offer, we haggled, and he finally bought it. Shorty and his family were dairy farmers. They used to take this colossal truck over to the 101 Brewery in Los Angeles to pick up the mash; on one of the runs back, the truck stalled on the railroad track, and Mr. Jendian thought he could get it started and out of the way. He played it too close; the train couldn't stop. I attended the funeral; now, the brothers had to run the farm. Shorty's brother Dave built dragsters. A few months after Shorty bought my car, Dave was racing. They had to change a wheel and forgot to put a pin in. He flipped the car and died at the scene, a real tragedy. I was a pallbearer at that funeral. It hits home sometimes. One of my other friends was working with a backhoe; he was at the edge of an embankment; it flipped, and he couldn't get out of the way. I lost too many friends that summer, and they were all good people.

For the next several months, I just concentrated on working. Besides working for my Dad once again building swimming pool equipment, he also took on a couple of other small businesses, which of course, I got to work.

We would put up and take down signs for the man running for Supervisor in the county. Some of the posters were large billboard signs. Just getting them on the truck was a chore.

Dad also bought a spreader truck and a small tractor. Bud and I took the equipment, cleaned out the chicken manure from under the hut, and brought it to the strawberry farmer. There we would spread it for fertilizer. When Dad finished with these enterprises, he decided to open a fruit and vegetable market. It was a good-looking store on Valley Blvd at Garfield in Alhambra. We now had the opportunity to get up at 3 AM to go to the wholesale produce market in Los Angeles. Come back to unload the truck, place all the products on shelves and bins and get the store ready to open. Dad's market was always organized and clean.

In one container, we would dump a lug of tomatoes, a case of peaches next to it. On the aisle, right across from them, I got one of my first lessons in marketing. In one bin, we would neatly pyramid the tomatoes. In the bin next to it, we would neatly pyramid the peaches. The tomatoes poured in the bin were 59 cents a pound, and the tomatoes neatly stacked were 79 cents a pound, likewise for the other fruits. The neatly stacked would sell out, then we would take from the bins where the produce was dumped and neatly stack it over in the other bin that sold out. We did that display with all the crops; they could either buy off the neatly stacked shelf or out of the dumped container. It was all the same product. But it was a tricky business and a lot of work, so Dad closed the store after a while.

I didn't want to work with my Dad anymore, so I got a job at Chrysler Corporation working on the assembly line. We worked at assembling gas lines and the clips to hold the tube in place. Let me put my experience at Chrysler in a nutshell; I found the scope of intelligence as low as I have ever encountered. One of the plans was to steal your lunch and fill your lunch box with nuts and bolts, or if that wasn't big enough, fill it with grease. My job required you to bend over slightly; their other joy was to put a grease gun in your back pocket and fill your pocket with grease. These were just a few of the high intellectual things that went on. After enduring this for about 3 to 4 months and watching the stealing and theft, I couldn't get out of there fast enough. Unknown to me, quitting Chrysler was at the opportune time.

My friend, Wayne, was getting married. He asked me to drive with him from Monterey Park, California, to Torrington, Connecticut. I was on my way—approximately a 3300-mile journey. Wayne forgot to tell me, though, before he gets married, we have five days to make our trip. Wayne had to be there two days before the wedding; that meant we had three days to travel, so 1100 miles per day. We drove 24 hours a day nonstop with our sunglasses on at night to stop the glare of oncoming traffic. Most of the roads were still country two-lane travel, freeways were just getting built. Wayne had a 1950 red Ford convertible with a white top. We had been driving nonstop; the only time we stopped was for fuel. While going through Texas, there was road construction of nothing but red clay, and it ended up all over Wayne's car. This was his pride and joy. Sometime the next day, we came to a stream, stopped, and washed the car before we could go on. As we were driving along, something didn't seem right. Wayne was driving, and I said the car didn't sound right; we better check it.

We were so tired; we didn't realize we had been driving in second gear overdrive for about the last 50 miles. Our speed averages about 70 MPH, with most of the highway's speed limits at 55 MPH, but we didn't get stopped. Fast food and lots of coffee got us to Torrington late in the afternoon on the third day. Madeline, his future bride, and her folks fixed us dinner. Immediately after dinner, we showered and went to bed. We got up a little before noon the next day, and her folks made us breakfast with beer. It was their custom, lots of beer. That afternoon, we all went to the church for the wedding rehearsal, and the following day they were married. After the reception, they were driving back to California. I hopped on a plane and flew back.

My cousin Andy is now a dentist; along with helping him build his office and set up the equipment, he decided to get his pilot's license. Andy thought I should become a dentist. I applied, carved the tooth, and was accepted by the dean of admissions. But the more I thought about it; I knew there would be no happiness for me going from one little cubicle to another looking in someone's mouth. I told Andy, dentistry is not for me. But Andy did talk me into getting my pilot's license; it was an easy sell. The instructor I had didn't care about his job; he was just working by the hour. On one of my last flights, the instructor had been particularly pesky the whole flight. We are landing; he says stop over there. I said I needed more of the runway, and he says, I told you to stop over there. So I pulled the hand brake and stomped on the foot brake; the plane swung around; it flipped to one wing, bounced back, and broke the strut. He yelled at me, "What the hell."

I was incensed, "You told me you wanted it stopped here; well, you're right where you said you wanted to be." I climbed out of the plane and continued getting my license with a different instructor.

Andy and I also had some close calls, one of them being when I was working in Vegas; I was having trouble getting a flight home. Andy said he would fly me to Vegas; he needed the hours for his license; as we were about to take off in the rented plane, it sputtered and choked. I told Andy this is not a safe aircraft; I found out later that the plane had just come back from Mexico, where it had fueled, and there's dirt in the fuel line. Another time Andy and I were up, the engine stalled, the prop froze, we were mid-air and falling. Don't think I was ever that scared. The ground is pulling you down. Everything you're trying isn't working. The plane is falling, you can hear the air the rushing, it's getting warmer as we are dropping. Andy pushes the choke, then he pulled the choke. There was a sputter, the prop turned and we were air borne. A few more feet, there would have been no return. When we landed we both headed for the restroom with wet drawers. I don't know if that was a close call, way too close or divine intervention.

Dad decided he wanted to move from the city. We kept the house in Monterey Park; my Grandparents still lived in the house we built for them. Dad purchased a 15-acre place on the upside of Lucerne Valley. It was about a half-mile off the main road with a solid house and a u shaped driveway. Properties there were generally surveyed but hardly ever fenced.

First, we would go up a couple of times a month for weekends, hunting cottontail rabbits. Seeing as Dad was a retired chef, he would make some fantastic meals. He wanted to turn the property into an income-producing venture. I was still in school during this venture. On Friday evenings, I had the privilege of driving for about 2 hours over Cajon Pass to Lucerne Valley to maintain the grounds. Everything needed water; I brought tools, supplies, and whatever was necessary to ensure all was well at the house. I've been driving a 36 Chevy ton and a half, and at this time, trucks and autos didn't have air conditioning. I went with the door open, propped my foot on the door and drove in second gear through the pass. Cajon Pass is long and high and extremely hot in the summer. It would be so hot they put out water barrels for all the vehicles overheating. The hills and mountains would rise on both sides of the road; it became a tunnel of heat spiraling down onto the road and the drivers.

Purina Feeds came out with a plan. You provide the housing, and they would provide all the chicks and the feed. When the chicks are grown to the fryer stage, Purina will repurchase them. To develop the chicks from chick to fryer, it would take one square foot per bird. Purina required that you have a minimum of 10,000 sq. ft., and Dad had a plan. Dad was going to raise fryers, lots of fryers. After receiving all the information, we needed to find a 10,000 sq. ft. building. He found a military base that had Quonset huts dismantled and for sale.

Each Quonset was 3300 sq.ft., there were 3, we were 100 ft short, Purina said they would accept it. We bought the three that were dismantled but made sure all the parts, nuts, and bolts were there. Dad hired a truck, we loaded. The destination was Lucerne Valley. We instructed the driver to follow the route up to the ranch. Very simple,

Los Angeles to San Bernardino up Cajon Pass to the Lucerne Cutoff. Dad, my cousin Andy and myself had already prepared the area for the buildings. Day one, no truck, day two passed no truck, day three, and the truck arrived late afternoon.

Dad was a little warm; Dad was short with thick dark hair, a nose to match his heritage, and likewise on his temperament. Dad was no slouch; he had a sixth-grade education and quit school because in Italy, the proper dress for a young man was knickers; in Rhode Island, the kids made fun of him. Dad did not come from a poor background and was a proud individual. At this time of his life, he could speak four languages: Italian, Spanish, French, and English. On top of all that, my father was not a patient man. When the truck finally showed up to unload, I thought Dad was going to explode, but he kept his cool. You never know when you might need that person or company again. The trucker went over the Lancaster Route, which was miles and days longer. It was late; we were all tired and needed a decent night's sleep. We are up early the next day, ready to work and start unloading the truck. The day was long, but the flatbed was almost empty. I said Dad; you better take a break; you look tired. I no more than said, take a rest; he backed up and fell.

My Dad falls off of the truck bed and breaks his arm. There are no medical facilities out here; we had to drive to Victorville for medical treatment. Once we got Dad taken care of, we went back to the ranch. Andy, I, and the driver finished unloading, and then the driver left. We spent the night and the next day, then drove home to Monterey Park. Not a word is spoken all the way home.

After the incident at the ranch, my Dad, not knowing how long it would be before he could work, decided to sell the buildings and the ranch. The contract with Purina had a deadline, and it didn't look like we would meet it. In a short while, the ranch sold. Dad purchased a newer Ford ton and half stake-bodied truck. We loaded all our personal effects, and after the numerous trips to this desert ranch in the middle of nowhere, there was no way to express the amount of disappointment.

A few days before closing, everything was packed; the following day, it closed. We spent the night and the day of closing to make sure we did everything. Everyone was happy, and it was late afternoon before we left. We didn't think about the time, but it was about dusk when we got on the road.

The decision was to take Lucerne Highway to Victorville Highway down Cajon Pass to San Bernardino and then home. Dad and I were tired, but he wanted to drive. We headed for home, not knowing what was about to happen. About halfway between Lucerne and Victorville Highway, which is a long stretch of barren road with nothing around for miles and very few cars passing us along the way, I happened to look back to check the load; it appeared the mattresses were on fire. Dad stopped, jumped out of the truck. There was no water, no fire extinguishers. The shovels are at the bottom of the load. Our belongings are tied down tight, and there's smoke. We had two cups and tried throwing sand, but a steady breeze was fanning the growing flames. I can smell the gas fumes; the fire is out of control. The truck and the fire groan; we only have a matter of seconds. I hollered to Dad, we have got to getaway. Dad didn't want to give up; this was all our worldly possessions; I pulled him to the ditch, away from the truck.

We heard a puff, puff, puff; the metal was buckling, and then it exploded. Truck parts, flames, everything is consumed. A car headed in our direction; said he saw what happened and said he would notify the Highway Patrol when he arrived in Victorville. We waited about an hour before we saw the Patrol car lights. No one lived out this far. There are no homes or lights to be seen. It's total darkness, even the stars weren't shining this night along this vast desert stretch. When the Highway Patrol finally arrived, they took out the fire extinguishers for the still burning tires. The fire was so hot, it melted the tires into the asphalt and left the black burn marks of the truck for years to come.

Incidentally, that was my 21st Birthday, April 25th, 1954.

Everything is charred; the truck, cab, bed, belongings. The Highway Patrol determined the cause of the fire was someone driving by, who flipped a cigarette that landed in between the mattresses, and because I didn't see it right away, the fire started. The Highway Patrol said forest fires get started here all the time; people just aren't careful. We got in the Patrol car, and they drove us to Victorville to an all-night restaurant; the Sheriff said they would call the tow truck to pick up what was left and have it towed into Victorville. The Patrolmen checked our driver's license and registration, and insurance in the filing process. The truck was just purchased a couple of days ago for the move. They asked us if there was any more they could do. We said no, we didn't think so; we would call family to come and get us.

So we called our cousins, it's now about 11 PM, they weren't thrilled. It's about a 3-hour drive. We just sat and waited. When Andy and his brother Jullian got to the restaurant, we bought sandwiches and then started home. There was little conversation, everyone was tired, and the events of the day weighed hard.

For the next couple of weeks, Dad was consumed with paperwork and dealing with the insurance company. The insurance agent had not filed the new policy. Dad spent two to three weeks arguing with the insurance guys and got nowhere. The truck, all the household belongings, files, tools, and possessions were gone and not insured.

Dad and I drove back to where the truck had burned; any tools that were left were gone, the engine stripped, nothing but a charred buckled frame. Now the towing company wanted $300 for towing it off the road; my Dad told them, "Go to hell."

This is a meeting, not a phone call; we are at a time of life when you meet your opponent face to face.

They said we needed the title to the truck. Anger is an understatement; he said, "You figure it out," and we left. The loss was tremendous, and we never heard any more about the insurance or the towing company.

Dad still had the house in Monterey Park, but his plans, his dreams were shattered. It would take time and effort to move on, plus replace a houseful of lifelong accumulation.

ME AND DANIEL

Chapter Five

———∞∞———

1954 LOUSIANA

AFTER THE TRUCK fire, I was unhappy with the way things were going at home. A friend of mine was checking out a new business in the south. He called me from Louisiana; Lou said, "There are some great opportunities here. I need your experience in this business I'm checking out. Can you come and see what we have?"

I am going to Louisiana at 21 years old, I haven't done any traveling except California, and most of my jobs have been working for my Dad. My first company would be in a place I've never been to and know very little. Lou was a good friend; I felt I could depend on him if needed. I made the decision.

Ray, a pool company owner in New Orleans, was building swimming pools he couldn't complete. The pools were not holding together; they were cracking and floating up out of the ground. Ray just didn't know how to complete the jobs, so Lou went there to help him out. The complexity of building in such a high water table was a little more than Lou had expected, so he called me, knowing I had the knowledge and the experience, and engineering to make this a successful venture.

I flew from LA to New Orleans, Moisant Airport. When I departed the plane, heat and humidity liked to knock me over. I had never experienced anything like it. It occurred to me; maybe I should get back on the plane and leave right now. I went into the airport cafe; I needed a good cup of coffee. A sweet waitress gave me a cup of coffee with half and half and sugar. I stirred it all and took one big sip.

I asked her, "How old is this coffee?"

She informed me in her lovely southern accent, "Sir, I just made this coffee special for you."

I said, "What kind of coffee is this?"

The waitress said, "Why Sir, that there is Chicory."

This California boy got his first introduction to the south and a multitude of experiences on the way.

For the first couple of weeks, I rented a place in the French Quarter. The opportunity to experience the nightclubs with some of the best music in the country. The cafes and restaurants with exquisite cuisine were any young man's dream.

Later I found a more convenient room at the Saint Regis Motel, with friendly owners. Unknown at the time, Bob and Jerry would become dear friends for a lifetime.

The next day I met with Ray and Lou to see some of the problem pools and solutions. From that point on, it was long days of work. We were able to resolve most of the problems and start on some new construction. I didn't know when I first arrived what the degree of the building would be. We were fortunate to have contracts with the elite of New Orleans. Each pool was custom with its unique design and landscape; no cookie cutters here. Contracting to the wealthy, like the Ceo of a pharmaceutical company who introduced us to his friends, was just the beginning, and the business took off from there.

One of my first introductions was to Blaise D'Antoni, a whole story unto itself. We hit it off from the beginning. When he heard my name, being Italian, we were off to a good start. We talked about food and family. How long my family had been here, and all the colloquial

Italian customs of that culture. The following day I met with Blaise at his home for breakfast. His estate was a mansion of grandeur located across the street from Lake Pontchartrain. There were things I had never witnessed before, such as white and black drinking fountains. I happened on an overloaded tour bus and offered a black lady my seat, and I was immediately informed I couldn't do that.

I arrived at the D'Antoni estate, rang the doorbell; the butler answered and said, "Mr. Daniel, Blaise is waiting for you in the dining room."

It was about 6 AM, and Blaise was having his breakfast.

He turned with a warm smile, "Daniel, would you like Chicory or coffee?" Blaise was an astute businessman and knew that people from California didn't know how to drink chicory. Blaise asked what I would like for breakfast; he pulled the sash cord, another butler came in, took my order, and served a delicious full course meal. After breakfast, Blaise explained, it was his daughter's 16th birthday. Southern tradition and culture dictate a coming-out event of maturing to young womanhood. Blaise's estate was sizable, and the construction I was here to bid on includes building a large structure for the orchestra, a dance floor, and within that same area, he wanted a swimming pool and not just any pool. He asked for several different designs in one week. It was to be completed in his time frame.

In one week, I met with Blaise to present three unique designs at his estate after lunch. As I soon learned, the typical southern style does not allow for conducting business during lunch. He selected the design for the pool, grounds, and structure, and to make sure it would be to his liking; we walked the grounds. Each angle and design would need to fit with the landscaping and the stature of the mansion. The enormous old southern oak trees cover part of the grounds, and I received instructions they were not to be disturbed. The pool's design was a three-leaf clover with three arches, each 30 feet in diameter, and the stem was the steps leading into the pool. The arches are at three different depths; one is at 3 feet, one at 4 feet, and one at six feet, each flowing into the next. Regular pool coping was eliminated—the entire perimeter of the pool to be completed with white and soft orange brick. Blaise selected a custom 6x6 tile, and we are to finish in a three-month window. When Blaise said finished, it meant ready for his guest to arrive. There would be nothing left undone.

The excavator for the pool was to be there at 8 AM sharp. It was now 9:30 AM. Blaise asked me who it was; he then picked the phone and dialed the excavator.

Blaise stated, "You will be here in the next 20 minutes, or you will never do another job in this town". The excavator arrived and was at work within the 20 minute time frame.

My men did a fair amount of the work, but when there was a need for extra supplies or another contractor, I only had to say this job was for Mr. D'Antoni, and I had no problem getting anyone out and on time. As the project came along, Blaise and I developed a great friendship; we respected each other. My respect for him was who he and his family were. I believe his respect for me was completing the project as he wanted, enhancing his estate. We were living up to our word. He wrote the contract on a cocktail napkin, and nothing more was needed. We both knew our part, and each of us had the integrity to complete it. My invitation to the coming-out party, a festive gala affair, lasted several days. What an honor; I was still a 21 year old from California and experiencing a culture and style of life unknown to me.

During the project and beyond, Blaise and I met at several social functions. Introductions were too many to remember of the same social standing as Blaise. Though, I'd like to bring up one in particular. I bought a seasoned boxed seat at the sports arena. Joe Louis was to be the referee at an exhibition charity bout. Blaise noticed me sitting in the box seat and waved to come down and talk with him.

I went down to the front row; he said, "What are you sitting up there for? Come on over and sit with me".

I said it's ok, Blaise. He said, "No, come on down, sit here."

We went down to ringside. Some of the reporters at ringside saw

Blaise and left their seats so Blaise and I could sit as close as you can get without being in the ring. After the match, I was introduced to Joe Louis and shook his hand; needless to say, I was impressed.

When I eventually returned home, I could only share small portions with the family; they wouldn't believe me. The first month I was there, I sent Dad $1,000.00 just because I could; it's still 1954.

Dad called and said without humor, "What did you do, rob a bank?" That was the last check I sent. There was no point trying to explain.

I was informed by those who know, Blaise D'Antoni and his family owned Standard Fruit and Freight Lines, a shipping company that included Chiquita banana orchards. Blaise's wifes' family-owned Jax Brewery of Texas.

While getting settled in New Orleans, I met Bob and Jerry. They were managing a motel in Metairie on the west side of New Orleans. They wanted a pool for the motel, and the friendship began. Bob said, You're working on our pool, might just as well stay here, and that was where I made home base. Every evening the three of us would get together. Jerry would make a pitcher of Martini's, and we would enjoy the hot summer nights and each other's company. It turned into a lifelong friendship.

Daniels dictation has ended here.

As Daniel was prone to do, he would wonder, one of his favorite pastimes was exploring the countryside. He frequently found a bar or lounge playing the Blues that you only found in New Orleans. The leisurely tempo, dark, smoky atmosphere, and heat are part of the southern scene, with one cocktail to sip through the evening and enjoy.

Daniel had more income at this time than he had ever known, no responsibilities, meeting a lot of the right people, not a care in the world. He and his friends took a ride on a wind boat into the bayou country and thoroughly enjoyed it. Daniel bought a speed boat, and with as much speed as possible, they are zipping along on Lake

Pontchartrain. As Daniel is on the skis, there's a log directly in his path, trying to jump it, the speed takes over. He skips along the top of the water like the sandstones tossed by the kids to see how many times they'll bounce before sinking. The following day he nursed his bruises.

On Friday evenings, after paying the crews, Daniel would buy a bushel or two of shrimp, a case of beer, and everyone could unwind from a week of hard work. There was one fellow, his name was Lionel, he worked slower than all the rest. Lionel was older, carried a bottle in his back pocket, and would stop for a swig every so often.

When the day was over, his work would be complete; he never complained, didn't ask for favors, and would always say, when receiving his check, "Thank you, Mr.Daniel."

Daniel had a couple of crews from Mexico, and after a few weeks of work, one guy got a raise. His work was superior, and now the rest of the crew was jealous; they didn't get a raise. The battle began, Daniel passed by the construction site, and two of the crew were down in the pool with knives and a lot of loud, angry Spanish language. Daniel grabbed a piece of rebar, jumped into the pit. He meant business, "Put the switchblades away, or I'll start swinging, and I don't ever want to see those again." Tempers were quiet for a few months.

A favorite time was to drive, always interested in the next corner or what's over the hill. One afternoon he took a long drive to nowhere in particular, and as he was going, things looked a little less prosperous and continued to get more and more sketchy. Finally arriving back at the motel, he told Bob and Jerry the excursion he had taken today. Bob said, "Don't ever go there again; even the police don't venture there. If they get a call because something happened, they just don't go. Word is you go there you don't come back."

Daniel said, "Ok, got the picture."

Late one evening, Daniel was walking to his car after dinner in the French Quarter when he felt this piece of metal at the back of his head. The guy holding the gun said, "Give me everything in your pockets."

Daniels replied, "Either pull that trigger or run for your life." As has been said before, "Someone up there likes me." The guy took off, and Daniel continued to his car and back to the motel. Is that luck or divine intervention?

When you have a single young man in a city that's new to him, a fellow who does not stay home to read a book, he generally goes exploring. Daniel had always been an explorer, loved to get out, see the neighborhoods, the countryside, and meet new people. One evening, he was on his way to dinner when a beautiful, very tall, well-dressed lady with olive-colored skin, stopped him.

She said, "Would you like some company this evening? I only deal in white studs." Daniel smiled, glanced at the beauty before him, and smoothly said, "Thank you, but I'm running late for a meeting; you have a nice evening."

He thought afterward, how tempting but not the thing to do.

After working in New Orleans for about a year, the tides started turning. The partners now felt they could continue running the company and design the pools without anyone else. Things started getting touchy as to who was getting paid for what, and after a couple of months of watching the attitudes and movements, Daniel decided it would be time to move west. He didn't have any real ties, the partners would buy him out at a minimal price, and he could be on his way. He didn't want to tow his boat back, so he traded it for a blue Aurora Diamond, which he later gave to his new wife a couple of years down the road.

Daniel has a brilliant mind which he worked at hiding from most. The desire to be liked, to not offend, was frequently in the way of his knowledge. His sense of humor and quick wit, compounded with expressive acuity, would put him out front and center stage. He didn't feel comfortable being the deciding factor, even though he was an in-charge type of person. The inner conflict was always there and in the way of many decision-making processes. So the business that is doing well is left behind with friends and lifestyle. Daniel was now on his way back to California, leaving Louisiana behind and moving on to the next chapter of life.

Chapter Six

WHAT TO DO NOW?

I'M BACK HOME, at the DiSandro household, working on cars, hanging with cousins Ray and Andy. I started looking for a job with some future to it.

I met a German couple through the pool industry, their joy in life was to go water skiing. They skied to Catalina, no small feat on ocean waves. I went with them a few times; they did the skiing, I stayed in the boat. Once, we went skiing at Lake Havasu. I would try the skis this time and have fun, but I couldn't compare to how good they were.

I went with another friend to Catalina to hunt Javelina; he got one. The hogs were overrunning the island; there weren't any predators, so they would issue hunting licenses to thin out the herds. It was an experience, but they are vicious animals, and I can't say it was that rewarding.

I tried dating a couple of girls, but it wasn't a good fit; nothing seemed to click. Andy wanted to date this one girl, but he wanted to double date, so Andy asked me, "Would you ask the sister out?" It wasn't what I wanted, but I caved and asked her out anyway.

Andy didn't hit it off with his date, but I kept going out with the sister. One of our evenings was at the Balboa Ballroom on Balboa Island, and Lionel Hampton was playing. My girl was an exceptional dancer, and I wasn't too bad myself. We were having a great time; one song, we cleared the dance floor. We were the only ones left dancing as the song finished and surprised to see no one else out on the floor. The applause was for the band and the two of us; what a memorable night.

I continued to date the sister, and by the age of 25, I was married. We started a family and bought a new ranch-style house in Anaheim, California. I was proud, put in a dichondra lawn, and the yard had an appearance of velvet, but I would never start another yard like it.

It's a specialty grass that doesn't need mowing, but growing is too tricky, especially with small children. After work and in the dark, I would be out there weeding and watering. The backyard had no landscaping, so the first thing was to plant an avocado tree; after a while, it produced more fruit than we could give away.

Before I was married, I purchased some apartments with the guidance of a friend. He was older than I, had good business sense, and introduced me to the world of real estate. Jake knew of someone that needed to sell his apartment buildings. The financing was easy; I took over the loans and gave him a down payment of $500 each, a 4 unit and an 8 unit studio apartment. Jake ended up being my friend for a lifetime.

I said, Jake, I need to paint one of the apartments, to rent it again. When I drove by after work, Jake and a young Mexican boy he had taken under his wing were just finishing the unit. Jake made a deal with his young protege'. You stay out of trouble, keep good grades, and at 16, the red collectors auto sitting in my garage is yours. In turn, I would help Jake whenever I could, and he did likewise.

After returning from Louisiana and buying the 4 unit and 8 unit, I also purchased a 17 unit, and 26 unit-they were the better-taken care of apartments. These newer units were more trouble, and someone always wanted something.

One night about two in the morning, a tenant calls. She says, "My faucet is dripping; I can't sleep."

My reply is, " Mrs. Jones, take two aspirin and call me after 8 AM" tomorrow. I didn't keep the 17 or the 26 units very long.

Another tenant in the 26 unit decided he wasn't going to pay his rent. I served him notice to vacate, and he just didn't leave. If I took him to court, it might be six months down the road before I get him out.

Early one morning, he gets a knock on the door. Standing in front of him is a big muscled Haitian guy.

"Mr. DiSandro says your apartment needs paint, and we are here to paint. Gather up your stuff; we are ready to get started."

The tenant says, "You can't do that." The painters pushed the door open, walked into the second-floor apartment. Sofa, TV, anything in their way went over the balcony.

The Painter, very soft-spoken, said to the tenant, "You don't want to make Mr. DiSandro unhappy, now do you?" The tenant left.

One of the renters was constantly complaining. Sap and leaves from the tree in the back of the apartments were getting on his car.

I told him, "You can cut a branch that hangs over your vehicle, which should take care of it."

About three days later, I got a summons from the City of Santa Ana to remove a tree from the alley, or they will remove it and send me the bill. The tenant cut the whole damn tree down, and it wasn't a small tree he left in the alley.

I cleaned up the street and took the tenant to small claims court. I explained to the judge about cutting one branch instead of the whole tree.

The Judge said, "Well, he cut it a little short."

I said, "Judge, if you went into the barber for a trim and came out looking like Yule Brenner, you would be a little upset."

The judge slammed his gavel down, "Mr. DiSandro, would you like me to hold you in contempt of court?"

"No, Sir."

"Next case."

The City was always after me about something. The trash pick-up would only take what was in the dumpster, and the tenants were constantly putting the trash on the ground, which the city considered a health hazard. So I would get a letter, I'd go clean it up, and next week the same scenario. The dumpster wasn't full, and I didn't know which unit put the trash on the ground. I'm on surveillance; early morning, Mrs. Rodreguez in unit 6 would send out her little son with trash before school. He wasn't tall enough to get the trash into the bin; hence he would put it in front of the dumpster. I had to knock on the door, tell Mrs. Rodreguez she needs to make sure the garbage is in the dumpster, or I will have to charge her what the city charges me for the cleanup, and it's not cheap.

One time I rented to a couple of Marines, and they decided to have a party. The police were called, for disturbing the peace. The party tore up the apartment and broke windows, toilets, and smashed walls. It was a mess. My friend Jake was a retired Marine Colonel; I asked him what I should do.

Jake said, "Daniel, let me take care of this." The next day, the apartment was put back in order, with new windows, paint, and doors, and the guys also spent time in the brigg.

Collecting the rents was a challenge; the tenants in the 4 unit building and the 8 unit didn't speak much English, or so they said and only paid in cash. Some paid twice a month, and some tried to get out of paying. Then I met Jose.

He said, "Daniel, You're a dumb gringo. Let me collect, and I will make sure you get your money." Jose did a great job; I had to make sure I didn't insult his wife, though. Once a month, I would go to their house to collect rent, and she would make dinner.

It was a social custom to respect and complement his wife's cooking and have dinner with the family. When Thanksgiving was close, I would bring over a turkey.

After Jose and I became better acquainted, he told me, "When I'm ready to retire, I'll sell my gardening business and move back to Mexico. I have a hacienda on the ranch with cattle that I've been paying on. The family in Mexico runs it for me, and the ranch will be paid for in a few years, and I will be ready to go home.

I told my Dad about the apartments after I bought the units.

He said, "They're old and not in a good neighborhood. It's a lot of work." Why do you want those apartments anyway?

Dad was right; they were a lot of work. But they also made money. When I first bought the furnished 4 unit, it even had utensils. I was a bachelor and didn't know about antiques or collectibles. There were Duncan Fife tables, Tiffany lamps, and the silverware was real silver, clawfoot tubs. It was a collector's dream. I gave most of it away, thinking, who wants all this old stuff. I'll update the apartments.

An elderly lady lived in one of the upstairs apartments, and she liked to imbibe now and then. Well, I get a call from the downstairs neighbor, the water is running out the door and down into her apartment. I rush over, knock on the door. No answer. I use my key; it's a flood. My tenant's in the bathroom. She's passed out on the toilet with no clothes. After leaning too hard on the back of the toilet tank, the water just kept running. I didn't know if she was sick or intoxicated; I called the ambulance, put a robe around her, and prayed she would be okay. As it turns out, she has diabetes; the paramedics got her stable, and I found her a motel room while the damage was being repaired. She is so embarrassed by the episode that our friendship was never quite the same.

I had these apartments for a long time, therefore a multitude of happenings. A young man rented a downstairs unit; I would stop by to visit, and I could tell he smoked by the odor, and it wasn't cigarettes. But he didn't seem to be a menace to anyone and was a friendly enough soul. He had been there for several months when I received a call from the fire department. They said there might be a gas leak. I leave what I'm doing and rush over; I open the door to his apartment because he

ME AND DANIEL

doesn't answer. The firemen go in and find him in the kitchen with the gas stove fumigating the place. We were too late. He left a note, just to say I'm sorry.

I am now working for Anthony Pools, the largest and most successful swimming pool company in any state. We were building pools nationwide. I was instrumental in setting up our cement plant, and we had our own trucking lines and sandpit. I supervised pools for people like Cary Grant, Sammy Davis Jr, Jane Mansfield, a pink pool; everything she had was pink, Hollywood producers, and more. These were exciting times and challenging pools. Most of the elite didn't want just a hole in the ground filled with water; they were building tributes to themselves. One pool, for instance, the bar was part of the pool; to mix a drink, you would swim under the bar to get to the liquor section. There were multitudes of waterfalls and hi-dives; some pools were indoors.

Another pool was built on a cliff, overhanging the Pacific Ocean. I designed it, created it, and no one ever gave me the framed piece of paper to say I was a certified engineer. The engineers came to me for advice. We built a pool on the 13th floor of the Holiday Inn in Long Beach, California, and they said, "It couldn't be done."

A pool we designed on Balboa Island was next door to the mayor of Newport. He did not want to be awakened too early or listen to construction too late in the day. There were special permits to build on the Island, cross the bridge, extra checking of the soil's stability, and the neighbors to sign off before construction could commence. It was a nightmare all the way through. We did complete the pool, it took twice as long, cost the homeowner a bunch, and the profit margin wasn't any more significant than any other pool.

Because of all the advertising we did, I became good friends with the Chandler Family, who owned the Los Angeles Times. I had the good fortune of meeting a federal judge through the Chandlers at one political party function. He gave me his business card and said."If you ever have a problem, just show them this card." He signed it; that was like carte blanc.

When constructing pools in Las Vegas, the entire design of business and work changed. Many people worked evenings and slept during the day; the complaints would be numerous if we destroyed the sleep time. We couldn't start construction until after 1 PM, the hottest time of day. There would be troughs of water to throw the tools in because they would be too hot to handle. When the sun went down, the lighting system for visibility kept construction ongoing—the number of jobs was enormous.

The casinos treated us royally. The crews and I would generally stay at the Flamingo Hotel. We would be assigned suites; I could use the VIP lounge, excellent food, drinks, and free tickets to any shows. I'm not a gambler; I probably didn't spend more than $50.00 the whole time I worked in Vegas.

Flying from Los Angeles to Las Vegas was an enormous amount of time; if the schedule were too tight, I would helicopter to Orange County airport from LAX. There were a few times where I would do no more than land and have to fly back. If I needed to get a flight right away, it was common for seats to get bumped at the last minute so I could get on a flight or entertain a guest at a show; whatever it took, the door was always open.

There was one time a flight was running late, and I missed the helicopter. I had to take a taxi 35 miles to Orange County. As I've said previously, an Angel is watching over me, that helicopter went down, and no one survived. I didn't pray a lot, but I wasn't so full of myself to think I had control over everything.

We built multitudes of pools in new neighborhoods; some would get started before the house is finished. On one occasion, I get a call, and the homeowner says, you haven't put the pool just where I wanted it. I tell him, I'll be out tomorrow and take a look; we'll get it squared away. I get to the job site, and there's no start of any pool construction. The contractor hadn't put house numbers on the homes yet, and my crew went to the first house on the second street, not the second house on the first street. As I'm trying to figure out where the guy who called me is, he comes walking over, shakes my hand, and says, my house is over here. Sure enough, he has the hole in his backyard for a new pool, with our construction sign in his front yard. He and I converse, and we come to an agreement that will satisfy both of us. We will build his pool at cost, no interest, and he will allow us to put a large sign in his front yard declaring what a fantastic company we are. We got a ton of business, and he had a new pool, with landscaping for less than half of what it would have cost him otherwise.

The amount of time spent working was horrendous, I knew the family was important, but I couldn't let the job lag. There was always someone shooting arrows, wanting my position. I was always looking over my shoulder to see which one was trying to get my job today. The tight rope to straddle was getting thinner all the time. I ordered my wife a living room set and had it delivered; I thought it would be a pleasant surprise. She didn't like it. She didn't get to pick it out; I can understand that. It was a gift, I didn't have time to go shopping with her, and she was not the kind of shopper I could hand a credit card to unless I put a limit on it. I had put new tires on her car, and not a month later, there's a flat tire. I'm at work; she's angry because I don't come home to take care of it now, and her flat tire is my fault. In my most diplomatic way, I say just get a new tire, have it put on. My wife bought the most expensive tire in the shop, I think out of spite, and of course, it didn't match the other tires. These types of problems were becoming daily events.

While working at Anthony Pools, the executives had a dress code. We are in the IBM era; we wore navy sports coats, ties, polished shoes. One must always look proper for a meeting. If it was a special meeting with clients or bankers, the dress code was Petrocelli suits and French cut or Florsheim exceptional quality shoes. Some customs, in other countries, you didn't cross your legs, others you shake hands with the left hand, and a whole series of items to be aware of for each culture. When we were doing business overseas, the proper dress code and knowing the customs for each country was mandatory. Education for business and etiquette was not a choice. Primary countries at the time were France and Japan.

On one morning meeting, I walked down the hall, jacket on my arm, tie loose at the neck.

Mr. Anthony walks up to me, "Good Morning, Daniel."

I say, "Good Morning, nice day."

He says, "You are attending the meeting this morning?"

"Yes, I am."

"Then you will straighten your tie and put on your jacket."

I looked at him with a smile and said, "Mr. Anthony, do you pay me to look good or for what I know?"

He replied, "I pay you for both," and promptly walked on.

So for that day, I put on the jacket, tugged up the tie, and went to a meeting I didn't want to attend.

My schedule was too hectic; I put in too many hours and started having asthma attacks. I slept in a recliner so I could breathe. The bout with asthma continued for a year. The local hospital had a standing ACTH order on file to keep me alive if someone brought me in. The medication could cause a heart attack, but it was the best they had at the time. I didn't know if my wife understood or cared, and the four kids were all too young to be of any help. The family I worked so hard to care for just didn't get what was happening. It was time to make a change.

I left Anthony Pools. There was a time when I worked three jobs at a time. I worked in a bank, the graveyard shift; it's called that for a reason. I'm employed at a factory where I had my hands and arms mangled by one machine. The doctors said I might never use my hands again. But with persistence and prayers, I recovered, and over the years, the scars faded. I worked at various pool companies over the years. Life was not becoming a satisfying daily event. Homelife slipped a little farther south each day, and after 13 years of trying to make things right in my marriage, I gave up.

There are four children, I wanted to raise two, and my wife could raise two, but she would have no part of it. I knew without asking; the courts would never allow me any custody. To put the icing on the cake, she hired an attorney, a friend of ours. I didn't even look for a lawyer and didn't go to court. I gave her the house, the car, and the bank account. My former friend and her attorney said they would take my apartments. The attorney never found an apartment.

I left with some clothes, and I told her I would help take care of the kids and do my best to see them raised. Remember the 1937 sh..t rental brown plymouth, my first car. Well now I have a 1963 plymouth station wagon, same color, leaks oil, smokes, but for the time being, it will get me around town. No matter, it was always a battleground and forever unbearable to even try to be a responsible parent.

After the divorce, life changed, and I decided to get a dog. The dog's name was Ursula, a brown Doberman. She was intelligent, disciplined, and a fantastic watchdog. I lived in an apartment, and if someone came to the stoop at the door, she would stand alert, but she could tell if they were just walking down the hallway. If you left work and there was food on the table, Ursula wouldn't touch it. But I could not get her to stay put if there was a cat. She chased cats anywhere and everywhere. We were driving down the street one great sunny day, windows open. Ursula saw a cat; I'm at a stop sign. She jumps out the window, and the chase is on. It took me a half-hour and several blocks to finally catch her. My son CM wanted to take her for a walk with a leash; she took off after a cat, dragging him behind her. CM should have let go, but he didn't. Fortunately, the cat went up a tree, and the dog stopped running. Ursula went most places with me; I'm in my truck, now I only roll the window down an inch, I get stopped. The officer walks up to the window and asks for the usual driver's license and registration.

I roll the window down just far enough to slide the paperwork through, and he says, "Roll the window all the way down."

I said, "I don't think that's a good idea."

"I told you to roll the window down, now."

I said, "Okay."

As I rolled down the window, Ursula came charging past me at the Officer, and he's shouting, "Roll up the window, roll the window up."

Of course, I did. He handed me back my papers through the space in the window and said, "Make sure you drive safely."

A friend of mine wanted to borrow the dog for a camping trip, I said Ok, neither he or the dog were ever seen again.

I started looking for something different and bought a Curry's Ice Cream shop with a sandwich grill. There were always deals to be found that could pick up for near to nothing. I tried working that for a while, but with all the unruly people, kids throwing ice cream on the floor or didn't like their choice and expected to get something else without paying. It didn't take me too long to find out; this wasn't for me. I sold the business.

So I found a liquor store by the race track, and my Dad helped me run it. It wasn't bad; you had to watch the customers so they wouldn't take off with a little something extra in their pocket. The inspectors were coming by to assure you weren't selling to minors. It just wasn't my kind of business. I sold and moved on.

I could always find a pool company to buy.

I struck up a deal with a country-western band to be their manager. It worked pretty well for a while, I entered them in one of the competitions for state country music, and they came in second place. We were all pleased; the Green, Green Grass of Home was their signature song. They could have continued, but like so many bands, the internal rivalry and who would play lead guitar grew to the point of no return. I knew when I got into it; bands had virtually no longevity; this one was no different. If they had stayed together, there was a good possibility for success, but apart, there wasn't enough strength. There was no working it out.

So moving on, I started up a pizza restaurant with a couple of brothers in Long Beach. It was a big restaurant, about 4000 sq. ft. with booths and tables. We rolled out our homemade dough, stewed our homemade sauce, and had a great lunch crowd from Douglas Aircraft.

After a time of doing well, the brothers decided they didn't need me. I had put our partnership agreement together so tight; I couldn't take it over or get back in the partnership. I outsmarted myself. There is an item known as retribution; the oldest brother got a brain tumor and died about six months later, and within a year, the second brother had cancer. I don't know what happened to him or the restaurant; I had moved on to other things.

While a lot of this was happening, my folks had moved into a travel trailer; they thought it might be something they would like—the first tiny house. Well, the first travel trailers were extra small. But they were in a lovely park by the beach, so for a while, it worked. Then I found them a place up the coast, a charming little town with a gorgeous beach, and a new mobile home park still under construction.

We took a drive; I said, "Dad would you like this?"

He said, "Yes, I think this might be good."

He even had a choice of lots to pick from since the park was new and just starting to get tenants. I bought them a new single wide, and Dad picked out a double-width lot. Now he could have his pick of several large lots anywhere in the park, and his choice was back by the train track. They had a fence up, so you couldn't see the track, but you could certainly hear it as it would come through about four times a week in the middle of the night. It didn't seem to bother my folks, and Dad could go down to the pier just a few blocks away and fish. My cousin Theresa, her husband Tom and Aunt Rena, my Dad's sister, decided they would like to move to Pismo Beach and be close to Mom and Dad; they had made the move with us from Rhode Island, so many years ago. I helped them get a good deal on the house, now they all had someone to visit, Tom got a job at a car agency, and best of all, it was a nice place to live.

Before moving my folks to Pismo, I had a cabin cruiser in Long Beach; they would come down and fish off the back of the boat and enjoy the water. A friend who retired to a condo that overlooked the dock; said he would keep an eye on the boat for me. My folks never took the cruiser out; they were satisfied just being on the water, dipping the pole, and occasionally catching a small fish or two.

However, my oldest son, his sister, and friends decided to make themselves at home. I always kept a full tank of fuel to keep moisture out of fuel. The following weekend I decided to use the boat and noticed I had less than half tank of fuel. This could only mean someone had taken the boat out. Talking with my friend in the condo, he says, "Ya, I saw your kids take the boat out, guess that you knew about it."

I addressed it with my eldest, but after that, I felt there was a need to keep it locked uptight. It wasn't long after that I sold it.

My oldest son turned 16; I gave him my truck; it had a few miles but ran well. With wheels, he could help his mom, plus get back and forth to school. The kid was a whiz; as I look back, he was too smart for his own good. Years later, I concluded he was educated beyond his intelligence.

I went hunting with some friends to Panguitch, Utah. It was fall and getting cold, but we were all going to rough it. Tent and sleeping bag, cook over an open fire pit. The first day there, we each strikeout. I head off in my direction; the sun is shining, it's comfortable, and I get tired. I prop myself up by a big Aspen tree and fall asleep. When I wake up, it is starting to get dark; I'm disoriented. I must have been so tired I couldn't discern where I was. Base camp was by a river, so I should find them if I head downhill and follow the river. I walked, what seemed like forever, and it was now pitch black, not even stars. It was also cold, freezing. At about 9 to 10 p.m., I could see the flicker of a fire in the distance because it was so dark the light from the fire looked like it was a whole lot closer than it was. I kept walking. When I finally arrived, they hadn't saved me any dinner; I opened a can of cold beans.

They didn't try to find me, just said, "We knew you would show sooner or later."

Who needs enemies when you have friends like these?

I was ready to go home. I was just glad I didn't have the kids with me this time. When we got up in the morning, our clothes were frozen.

I am not having a good time.

After the divorce and some time down the road, I struck up an association with a gal, a friendly person, but again my choice of getting together wasn't the right one. We both agreed on one thing; it didn't work.

Life has moved on, and I'm now forty-two years old, a partner in another pool company, working my butt off and trying to make heads or tails out of what I'm doing and where I'm going.

Then I meet this gal, she's younger than me, but seems to have fair head on her shoulders. I think I'll get to know her, you never know, there might be something there.

Chapter Seven

———∞———

DIANAH

A TIME OF turbulence and disaster like the world had never seen. The year is 1945; Dianah Lee Hodel, born on April 4, at Berlin Memorial Hospital, in Berlin, Wisconsin. My Mother, Ardell Elaine, and Father, Willard Edward Hodel, are young, and just beginning a family life. My mother told me, when she was in the hospital, and everyone was listening to the radio, the populace was drawn together in anticipation of a war to end all wars.

They watched the newsreels at the movie theatres, read the newspapers, and listened continuously to the radio for what was next.

Ardell is in the hospital giving birth. She's a young bride of 20 years old; listening to the radio broadcast stating President Roosevelt is very ill; he is now in the hospital. The President had been voted in for the fourth term, the people of this nation thought he was above and beyond the best we had ever had. While bringing the nation through the depression and getting the country through this war, the patriots are praying for him.

The United States is on high alert; we have two wars confronting us, Europe and Japan. President Roosevelt, his 4th term in office, is suffering from the after-effects of polio he had as a young man. Most citizens didn't know about his debilitating disease, and under the president's direction, the newspapers shaded the real picture. The country's leadership is in dire need, the historical significance of so many events in one year is beyond the comprehension of most.

Dianah is born into this world of turmoil, and with all this upheaval, many everyday items don't run smoothly.

The family wrote her name as Dianah on the registration certificate, the state arbitrarily changed it to Diana. It was not an uncommon occurrence for the recorders to assume they knew better. The government at all levels had taken control as never before. The politicians would make choices as they saw fit. Friends, neighbors, and family are reporting each other if there was the slightest thought of someone as a communist, a nazi, or any other affiliation which might be against the US government.

I came into the world as a healthy, loved child on her way home to the 200-acre dairy farm in central Wisconsin. Not only am I the first child but the first grandchild. Grandparents and parents, plus two aunts for a short while, all live together in the original farmhouse. During the first year, all hands and eyes were watching over me. My two aunts moved after a short while to be on their own. Dad's sisters and brother moved from the farm when they were 13 to 14 years of age. Grandpa believed that children were to be used as workers if you were a female that brought on a whole other set of circumstances. Uncle Merlin went into the army, stationed first in the Japanese area, after Pearl Harbor. Merlin came home on leave and brought a pretty little dog, which Grandma named Queenie. I was told by Mother, Merlin got the dog for me and I was too young to care for it. I always thought it was my grandmother's dog until I was about fourteen when Queenie left one day and didn't come back. Mom said that's what animals do when it's their time. I was told then, the dog had been for me.

My Paternal Grandfather is from recent German immigration; my

Paternal Grandmother is of Irish descent. Grandmother's Uncle homesteaded and built the farm that she inherited. My parents, Willard and Ardell, who never had a childhood of their own, are now hoping for a future and praying the war will end soon.

Ardell was one of 12 children, one of the middle children. Her parents were a combination of nationalities, English, Irish, French, American Indian, and German. My maternal grandmother passed when my mother was ten, and most of the older siblings were moving to make their way in the world. At the age of 10, Ardell needed to stay home; school became a part of her past. Ardell now is the cook and caregiver; to her siblings who are still at home. The youngest brother Ronnie was still a baby. Once Ardell married, Ronnie moved in with Blanche, an older sister, and her family. My Maternal Grandfather was in his 80's at this time.

Willard attended school through 8th grade and wanted to continue into high school, hoping to become a teacher in one of the local schools, but the farm needed his help. It's wartime, the army draft notified the family for Willard to join, which he willingly wanted to do. However, Grandpa applied for an exemption, which Willard didn't know about until after the fact. It was a family of very few words and no explanations. The exemption as a necessary home business to provide food for the army was granted, and Dad was the primary worker. Dad would stay to work the farm for the next 22 years.

During the Year 1945
Franklin Delano Roosevelt has his 4th inauguration in January; he dies in office on April 12th.
Vice President Harry S. Truman is sworn in.
We are part of World War II.
Adolf Hitler moves to an underground bunker.
A day later, Adolph Hitler and his wife of one day Eva Braun commit suicide.
British troops liberate the Belsen concentration camp; thousands are dead

Dachau concentration camp is liberated

Joseph Goebbels and his wife commit suicide after killing their six children.

William Joyce is captured, charged with high treason in London for his wartime broadcast on German radio. He was hanged in 1946.

The Soviet Union reaches Berlin in April.

The three prominent leaders meet to discuss the end of World War II, Soviet leader Joseph Stalin, British Prime Minister Winston Churchill, and US President Harry S. Truman. The meeting included a commitment to end the war with Japan with a threat of destruction to the still belligerent country.

Italian partisans execute Benito Mussolini

Germany is divided between the allied forces.

The USS Indianapolis is sunk by a Japanese Submarine, killing 883 seamen

The USS Franklin was severely damaged, with a loss of 700 lives

The United States detonates an atomic bomb on Hiroshima, August 6th.

The United States explodes an atomic bomb over Nagasaki, Japan.

Emperor Hirohito announces Japan's surrender on the radio.

The Philippines and Burma are liberated from the Japanese

V-J Day is celebrated

The United Nations Charter is signed by 50 nations creating the United Nations.

The United States Navy Flight 19 disappears over the Bermuda Triangle

HoChi Minh declares the independence of Vietnam from France

Day to Day news

Percy Spencer accidentally discovers microwaves heat food

Only 5,000 homes have television sets
The world's first general-purpose electronic computer is completed, covering 1800 sq. ft. of floor space. The first set of calculations is run on a computer.
Arthur C. Clark puts forward the idea of a communications satellite in a Wireless World magazine article.
Orwell published his anti-Stalinist allegory Animal Farm

The Cost of Living -
a new house average $4,600
Wages $2,400
A gallon of gas 15 cents
House rent $60
New car $1,020
Ladies fur coat $70
Men's shirt $2.50
Portable typewriter $68.37

Men are coming home from the war, and many are not coming back. New inventions, new ideas, new government policies, and a new version of war is about to set in, known as the Cold War.

I am the apple of the family eye. I could do no wrong, as the pictures portrayed, a healthy beautiful child, and fast to learn. It wasn't until brother Frank was born that sharing became a part of my world. Because farm life is hard work and you're never done, there's never much time for a child. I became my own best friend and didn't care for dolls. I created imaginary playmates. I made up stories and I was the heroine. As siblings, Frank and I got along well, we treated each other as childhood friends. Neighbors were far away, and there were no other children to associate with; our only reference to growing was the adults on the farm. So it would seem my life was rather charmed.

Around the age of five, Grandpa chose to have electricity installed on the farm and in the house. Until then, we had a generator in the machine shed. When the electrician had finished outdoors, he started making a real mess inside. The walls were torn apart. What a mess for days. While the wires were being installed; there was plaster everywhere. I don't think he was a real electrician, just someone the family knew and said he could do the job. Each room had one or two outlets installed. Of course, we didn't have much to plug in at that time. He set up a plug for an electric stove in the kitchen so Mom and Grandma wouldn't have to cook on the woodstove anymore. Mom said the old wood stove made better cakes and bread than the new stove.

The man, who was doing the electrical, was always so dirty; even in the morning, he looked like he just came from the coal mine. He was tall and skinny, smoked a corncob pipe, and didn't talk much. When he did talk, you could see a lot of his teeth were missing and the ones he did have were as dirty as the rest of him. I asked Mom why Leo was never clean. Mom said, "Shhh, that man was once your Grandma's boyfriend, but she chose Grandpa instead, and when she did, Leo never married. It took Leo forever to get everything done and the plaster back on the walls, but eventually, Leo was gone and we cleaned up the mess.

Grandpa could be mean sometimes, but he was neat and clean. He had diabetes; I would watch him every morning after breakfast, give himself an insulin shot. I felt sorry for him; when one arm was sore, he would switch to the other arm, and then sometimes Grandma would have to give Grandpa a shot in his leg. Grandpa didn't complain, but much of the time, he wasn't feeling well.

It wasn't too long after the electricity was brought to the farm; they installed a milking machine in the barn. Grandpa paid the neighbor's share for the electric line from the main road over their property to ours; the charge was by the number of feet of road frontage and the closest electricity was at the mailbox one-half mile away. Still, with an electric milk machine, much of the work continues by hand milking. It didn't save much time, and Mom and Dad had to carry the machine

The farm

buckets to the strainer still, put a strap over the next cow, and get her all set up to milk.

The only part I liked about the barn was the cats. Mom would fill a pan of milk; no matter how many there were, they would be there waiting. Sometimes we only had one or two cats, and other times there could be a dozen. As a kid, I never figured out where all the cats disappeared, but it wouldn't be too long before there would be another bunch.

Then the dairy people, who picked up the milk, said we had to have a milk house to keep the milk clean and cold in the summer. So we built a milk house, a concrete floor, and a water tank for the carboys. There was enough room in the milkhouse for a kerosene stove to heat water for washing clothes. Mom used to wash clothes with the wringer washer in the kitchen, there wasn't enough room for one person and that was the room everyone congregated to. When the milk house was finished, the washing machine moved out there. We no longer had to carry the five gallon pails of water from the well to wash clothes. Still

ME AND DANIEL

needed to carry the water for the kitchen and drinking, but one is always thankful for small blessing. I can tell you carrying five gallons of water up five steps and about hundred feet several times just to wash clothes, will get you to say, Thank You. A water pipe was put in from the well to the milk house and into the carboy tank. It was another item I pondered. I understood the milk remaining cool, but Mom had to carry water in the house to wash clothes for years before installing the water pipe, which I considered an insult to humanity. The story goes, on a farm, the barn, equipment, and animals come first. The house and women's work is last in priorities.

Even as a youngster, I thought the plumbing was supposed to go in the ground, but Dad and Grandpa didn't want to dig down six feet below the freeze line, so they put the water pipe way up in the air to run from the well down to the milk house, a length of about 200 feet. They told me we didn't need to worry about freezing in the winter because the water pipe was at a great enough angle for all the water to drain, so nothing would freeze in the line. I understood but said it sure doesn't look good. I am told it works; that's all that matters.

In the summer, Dad would use the milk tank to take a bath after haying; none of the rest of us did; the water was always super cold coming out of the well.

We'd use the wheelbarrow from the milk house to take the clothes over to the clothesline on the backside of the house. There were four long clotheslines, and it wasn't enough, so we strung another line between the trees with a big prop stick in the middle so they wouldn't sag to the ground. Mom used a wash stick at the washtub, about 4 feet long to move the clothes around in the tub, and it was smooth and bristol white from the bleach. One of my mother's things was to have sparkling clean clothes. As summer bloomed, birds sang, and the squirrels ran through the trees, it wasn't too bad hanging up the heavy clothes, but as winter came and the wind blew, your hands would freeze, pinning the wet clothes to the line. If the wind didn't blow, the clothes froze stiff on the line. The overalls the men wore were larger than I was and heavy, and hanging them around the stoves inside left little room for anything else. Wintertime would be so drafty; we'd have a wood stove in the kitchen, a coal-burning potbelly stove in the dining room, and an oil burner in the living room. Before the clothes were put away, everything was ironed, even the men's shorts and including the bib overalls; they were the worst. Grandma had an old iron, it was heavy and I burned myself every time I had to iron.

In the beginning, Mother would sew, and she made her own patterns. Mom took apart

Frank and Dianah, first day of school

old coats the adults couldn't wear anymore and cut them down to make me a coat. Along with all the other cooking, cleaning, and help with the farm work, she made time for me to study the alphabet to write my name and numbers before starting First grade. There was no kindergarten, and preschool was an unheard-of event. I attended the two-room school from first through eighth grade. There were two teachers, Mrs. Davis 1st thru 4th grade and Mr. Nickolas 5th thru 8th grade. The bus would arrive at 7 AM, and I would return home at 4:30 PM. There were years that I didn't miss a school day; I preferred being at school to home life. I was the only child that had the advantage of one on one time with Mother. But that was short-lived. It then became my job to help Frank get ready for school, it's a guess, but I probably didn't help advance his education. In my defense, we both needed to put effort forth; I don't think either of us gave it a good try.

Until I was seven or eight years old, the summers were good, I didn't have any friends, and Frank was still a baby, so I had made up

ME AND DANIEL

friends. I pretended I could dance and sing. I was always in charge. I could barely carry a tune, had no rhythm, and had no idea what I was in charge of, but I had a much better time than playing with dolls, which was what some of the adults thought I should be doing. The closest I came to enjoying dolls was when I received paper dolls and designed their clothes.

By the time I was eight years old, brother number two arrived, Danny. My time to become a caregiver now began. I had started washing dishes at age 5, a stool at the sink; they said it was time I learn to make my way. On a particular cooking and baking day, I decided it is now time to disappear. I hid in the back seat of the car on the floor for at least 3 hours, assuming the kitchen must indeed be cleaned by now. Mother knew what I was doing; when I strolled into the kitchen, it was a disaster. The dishes were waiting, piled in the sink, on the table, the stove. By the time I finished washing and drying, it was time for dinner, and the process began all over again.

Once it was determined I could help take care of siblings, besides washing diapers and the other clothes, the addition of feeding the baby with a bottle and spoon, changing diapers, and giving the baby attention for a quiet time became my job. Quiet was essential; the grandparents had no desire to listen to crying babies.

Occasionally my parents went out to get away; I also became the babysitter. By the time I was age nine, brother three was here. Each time a new baby was on the way, Mom would say, I have something important to tell you. She never told me anything that was going on except for a new addition to the family. So whenever we were alone, and the statement started, "I want to tell you something," I would think to myself, oh no, not again. There was a year when the only place I went was to school and home. Not to the grocery store, not to see a friend; summer was only to take care of children and work around the house.

During the early 1950's Grandpa neglected to pay the taxes on the farm for three years, and the dairy business failed to support two families. To keep from losing the farm, Dad went to work as a milk truck driver. He could pick up the carboys, one in each hand weighing close to 100 pounds each, and throw them in the truck. Dad's height was five ft. 7 inches and strong. When he finishes the morning run, the rest of the day is allocated to the farm needs in season. The cows are milked and fed before he leaves for the milk run; Mom would help. She would come in from the barn, make Dad's breakfast, and make sure we were ready for school. Grandpa would feed pigs and spread the manure; Grandma fed the chickens, fed the dogs, and made Grandpa's breakfast. When Frank and I came home from school, we would go into the silo, shovel the silage down for the cows, sometimes it was frozen, and we had to dig it out. The cows were fed silage, grain mix, and alfalfa twice a day. The milking process was twice a day, and shoveling the manure out was generally twice a day. In the spring, the plowing, planting, and cultivating began. Grandpa cultivated the corn; I rode on the corn planter; at the end of each row, the corn planter was manually raised, and seed flow stopped for the turn to prevent any seed waste. It also kept the crows from finding the grain. Strawberries were picked in the early summer, then taken door to door in the city by Frank and me to sell. Grandpa or Dad would drive the truck; we would ride in the back of the pick-up with the berries about 40 miles. We usually looked like poor orphans asking for a handout. Grandpa said it is easier to make a sale if you don't look too good; they buy more if they think you're poor. Nobody bothered to tell us we were penniless. All work on the farm was to make a living. There was no pay, no allowance, no pay for extra work.

About age 10 or 11, I discovered Doubleday Book Club, and I'm not sure where I got the money; the first dollar wasn't too hard, that was to join, but the month after that first order was probably from Mom. I ordered the most extensive and fattest books I could for the least amount of money. That summer, I read the entire series of Nathaniel Hornblower. My Dad's youngest sister was visiting; she asked what I was doing upstairs for so long.

"Reading."

She came back upstairs with me to see what I was reading, thinking I must be reading a romance novel of seductive content. Aunt Evelyn liked those kinds of books.

When she looked at the thickness and content, Aunt Evelyn said, "Are those the books you ordered? Do you find it interesting?"

"Yes, some of the words are kind of big, but he gets to travel all over the place."

I could tell she didn't understand, and she went back downstairs.

One of the summertime crops is cucumbers; we all picked cucumbers; mother made dill pickles and relish. After everyone finished the main picking, Frank and I would pick the pickles to sell at the sorting station. It's our spending money. We earned $1.20 for 50 lb. bag for little pickles, oversized pickles were sorted out, and any turning yellow was discarded. I picked and saved one whole summer to buy a high school class ring for $28.00. It seemed important at the time; all the kids at school had one.

By the end of summer, it would be time to harvest the sweet corn; unbelievably good. The corn is picked just before dinner, shucked, put in a massive kettle of water, some salt, and brought to a boil, served with lots of butter and salt accompanied by pork chops or side pork. No corn skewers, just our fingers, and be careful because it's hot. Frank and I would have a contest to see who could eat the most. It wasn't a fair game, Frank was younger and smaller, but he always did an excellent job of keeping up.

As Autumn came, the hogs were ready to ship to market. One frigid day, everyone participated in catching the yearling pigs. It was a cold, dreary day, and it looked like snow was on its way. The pasture is over an acre with wire fencing, and the animals are healthy and fast. As directed, Frank and I went to the far end of the frozen rutted field. We chased the pigs toward Dad and Grandpa; they would catch and sling them in the trailer for sale. A couple of the hogs maneuvered better than the catchers and started running back toward us.

Someone is calling to me, "Dianah, catch it, quick."

It was stronger and faster than me; as the pig ran through my legs, I plopped down on its hairy back as hard as I could, thinking I would knock the air out of it, and the pig would fall to the ground. Mr. Pig kept running; I didn't slow it down even one step. I'm hanging on to his tail, not to fall to the frozen ground; I can't see where I'm going. The pig is running in one direction, and I'm facing in the other. I know the fence is close at hand; I do not want to be tangled in the barbed wire. This pig is strong and keeps running; my feet are up so as not to scrape my knees on the frozen ground. Everyone is laughing; Dads Yelling, jump off; jump-off it now. I couldn't get the pig to slow down enough to jump off. I finally rolled off into the frozen, bumpy mud. The family was still laughing; I guess it must have been a sight and probably didn't take 5 minutes; I could have sworn it was 20 minutes. The one and only pig ride I have ever taken or want to take. After the family finishes all their laughter, it's back to work.

The field corn needed to be cut and bundled. We would all work at shocking the corn to dry. Shocking the corn is standing the bundles up and leaning them against each other, like making a teepee; once dry, it would be fed through the shredder and shot up the funnel into the silo. It was a dusty, dirty job, with lots of pollen and sometimes mice.

One year a neighbor was helping; he slipped and fell on the conveyor belt into the shredder. By the time they could turn off the tractor that turned the belt, it was too late. The nearest hospital is 30 minutes away, with no phones and no ambulance. Most farmers didn't have insurance; everyone chipped in to help the man's family as much as they could.

Before the corn harvest, the oats would be ready. I would ride the grain threshing machine, which cut and bundled the oats. At the end of every row, the sickle had to be lifted and then put back down to start the next row. When the cutting is complete, a day or two on the machinery, it would be necessary to shock the oats. The process was required for drying. When the threshing season is ready, the neighborhood farmers will gather all the oats from the field, and the threshing

ME AND DANIEL

Grandparents on the farm

machine would blow oats out of one pipe and straw out the other. Everyone worked as hard as they could to finish in one day.

At the beginning of the 1950s, the recession was here, hard times. The weather was upon us, heavy snow up to the electric lines, no phone lines to the farm. When the snow is this high, to open the back door, you use the front porch because it has a porch roof; open that door and carefully make your way around to the rear porch and shovel the back door open. Then dig a path to the windmill so you can take a kettle of boiling water to thaw the pump. When the pump has started the water to the cowl tank, you quickly shovel the snow path to the barn, break the ice water in the tank so the cows could drink, and start the milking day.

After breakfast, no school, not even the snowplow could get through on the roads, it was up to us kids to shovel out the machine shed, to use the tractors. We shoveled to the outhouse, the chicken coup, and the pigpen. One never thinks of things being too far away until your shoveling snow, and it just might snow again tonight. After a day or two, the snowplow came by and opened the roads. But we need to shovel again where the snowplow pushed the snow into the wide driveway for all the different machinery.

The little kids wanted outside and Mom was glad to get them dressed and out her hair. Frank and I are shoveling, Dan and Joe are building a snowman and an igloo. Linda wanted to get on top of the snowbank, we all said, "Don't go up there, you might fall into the bank, it's not solid. But Linda usually did as she wanted. She's up on the bank and I hear a scream. The snow was up to her shoulders, she couldn't move. I don't know if she was cold or scared, I said to Dan and Joe, "Go help your sister out of the snow.

"We're not going to get her out of there, you told her not to go up there."

Frank and I went back to shoveling, and Linda continued to scream until Mom came out and made us get her out of the bank. Mom took her into the house, dried her off and she was back out in no time.

The year of all the snow brought flooding in the spring. The cows were standing in water up to their udders, trying to milk is next to impossible, and getting the milk cans to the milk house through the mud; only my Dad had enough strength. The only place on the whole farm out of the water is the house. It took a week for the water to subside, I couldn't use the wheelbarrow, it sank in the mud. Dad put on his wading boots for fishing and hooked up the hay wagon to the tractor to get from one building to the next. We had to find dry spots for the cows or their hoofs would rot, the feed and hay were wet. The cows had to be coaxed out of the barnyard or they would be stuck in the mud. It was a mess, and somehow we managed.

My brother Joe arrived when I was nine, the workload increased. Dan and Joe become almost like twins, though they are one year apart in age, they formed a bond. Wherever you saw one, the other would be there. By the time the two were able to run and play, they were inseparable, and because of that when you called, it was always Dan-Joe come to dinner. After some time we discovered Joe thought his name was Dan. Joe was the most important person in his life and we always called, naming Dan first. After a short time, it was corrected in everyone's mind, including Joe.

The family dynamics were starting to get stressed. Dad didn't drive the milk truck now. He worked in a small town of Poy Sippi, about 6 miles from home, at the creamery, where they made rounds of cheddar cheese. Frank and I went to see the vats with the floating curd. Once I slipped, fell in the vat, in my Sunday dress. I would have to endure the day, no one was going to drive home just because I was wet and smelled of curd cheese. I wasn't too fond of the creamery, didn't care for the odor, and it was always wet and damp.

After a day's work, Dad would go across the street with the guys to the bowling alley. He was in the bowling league and won two trophies, but the beer drinking was increasing.

The school bus went through Poy Sippi at about the same time Dad got off work. Frank and I could get off the bus at the corner and walk to the creamery; if dad wasn't there, we walked across the street to the bowling alley. One afternoon, we made the stop and couldn't find Dad.

I asked a couple of the guys Dad worked with if they knew where he was; they said no, and wouldn't consider driving us home.

I told Frank, "Guess we'll walk."

Frank was short for his age. He looked up at me. I could tell he didn't think this was a good idea. I remarked, we can't stay in the bowling alley all night, and our farmhouse doesn't have a phone.

Winter is upon us; it's now around 5 PM, getting dark and colder. We started the walk; I said to Frank, "Both of us need to stay aware of anything unusual around us, be it two-legged or four-legged. Dusk always seems to be an intrepid time of day. It didn't take more than a few minutes, and we were out of town, walking on a country dirt road that would run through the woods all the way home, around 5 miles. I didn't want to think about how cold it would get and was hoping there was no snow on the way. Every time there was a movement in the trees, we would both stop, hoping it was just the wind. I was more concerned about the trouble I would be in from the parents than walking home through the woods. About a third of the way home, Dad found us. When the school bus didn't stop at our place, Mom thought we were with Dad, but then Dad came home without us. So Mom sent him back out. I admit there was a moment of relief not having to walk all the way home. I didn't get into as much hot water as I thought I would, but that was the last stop in Poy Sippi.

Dad heard they were giving accordion lessons in the evening in a cold damp basement in town, and he liked the accordion.

Mom knew how to play; she also played the piano. We had a grand organ, it even had candelabra holders, and Mom would play; she had a good rhythm, and very seldom missed a key. Mom, Dad, and Grandpa could all do the harmonica, but none of the family could read music. The accordion lessons weren't expensive, and they decided I should have lessons. Oh, what a disaster for a nine-year-old. The accordion was too heavy, too cumbersome, and I didn't like the sound. I couldn't coordinate the keys with the buttons plus the air compression movement. I didn't know what synchronization meant at the time; I just knew I didn't have it. I was supposed to read music while playing the accordion, none of it fell together. Reading sheet music made no sense to me. I might as well try to read Greek. They all expected I would catch onto it just like I had been reading all my life, which by the way, I am nine years old.

After about three months my family and teacher gave up on me. I didn't have to endure the torture of the accordion any longer. Not being able to play did make me feel as though I had let them down. I failed, I wasn't smart enough to figure it out, and the family could play music without thinking or reading.

Our cousins Jesse and Roger came to visit during the summer, they were city boys, so it was always interesting to hear the stories we could share about our different experiences and lifestyles. One of the days we decided to do our favorite pastime, go up the North Road, the one that was no more than a wagon trail, and build us a fort. We all agreed if we used a few tools the fort would come out better than usual. Using

Grandpa's tools was something that was never, ever done. But today we were brave and foolish. We helped ourselves to a couple of saws, and hammers and very carefully went behind the buildings to get to the road unseen. We are sawing away, hammering, there are no nails, we cannot be wasteful. Grapevines as lashing is the plan. We are making a general mess, but we'll clean up later. Our forte is under construction. Jesse says to me, "I can't get this limb sawed; it keeps moving. Will you hold it while I'm sawing." I grab hold of the limb; I'm not strong enough to hold it steady and not wise enough to keep my hands away from the saw. The saw jumps and slices twice along the top of my thumb. We both jump; Jesse is scared; I tell him it's not that bad, except I'm bleeding all over the place. I decided to go back to the house to wash it off and get a bandage to stop the bleeding.

Before I could get in the house, Frank and Roger were already telling Mom, and Grandpa was there too, "Dianah got cut with the saw."

I was holding my hand behind me when Mom said, "How bad is it?"

"Not bad, just need a big bandaid." I could have hidden it, except the blood kept dripping, giving away the secret I was doing my best to hide.

Mom and Grandpa took a look at my hand; no doubt, I was going to the doctor. Grandma would drive, they brought out a towel, and off we went.

The old country doc looked at me, "Can you move your thumb?"

"It'll bleed more if I move it,"

The Doc smiled; he knew I was in trouble.

Mom told him she thought I needed stitches.

Doc shook his head, "No, we'll use some tape, keep it dry for a couple of weeks and change the bandages every so often. It might leave a scar, but it's probably bled enough so that she won't need any shots.

Everyone is quiet as we drive home. There was a lecture about using tools and cleaning up the roadway. I couldn't wash dishes now and razzed the boys about them having to do the cleanup. Jesse and Roger's,

Mom, and Dad were none too happy about the events. There were no more summer visits.

During the eight years of grade school, there was generally a choice of 5 or 6 girlfriends you could have. As the years passed, the friendships seemed to change. In the beginning, the closest friend was Dawn. Her family was the town's founder and owned a large portion of the village and farms, even the general store. Participating in Dawn's lifestyle became a trial with her parents; they lived a much different lifestyle, and the association drifted. Barabra, small for her age; her hair was so blonde it was white, and she wore glasses even in first grade. She was not the go-to girl; kids would automatically drift to when looking for a friend. She was quiet, academic, and intelligent. I appreciated her wanting to get the most out of our schooling. But Barabra and I drifted; I think it was after I started noticing boys as the opposite sex. Then there was Janice, who was much more worldly than I—new about relationships with boys. I didn't have a clue.

I did a sleepover at her house one night and asked, "Janice, how does that all work between boy and girl." Janice explained the whole thing to me; I thought it sounded pretty disgusting and was quite pleased I didn't have a boyfriend as she did.

There were summers before all the children started arriving; I could spend two weeks in Milwaukee with my aunt and uncles at their homes. It was an extraordinary time; I thought their homes were grand. They had indoor plumbing, television, room for everyone to sit at the table, and besides that, they were happy to see me.

After age 12, the visits to Milwaukee ended.

While on this last visit, my aunt said, "You need to wash dishes."

I was insulted; and said, "No."

Aunt Iness thought I was a belligerent upstart. She gave me that look, which said, you are in my house, a guest, and you will behave as expected. I, therefore, explained to Aunt Ines, "I wash dishes every day without fail; I change diapers, wash clothes and carry babies. There is no time off. I thought this was my vacation, my only vacation. I could tell she still wasn't pleased but said that as you grow and have a family with daily chores, there are no vacations, especially for women. Once again, I was left wondering about the inequities of life. The episode dampened the pleasure for the rest of the trip. I knew I should have washed dishes; I was too stubborn for my good. I didn't realize at the time I was an ungrateful guest. I was thinking of myself as an adult; after all, I did grown-up labor.

The amount of reading also put me at odds with the family. I read that a proper hostess doesn't ask or expect her guests to help with chores. Then there were the situations of good English; the lesson not to correct any of the adults was taught by age 6. I spent a lot of time being on the wrong side of the family dynamics. Either I didn't do enough, or as the family would say, I was too big for my britches, which made little sense; I am continually told to eat more, you're skinny.

The family visits had now ended; I needed to realize specific etiquette and manners are necessary, which I had not excelled at and had not been part of my education. The adage "Children are to be seen and not heard" was a daily mantra. We didn't have visitors, so very little interaction. One difficult task, I had a habit of saying what was on my mind; if I felt it was true, I said it. One lesson learned, speak when spoken to. Slowly I was learning to be quiet, which I didn't find out until much later in life labeled me as an introvert. But at age twelve, I only knew no one wanted my opinion, and I was better off not stating it.

At age 10, July, Mother came home from the hospital with a baby sister, Linda. My interest in child care was waning, and Linda is a more difficult baby to care for. She was heavier and more demanding. Linda required more attention, or maybe it was; I wanted to give less. It was harvest season; all the neighbor men were at the farm to help with the silage. It was the women's job to feed them. The day after Mom was home from the hospital, she was helping in the kitchen to prepare the meals. I didn't think it was right, but I was ten years old; keeping the little kids out of the way, and setting the table was my job. It was hot and humid that summer; the mosquitoes were plentiful, and the flies were unbelievable.

We worked hard all summer when it was time to harvest the oats, the same series of events with neighbor men, and food prep. Only this time, Frank and I are in the granary over the shed, shoveling the oats away from the shute. The dust and chaff from the oats were so thick you couldn't breathe even with a scarf over your nose. The oats would come pouring out of the shoot, Grandpa would come up and help once in a while, but he couldn't stay because he couldn't breathe. I was so relieved when the job was finished, and I don't think I ever felt so dirty. There is dust in my eyes, nose, ears; you could hardly see my hair because of the dust. The chaff and dirt in the air is so thick you couldn't see from one end of the shed to the other, even with the sun trying to filter through.

We had one more harvest that year, alfalfa. The bails were heavy, about 80 pounds, with the bails, hauled from one place to another two or three times. The bailer pushed the alfalfa on a conveyor onto the wagon. The hay was thick; the bails came out faster than we could stack. Grandpa is going as slow as he can, with tractor pulling the bailer, it will stall and the bailer doesn't make the bails if it's moving too slow. Rain is on the way, we need to hurry before the hay gets wet and the alfalfa will mold. Stacking carefully at the back wagon brace, four tiers high, then from the wagon up into the barn, another place filled with pollen and dust. One year, after working in the hay most of the day, I went into the house, told Mom I couldn't breathe. She gave me an aspirin, a washcloth to remove the dirt from my face, and said, sit here in the kitchen until you feel better. A half-hour later, I went back out to finish the day's bailing.

The barn was leaning; we propped timbers to avoid it falling over; for that reason, we had to stack more on one side of the barn than the other. Whatever didn't fit in the barn was stacked outside in a pattern, or the stack would tip over. It was a long summer.

The family decided they should build a calf barn to increase the size of the herd. Dad and a couple of uncles from Milwaukee helped on the weekend, up went the calf barn. It wasn't beautiful but served

ME AND DANIEL

the purpose. Frank and I have another job, clean out the manure. On Saturday, it was taking us so long Grandpa came out to see what we were doing. Frank and I sat on the rail telling stories; the smell in the barn was so bad; breathing was an effort. There was no ventilation; the acrid urine odor made our eyes water; I didn't know how the calves tolerated it. Grandpa shook his head; he said, "You can get out of here if you get the job done." Frank and I looked at each other after he left and simultaneously said, "But then we'll have to do something else."

Grandpa bought a power lawnmower; before, I would use the push reel mower. There was about an acre of grass around the house. On a nice day, the squirrels would be running, and the birds would be out. I didn't mind walking behind the power mower; if I timed it right, I could be out there all day and not have to do anything inside the house. It would look almost manicured when all the mowing was complete; I could look at it and feel I had accomplished something that made me feel good.

It sounds like an excessive amount of time is spent trying to get out of doing the daily chores. Most chores were ever so dull, my indoor

Siblings Joe, Dan, Linda & Anna

activity was either washing dishes or caring for brothers and sisters, plus the amount of tension was growing.

There were times we would scamper off for most of the day, go up the north road, which was nothing more than a wagon wheel trail. No one cared what we did there. Because they were smaller, the boys would swing from the grapevines, pretending to be Tarzan of the Jungle. I would start the building of a forte. There were a few incidents when I was alone to wander into the north 40 field, and in the corner was a stand of birch trees. If it was summer, the leaves were a baby green, twinkling in the spring breezes. If autumn is here, the leaves had turned yellow, the grass under the tall birch was soft and willowy. The yellow leaves slowly fell to the ground like butterfly wings or angels waiting for a blessing to occur. It was a special place God made to let the breeze whisper in my ear; no one else went there except the whitetail deer and the forest birds. Gazing at the clear blue sky through the fluttering leaves allowed me to convene with Mother nature while feeling the Lord's blessings shine upon me.

At age twelve, I thought, almost a teenager, and for some reason, I thought that would make a difference in my life, but it didn't. In November, Mom came home with sister Anna. That winter was frigid; we had three stoves going, wood in the kitchen, and an electric range for cooking. The converted ornate cast-iron potbelly stove in the dining room went to coal. The living room oil burner stove gave very little heat to the second floor with its one lone stove pipe. First out of bed would have the advantage of being closer to the stove pipe, too hot to touch but any warmth stayed right there at the pipe and up to the chimney.

The farmhouse has three bedrooms —a small bedroom downstairs for Grandpa and Grandma, and upstairs provides a landing, one a tiny room, and one large room. There are no closets anywhere. All the children slept in three double beds and a crib, in one room. The infant sleeps in a smaller crib with Mom and Dad in their space. The smaller bedroom is large enough for a double bed up against the wall, a dresser, and a crib. Grandma and Grandpa had the same size room downstairs and a vanity which Grandma managed to squeeze in.

The house, every few years, would get some new wallpaper; you never wanted to be around for that event. It would become very testy in the best of circumstances. The kitchen floor would get new linoleum because the floorboards were warped and uneven, and the ridges would wear through. My mother would do a little paint here and there as time and energy allowed.

One time Mom said, "You and Frank need to help," it was after dinner and milking, but still daylight.

"We need to take the tractor and little trailer to the pasture. One cow didn't come in for milking, and it's calving. She might be having a problem."

This week, the pasture was over the hill, and the sun was starting to go down. When we got to the field, the cow was still trying to calve, but the feet came first. Frank held the harness on the cow and Mom, and I pulled until the calf was out. I didn't know about afterbirth and thought there was something terribly wrong. Mom assured me everything was fine, we put the calf on the trailer, and the cow followed us to the barn. Mom got the cow set up in her proper stanchion with the calf; they would be safe. Come morning, the calf was sucking just fine; we watched carefully for about a week; this was the cow's first calf, and both were well.

I'm now 14 and have started high school. It's an adventure. The school is larger than the grade school; there are about 300 students for four grades; the grade school had 50 students for eight classes. At first, I was overwhelmed, finding a room for each class and a different teacher for each category. No one tells you or introduces you to these nuances. My first impression, this school is enormous; it was the largest in the county. How do I establish new friends, the kids I had gone to grade school with all attended a different high school. My schedule on the school bus was still about the same; we just lived farther away than most. The bus ride now was with only high school kids; some guys smoked, the foul odor of smoke, so unpleasant. It would be a long ride if I had to sit close to a smoker, even though they couldn't smoke on the bus.

I started dating in November of my fourteenth year, the 1st year of high school. The first night out was for the Junior Prom; the boy was a junior. He was a friendly enough guy, but Gordy smoked, and he didn't do all that well in school. But I wanted to be out and having fun like the other kids. The Junior Prom is a big deal, and everyone stays out late; Dad said even though it was a special dance, I would be in by midnight. This night is my first actual date; I came in at about 2 AM. Dad instructed Mom to tell me I would not be going anywhere for the next three months. After about two weeks, I talked them into letting me date again.

I found out from one of the students that if you used your study hall time to work in the cafeteria, lunch was free, and they paid you about $10.00 a month. That was a great deal for me; I didn't need a study hall. I never cared for peanut butter or bologna sandwiches, which we always had from home. I signed up immediately, and the food was excellent. The lady in charge of the kitchen was a good cook, she made sure I washed the dishes, but it was better than being bored. The senior, who was the hall monitor, and I became friends. The cafeteria wasn't all work. Chauncy, the hall monitor, was a fun guy; he didn't get in trouble, just always at the edge. We dated a few times, nothing serious. After moving and graduating, Mom told me Chauncy came by the house; he had gone into the Navy and asked where I was and said he wanted to marry me.

"Mom, I can hardly believe that we haven't talked in a year, maybe two". I never did see him again.

Just about end of school year, Mom says, "I need to tell you something important."

"Mom," I exclaimed, "Not again, our family is too big already."

My mother did not want another child either, but there was no doctor to help her.

I asked, "Can't you say No to Dad!"

"It doesn't work that way."

I let it go. My parent's relationship was something that I couldn't change. Each pregnancy became a more difficult delivery. The evening battles between Mom and Dad were growing. I would be washing dishes and could hear them from the barn. It was always the same fight; Dad would accuse Mom of sleeping with someone else, usually my Grandfather. Mom and Grandpa didn't even like each other; they avoided being in the same room whenever possible.

The baby was born, things continued as they had been. There were now four boys and three girls. I was the only one required to do much. Frank didn't have to do much because he was a boy, and boys didn't have to do women's work. This last time Mom came home, the doctor wanted her to rest, so Frank went out with Dad to milk while I made coffee and breakfast and packed lunches. Created the formula and heated the bottle for the baby.

Someone told me once I was supposed to have been a boy, being the first child. It explained why I always thought I should have been a male; life would be so much more clear-cut. Women on the farm were obligated to do women's work and any farm labor possible. From the beginning, I couldn't see anything rewarding about farm life.

I dated as much as I could, but never with one boy for too long. It seemed inevitable; after a short time, the boys seem to think there were liberties they were entitled to. Not with this girl; I have been watching the girls in school and getting married because of pregnancies. So each time the hands started wandering, I ended the relationship.

My first year in high school was Wautoma. Then, they changed the district lines. The second year was then in Wild Rose, where some of the kids I went to grade school with attended. I would have a whole new set of friends. I was studious and always determined to have good grades, and as boyfriends came and went, it was just enough attention to get out of the house. There were some courteous, kind guys, some that were even fun, but I never let go of being ultra-careful.

In the summer of my sixteenth year, the family is having an auction. Not one of us kids knows what or why. We are told on the day of the auction to stay out of the way. There is no indication of ongoing plans. The auction is over, and the farm has been depleted of a lifetime of work and struggle.

Within a few days, Mom said, "We're moving."

I asked, "Where?"

"Omro."

"Where is that?"

"About 20 or 30 miles from here."

I already knew it meant a new school; I didn't ask any more questions.

The week following, Mom and Dad went to buy used furniture for the house that Dad bought. Mom hadn't seen the house yet, and we knew nothing about what was going on. It was all very hush, hush. I didn't realize that all the furniture in the farmhouse was Grandma and Grandpas. All these years, Mom had nothing.

It was a Saturday; we were ready to leave. Mom said, "Say Good-Bye to Grandma and Grandpa." Being inexperienced and not understanding the full scope of what we're doing, we knew we were excited about being on a new adventure. We said our Goodbyes to the Grandparents but had no idea about the reality of leaving and the possibility of not seeing them again or the farm. All the animals, tractors, and equipment were gone, and we didn't understand as kids; there was no coming back; life was changing.

The nine of us loaded in the car and drove to Omro. The first time for everyone but Dad, and pulled up in front of the house. The house's appearance from the outside was okay, but the yard was tiny, and all the other homes were so close. On the farm, there was a huge yard, and you couldn't see any neighbors. We walked in through the front door. Now keep in mind the farmhouse was no jewel, but this house was ugly. Former homeowners added on to the house several times without any forethought. The living room didn't have any windows, so it was

ME AND DANIEL

very dark and had lots of dark woodwork. It was open to the kitchen, but the kitchen sink is in the pantry around the corner. There was one room I liked; it was a sunroom with all the windows on two sides. No one else wanted it because there was no heat and the coldest room in the house. I claimed it as mine.

That first year was tough; starting another new school seemed different; these were not farming kids. If I didn't dress right or look a certain way, I didn't fit with the in-group, I didn't care about the group, but it seems they ruled the school. Had there been an in-group at the other schools I went to, no one told me.

Mom was pregnant again, and Mark was only about two and a half; she got the mumps and was extremely sick.

I was getting ready for school when Mom called, "Dianah, you need to stay home today. I need help; I can't get out of bed."

A little later that day, I walked to the doctor's office and told them what was going on.

The gal at the desk said, "Go on home, and the doctor will be there in about an hour."

When I arrived home, I checked on Mom. She said, "You need to get some clean towels and sheets and hot water." I started doing what she asked, not knowing why. Frank answered the door as the Doctor knocked, and I took him in to see Mom. I asked Frank to keep all the kids quiet in the kitchen. The Doctor asked for the items Mom had told me to get, which were almost ready. So I brought everything into the bedroom, then the doctor asked me to leave. In a short while, he came out, gave me a prescription to get at the drugstore, and said Mom would need to stay in bed for about a week.

The Doctor handed me a towel, I wasn't sure what it was, and he said, "You need to take care of this."

After he left, I went into Mom, and she said, "It's a miscarriage because of the mumps."

"Mom, do I go to the garden and bury the baby?

She said, "No, go down in the basement, use the toilet down there and flush it."

I'm holding a tightly wrapped towel and I haven't looked inside at the miscarriage yet.

"Are you sure?"

"Yes, and don't put the towel in the toilet."

Doing as I was told, I went down to this damp, dreary dark basement and this old ugly, stained toilet. I looked at the baby, there was no life, but this didn't feel right. It was wrong in many ways, but it was against the law to bury it in the garden, and we couldn't afford to have the mortuary do anything next door. I looked still at this lifeless being in my hands and decided I would do what I was told to do; it was not my child. It had been my mother's decision. I flushed the toilet, went upstairs to start dinner for the family.

"Mom, do you need anything?"

"Not right now. Did you take care of everything in the basement?"

"I did like you asked, and I put the towel in a soaking bucket with the other bedclothes that are soaking."

"With a sigh of sadness and fatigue, "Good, take my wallet, go to the drug store for the medicine, and I'll take some when you get back. Then you need to make dinner for everyone; there's meat out in the pantry thawing."

I managed all that was needed for the family to get through the day. I must have been processing because other than a few words with Mom and telling Frank what had happened. I don't think I spoke to anyone. Somehow we made it through the week as a family; all the children that attended school continued as before. I fixed breakfast, Dad's at 5 AM, his lunch for work. I checked on Mom, made lunches for school, and cared for the little ones. I washed clothes, and Mom told me what she wanted to have prepared for each meal. After about 3 or 4 days, she got up to check on things but not doing too much.

The following Monday, I explained to the school secretary why I hadn't attended classes. She wanted me to bring a signed statement; since I always wrote the messages anyway, I could have taken care of it right then, but I knew better. All my classes were fine, except one. Physical Ed, the least critical, or so I thought. I had missed a test, and I couldn't do a makeup test under any circumstances; it was going to lower my grade. Explaining the home events to the instructor made no difference; she said I could do extra classes, which would help, but my grade would still be lower. I wanted to go to college; keeping my grade average as high as I could was important. When I started at this school, the secretary said I hadn't taken the required classes for this district, so I had extra classes from the beginning as it stood. I also needed to get home ASAP after school to take care of things at home. Somehow we all survived, and my memory of that period is a blur. I just drifted through the days, doing the necessities of child care, cooking, and school.

Not too long after this, Grandpa got sick. We didn't know about it until he was in the hospital. Dad and Mom went to see him; I couldn't go because I needed to watch the kids, and the kids couldn't go because they didn't allow children visitors. He passed away of kidney failure within two days because he wouldn't go to the doctor for a urinary infection. When he couldn't get out of bed, Grandma had to drive to the neighbors to use their phone, and then it took about an hour or two before the ambulance got there and another hour back to the hospital.

The funeral was three days later in Berlin, with a large attendance. My mind was attempting to process the events surrounding us, and as we were sitting in the church, my brothers and cousins were saying, well, at least he's gone, and then they would laugh. I was one of the children; therefore, it was deemed I sit with the children even though I am no longer a child, and the designated place to sit was next to the boys, who were anything but respectful. I assumed an adult would say something to the boys, at least to be quiet, but no, it didn't happen. I wait for the service to end, to be away from all these people. It is almost more than I can bear, plus none of them seem unhappy, even the adults. This man, no matter how much the dislike or the hatred, he is gone forever. He's dead; a bit of respect is in order. Even the adults didn't understand my disturbing demeanor.

Grandpa was a hard man; he wanted things orderly and a specific behavior status; he could be mean if things weren't his way. But he wasn't always wrong. Grandpa suffered from sugar diabetes most of his adult life, and I grew up in his house until sixteen. He was a part of my family, and I mourned.

As I was to learn, life continued, and after a short while, Grandma came to live with us. One late afternoon, she was going down in the basement to get some home-canned green beans; the basement steps were steep, she slipped and broke her leg. It wasn't too long after the basement incident that Grandma decided to live with Aunt Agnes. I think it was a combination of the cramped quarters, and now that Grandpa was gone, and Dad was usually not home; there was minimal discipline with all the younger kids. Now you have five or six kids doing pretty much as they want. It was too much noise and confusion for a grieving widow in her 60's. I was gone as much as possible.

School continued, the months moved on, and there was a buzz about the Harvest Festival in the coming up months. They had elected who the king and queen were and those on the court to be honored. I was minus a boyfriend and decided if I were pleasant to the guy in my class who was on the court, maybe he would ask me to the dance. He was studious, class treasurer, a bit of a geek, but a good guy. He did ask me to the dance, and now I was obligated to associate with his friends. I hadn't thought this through very well. We went on a double date with his best friends, I wasn't influential enough to live up to their standards.

Another problem was that I was on the court, and I didn't have a dress. I went shopping, the prices for long fancy gowns were way out of my budget. I told my date if you have someone else in mind to take, that would be okay with me. I thought I was kind; the two of us did not have much in common, our life styles, friends and family were so very different. But he didn't have anyone else he wanted to take to the dance, but now he felt stuck with me. Then he told his friend what I had said. This friend of his, thought I was probably the worst person she had ever met, and told me so. Looking back, I didn't use the best judgement, but I was more caring than the confrontation I had just experienced. I didn't feel good about the situation, but I was beyond caring what she thought. But somehow, I had to make this work. Two weeks before the dance, an envelope appears on our doorstep with my name on it. Mom picks it up and opens it; she always opened all the mail no matter who it was for. Privacy, there was none. In the envelope were two twenty-dollar bills. No name, just the money. I had a good idea where it came from. I told my best girlfriend about not going to the dance because I didn't have a dress, and she told a friend we both knew, a fellow I had dated. I tried to thank them, but they said they didn't know anything about it. I bought the dress, went to the dance, was on the court with the upper group, and had a miserable time. I guess trying to fit in at times isn't worth all the effort. Another lesson.

Summertime is here; I need a job. I wanted the income, but more than that, the ultimate goal is to be out of the house. I found a job babysitting three spoiled little girls. My job was to watch the girls, entertain them, make lunch for the whole family daily, mop the floor once a week, and iron the clothes. I knew they were taking advantage of the situation, but it started at $17.50 a week. I made it through the summer, and just before school started, a friend mentioned another job. The local restaurant needed another waitress and didn't require experience. During the last three weeks of summer vacation, I worked two jobs and tried to keep up my dating life.

Since I now had some income, I asked Mom if I could have a phone installed. I would purchase the phone, pay for installation if she would pay the monthly bill. We agreed, everyone has a phone and needs one for emergencies. I used it more than anyone and thought, it's one small convenience that could last.

I spent very little time at home, but Dad caught me on my way out. They had to get a plumber, and I was the only one in the house with any money.

Dad said, "I need $60 for the plumber, and I'll pay you back."

Of course, I wouldn't say no. But there was no payback, though I wasn't surprised.

My latest boyfriend was good-looking, with dark curly hair, olive complexion, nice build in college, and an attitude. It sounds like I've become very opinionated, maybe so, but then some people are not courteous or pleasant. When another fellow I had dated a couple of times asked if I would like to go for a boat ride, I jumped at the chance.

We double-dated and had a good time when the sky started getting dark, and the thunder was rumbling. My date, a responsible guy, no longer in school and worked for a living, stated we better head back. The weather is not favorable. We headed home, and none too soon.

It's a Sunday afternoon; the rest of my family is attending a family re-union. I'm now home alone; the wind is blowing, thunder and lighting are rattling this old house to the point; I thought the windows would break. We indeed have a tornado. I knew all the things to do when the weather is this bad. Some limbs came down. After the weather cleared, the family came home from the picnic. Mom said she was worried I might have been in the storm. I assured her I was responsible, as were my friends.

The following week, the college boyfriend discovered I had dated someone else over the weekend. My explanation is that you never mentioned not seeing anyone else, and you didn't mention being a couple.

I stated, " You will not take me for granted. We were only dating." We split, went our separate ways, and it was a good thing.

As my senior year started, the school was sponsoring the Miss Omro Pageant. The girl chosen for Miss Omro could then try out for the Miss Wisconsin title, and the winner of that pageant would go to Miss America.

The day it was first announced, several friends said, "Dianah, try out. You would be great."

"I don't have a talent; my figure isn't good enough."

To one friend, I said, "You should try out. You could do this much better than me."

Surprise is my first reaction; I never thought of myself as pageant material. My friends didn't stop there. They were pretty insistent I should do this. The Pageant is being held in the school gymnasium and will be standing room only. It would be an undertaking of enormous proportions for me. Others may not think of it as a big deal, but I honestly did not have any ideas for talent or muster the courage to do this.

The following day I signed up for the competition. The obstacles are numerous. I didn't have a good bathing suit, still didn't know what I would use as talent, and was scared to death. One of my biggest fears was being in front of many people, all expecting something from me. I was not working at this time, so I had no money to buy anything.

I kept telling myself, "How bad can it be?" I can make a fool of myself, but not trying meant I was a coward. I needed to prepare and had one week to get ready. My plan came into focus; the art department would let me borrow a large easel. I can pre sketch an outline of what to draw while on stage. While drawing, the topic is discrimination of obesity. I have an old black swimsuit; it will have to do. My heeled shoes have seen better days, and my prom dress is the only part of this whole ensemble that makes any sense.

The dress rehearsal is two days prior; all the contestants are there with props and ready to strut their stuff. My turn came, and I could not get up on that stage. I told the coordinator my supplies hadn't arrived; I would get everything together tomorrow and be ready. There was no way I could fumble about in front of my peers.

The evening before the show, my mind was on a downward spiral. What had I been thinking? I simply can't go through with this. Sometime during the night, there is a vision telling me that I cannot only do the show, but everything will be fine.

The day of the show is a blur. I did the walk, swimsuit, formal gown, and dress. The talent portion could have been better; the audience was having a difficult time hearing me. During the question and answer portion, I'm not sure it even happened. I remember my knees were physically shaking; I must have had the long dress on because I thought no one could see the trembling. The awards were for the most likable, then second place, first place, and winner. I came in second place and was thrilled, not believing that I would place at all. There were eight contestants, each one talented and more surefooted than I.

Mr. Nielsen, the principal, announced anyone missing classes the day after the pageant would receive three days of detention. The exhaustion, with all the trauma I put myself through, and I couldn't tell anyone about the fear of being on stage, I was physically worn out.

My first class the following day was architectural drawing. When class was over, Mr. Jacobs asked to talk to me in his office and proceeded to tell me I had done a great job, and these were the reasons I didn't win, but I shouldn't feel bad. He didn't understand; I didn't feel bad; I was tired. As I walked out of class, someone else gave me a pep talk; it seems no one got the big picture. There was no disappointment; it's exhaustion.

Walking to the second class, I am stopped again; that was when I said, "This is too much, and I left the school grounds."

But now I couldn't go home. Walking swiftly out the school door, it's raining and frigid. Our house was so close to the school that I had to walk in the opposite direction, ending at the boyfriend's house I went with on the boat ride. His parents had a comfortable farm; Butch worked nights. I knocked on the door, no one answered, and I didn't want to stand in the rain, so I went inside.

I said "Hello" when I could get no response; going upstairs seemed a logical choice at the time. Only one door was closed; I knocked and opened it. Butch was in his underwear, just finished a night shift at work.

"Dianah, you can't be here."

"Butch, I have four brothers; you think I haven't seen underwear before." This is also stupid; I didn't say that.

"Why are you here?"

"There was nowhere else to go."

"You go downstairs; you are wet and cold. I'll make some hot cocoa and take you home."

Butches Mother was in the kitchen at this point; she made the cocoa. It was hot and tasty. It felt good; no one did those kinds of things for me. I tried to explain, but it seemed like a useless attempt.

I ended up not explaining anything to anyone, neither parents nor friends, either believed or not understood. The principal called me in, asking why I left.

I said, "I didn't feel well."

He states, "You were forewarned, which means three days of detention."

"Okay."

No one talked to me about it after.

I worked after school at the restaurant, now in my senior year of high school. On weekends, I worked until 3 AM. All the people from the bars would come in after 2 AM when the bar is closed. After closing the restaurant, I would walk home, about 6 or 7 blocks, there are only a few street lights, and past a mortuary. I always made sure I walked as fast as possible, looking for anything out of the ordinary.

There was going to be a school play; thinking I am over my stage fright, I'll try out for the part. And I did, I was accepted, but when they asked me about scheduling after school, I would have to quit work. I made a choice; work was more important.

I went with a friend and took the entrance college exam in Oshkosh, 10 miles away. I had saved just enough money for the first year of college and books; I asked Dad if I could ride with him in the morning on his way to work and then wait for him on his way home. I knew it would make him obligated, but I had no other options. I didn't have enough money for a car and certainly couldn't afford to live by the college. Dad said, "You don't need to go to college; you'll just get married and have babies."

"No, Dad, I plan on working."

"Dianah, I leave for work too early in the morning."

"It's ok, I won't make you late, and I'll just wait by the school until it opens."

"You don't need to go to college to get a job as a secretary and just sit on the boss's lap to get paid."

"Oh, Dad, that's not who I am."

I continued working at the restaurant, and high school graduation happened. There wasn't much to it. One day I was in High School, and the next day I wasn't. Mom and Dad didn't attend, but Mom and Grandma bought me a hairdryer for graduation. They tried to do what they thought was right. To myself, I thought it was a strange gift for graduation, but I thanked them both very much. Neither Grandma nor Mom had gone past 4th grade, their concept was different from mine, but I was grateful.

I met a cute guy; his father had drinks with my father. Italian heritage, he had a great sense of humor and did different things than going to the movies or the drive-in for burgers. Our first unofficial date was early on a cold Saturday morning; we went out on the frozen river muskrat hunting. I had never experienced anything close to this. I thought it was pretty exciting. He and I got along just fine, but it was time for me to make future long-term plans. I couldn't and wouldn't settle for a fellow who worked with his Dad as a garage mechanic in Omro.

Now I was no longer in school; Dad said, "You're an adult and out of school; you have a choice to either help your Mom at home or pay for a room and board."

I talked with Mom and kindly let her know that I would rather pay for room and board. I would give the money directly to her in cash, "Mom, I know you can use the cash more than the little bit of help I would give; all the older kids can learn to pick up after themselves. Mom didn't say anything, and I started paying rent.

The summer of 1963 began.

Chapter Eight

LEAVING WISCONSIN

HIGH SCHOOL GRADUATION day, everyone else in my class is excited. Most of the grads would have a huge party and go to college at the end of summer. I was still working at the restaurant. Room and board at home will be an ongoing expense until I discover the pathway to my future. There's no boyfriend, and the girlfriends are either getting married or going to college. I wanted college and a career, but with no car and only enough savings for one year of college, the amount of income from the restaurant would not get me far. While biding time, saving what I can, but there is no plan. The whole last year of high school is such a waste; you know you will graduate, there isn't anything new in the curriculum. You are just treading water until they say, okay, here's your paper that says you put in your time.

My friend Dotty called one evening in a cheerful tone, "How would you like to go on a blind date?"

"I don't think so; I've never been on a blind date. No, it just doesn't sound like my thing."

Dotty explains, "He is Ames' cousin from California; he's kind of cute, tall, and doesn't know anyone here. It would be fun; we'll just go for pizza and maybe a movie. You're not doing anything; I know you don't want to sit home on your night off."

I give up, "Ok, but you better be giving me the real picture. If he's a dud, I'm going to blame Ames for his choice of the family."

" Thanks, Dianah; I'll see you tomorrow night."

The following evening, he's at the door, introduces himself, and I let Mom know I'm on my way to the movies. He wasn't what I expected, but I'll make the best of it. The evening went as planned; I came home at a reasonable hour and went to work the next day.

My blind date is over at the house or on the phone almost every night after our date. About a month passes by, and Rick tells me his mother expects him to come home. She's been sending money, but he's been spending it. He can't get home because she isn't sending any more, and his aunt and uncle are not going to support him.

Rick said, "My uncle and aunt can't continue my stay at their house."

The more we talk, we conclude, both of us can go to California. I will use the money I saved for college, and when we arrive, his Dad will pick us up. I can stay at his folk's house until I find a job. The train was the cheapest way to travel if we got tickets at the lowest fare possible. The lowest fare meant you sat in the same seat day and night for three and half days. I gave Rick the money for the tickets and bought some suitcases for myself. I let them know at the restaurant when I would be leaving. I was considerate of the owner by telling him when and gave him a three-week notice. After two weeks, he said, "I have your replacement; I don't need you anymore. I was planning on that one more week of income. Disappointed, but I can put the time to good use.

I told my mother the plan; she didn't tell me not to go but didn't want to see me leave. Then I found out she was pregnant again.

I said, "Oh, Mom, I'm so sorry, but I can't stay. If I don't leave this town now, I might never get out of here."

When Dad was told, he said, "Who will take care of Mom and the kids when the baby comes."

I had thought that through, "Frank is 15, old enough to be in charge, and the other kids can help. You had me taking care of babies at eight years old; you have four children over eight years old, and just because they are boys doesn't mean they have to be served by a female. It's high time they learn to do something."

My Dad blew his top, but he knew he wasn't going to bully me into staying. I felt sorry for Mom, but me hanging around Omro would not make her life any better. The older I got, the more of an irritant I became to my Dad. I knew I was going whether it was a good thing or not.

As I was packing, Mom brought me some towels and a couple of blankets.

She said, "I wish there were more to give."

"Mom, you don't have to do this; I'll be alright."

I was packing clothes, records, and a portable turntable, the hairdryer Mom and Grandma gave me for graduation. I didn't give the slightest thought to housekeeping items. I thought I knew what I was doing, but I really didn't have a clue. There was only one reason this was going to work; the fact that I didn't know of any other way.

The friends I worked with and the customers who had become friends expressed concern; Rick and I have known each other only a couple of months. But no one was trying to talk me out of leaving, except for maybe Dad. But his motives were his own self-concern.

Shopping is on my to-do list. As conversations would start, the older women were excited for me. They all expressed, it was a bit risky but conceded they would not hesitate if they had the opportunity to move to California. The lady at the shop helped me pick out a traveling suit and suitcases. I thought the white fiberboard luggage looked great, and I didn't spend much. The sales clerk asked if the plan was for a one-time trip; she probably figured that's about as long the luggage would last. I should have picked my clothes and baggage myself, but I thought she knew better.

"Yes," I knew in my heart this was a one-way trip. Returning was not an option.

Rick and I spent as much time together as possible; I asked myself if this was love? I knew the desire, the wants, but love was hard to say. Even if we said the words, did we understand the meaning? Once I move, then what? I think I want to be with him. He was innovative, not very practical, but I felt he had good potential for a comfortable lifestyle. I have many hypothetical thoughts, my mind is a blur, and I can't put my finger on any definite statement of fact.

The morning I was ready to leave, Dad came into my bedroom as he left for work.

He whispered, "Dianah, wake up. "

I sat up on one elbow, "Yes?"

Dad said, "Are you still leaving this morning?"

"Yes."

Then Dad said, "When you get to California, and you don't have a roof over your head and nothing to eat, don't call and don't come back."

"Okay, Dad, I'll remember that."

He left for work, no goodbye, or have a good trip or let us know when you get there. I was taken back; I thought there was more to our Father-daughter relationship than what I just witnessed, I knew what we had wasn't great, but I wasn't going to dwell on his opinions. Since Dad was such a small part of my life, he wouldn't miss me, and I was onto a whole new adventure.

I was ready to leave in no time. Said goodbye to Mom and Grandma with a hug and kiss. Hugged Frank, told him I would write. Rick arrived at 7 AM; Ames is driving us to the bus depot in Oshkosh. The butterflies in my stomach continued on the bus to Chicago with the anticipation of the unknown.

We checked in our luggage at the Chicago train station; it's close to noon. The station agent informed us our train doesn't depart until 4:30 PM. I wondered what Rick thought we should do next. Going to the movies was his plan.

"How will we get there? Is it walking distance?"

Rick thought, "We should take a taxi to the movie theater, where Cleopatra was debuting. The movie is long enough to spend most of the afternoon."

I thought this was extravagant, but I guessed it was the most economical way to spend a whole afternoon.

I was astonished by the skyscrapers and the traffic, never having been to Chicago or any large downtown city. In my first taxi ride, the traffic maneuvering from one lane to another is exhilarating and frightening. At the downtown theater, the vast marquee and brilliant lights caught my breath. There is nothing like this in the small town I'm leaving behind, and we only had lights at night.

The lobby is an expanse of plush surroundings decorated in reds and gold. I am trying to take in all that I see. We picked out some candy and popcorn, just in time for the movie to start. Halfway through the film, I start worrying about the need to get back to the train, even though I knew we had enough time.

The four-hour movie is over; I feel tired. We step outside to the hustle of people and traffic; I'm now back to being alert. Rick hails a taxi and tells the driver to take us directly to the train station. As the taxi driver pulls out of the parking space, a city bus sideswipes us, not just a little bump. As I look out my passenger door window, all I can see is this colossal bus right up against us, and everything is moving in the wrong direction. The bus driver could see the yellow cab; he just kept pushing and sliding along the side of the car. The bus shoves us to the curb. There was a light standard that would hit the other side of the taxi. Fortunately, this 3-minute episode, which seemed like 15 minutes, wasn't hard enough to hurt anyone. The cab is damaged on both sides, but no broken windows.

The driver turns to check on us and says, "This is my first day on the job."

He looked like a nice enough guy who needed the work. I thought, this is how my new life will start, but I only said, "What now?"

The driver replied, "I have to get you to the train station right now, or you will miss your ride."

Wow, a person with a conscience in this vast city was concerned about us getting on our way and what he would face when he returned to his workplace. Rick says the company has insurance; he'll be fine. I said it's his first day of work; he may get fired.

We pay and tip the taxi driver, hurry through the train station, pick up our luggage, and rush to the designated train. Barely making it up the train's steps with suitcases, we find our seats, stow the bags, and take a deep breath. I can now say to myself; I am leaving home. I wonder if all the advice given about not going might be correct, it's too late; the train has started. I put on a brave face and muster all the strength within me.

As I sat down and had a chance to look around, there were no spare seats. It's like a beehive, everyone moving about, getting into their assigned seating. Noticing the seats are blue, the floor is the same color, and the walls are white with windows by each row of seats, three to a side with an aisle down the middle, I was trying to memorize where my place was so that I wouldn't get lost. Now I realize the lack of comfort, which will continue for the next three and half days. A middle-aged woman directly across and facing me with a child is trying to get comfortable. We need to sit at an angle while stowing our bags under the seat so our knees don't touch.

We had been riding for about 2 hours; when I thought it was time for at least a small dinner, we could split. Rick said we could get some coffee; it doesn't cost much, and have a cigarette.

"I don't smoke and haven't taken a liking to coffee."

He said, "Train food is expensive, so give coffee and cigarettes a try; you won't get so hungry."

This should have been my first wake-up call; we could get a taxi and movie, but not food. We could drink coffee and smoke, which I didn't do, and it was my money.

"Hello, Dianah, what are you thinking?"

Obviously, I wasn't thinking. We had one and a half meals in three days, no showers, of course, plus the weather was warm to hot the longer we traveled.

About mid-trip, the train stopped at a rural location for no apparent reason. I overheard another passenger telling the person next to them; a child had stuck his arm out while walking between the train cars; the signal lights on the track are within inches of the train. The boy lost his hand, they were looking for a doctor on the train or any medical help, and then we were on our way. No further mention of the incident comes forth, just an unscheduled stop shortly after.

I missed much of the scenery in the darkness, and as we went into New Mexico and parts of Arizona, what I saw from the train was not rewarding. Many of the shacks along the rails were piled high with junk; I wouldn't have my farm animals living in that squaller. The landscape is dry and barren; I pictured myself being out on this vast horizon; how would one survive.

The train is speeding into California; as I gaze out the window, everything is brown. There was a sign; it said National Forest; I don't see any; I mean no trees. I thought a forest meant acres of trees; there is not one tree in sight. I can tell this life will be different in many ways. For all the beauty they've talked about out west, I've yet to see anything green. We arrive at the train station in Los Angeles, and it is a beautiful station, a magnificent building. The sun is bright, but I think maybe I'm getting sick. My eyes are burning and watering, and it's hard to see. I have a headache.

Rick indicated, "It's smog; you'll get used to it."

We collected the luggage and stepped off the train; Rick saw his Dad and Uncle Tommy. We hurried toward them, they introduced themselves, and we were on our way to Torrance, his family's home. I met Rick's Mother, Jean, his brother Tim, and twin sisters Jane and Jill on arrival. They were in the throes of arranging bedrooms to make accommodations for me.

I have put the household in a state of upheaval, which I didn't mean to do and hadn't thought about before arrival. I was under the impression before I left, they had plenty of room. Also, Rick didn't tell me his mother, Jean was sick, had just had a hysterectomy, and expected me to do many household chores.

Didn't I just come from there about four days ago? Thinking to myself, do I have Maid tattooed on my forehead? Helping would be okay, but I don't know what the family eats and their schedule; I can't barge in and do things my way, mainly when I'm unsure what my method is.

Beyond those considerations, I am watching two grown males, ages 16 and 18, who are healthy and robust, telling their sisters to make them sandwiches and bring them drinks while they sit and watch television. Oh, No, this is not on my itinerary.

Rick took me for a drive to the observatory and along Mulholland Drive, through Palos Verdes, things we could do without money and still enjoy ourselves. It was all part of my adventure in this new world. He asked me if I would like to have a taco, and he needed to explain what a taco is. I didn't even know what a tortilla was. Along with new terrain, moving from country to city, I was introduced to different foods and vocabulary. I heard someone talking about gays; I could tell by the sentence structure they did not mean happy.

In two weeks, with some help from the family, I knew I needed to move; the household atmosphere said it was beyond time to get going. I have acquired a job at the hospital cafeteria. There's nothing friendly about my new job. Also, Rick and his Dad found me an apartment within walking distance of the hospital. A furnished apartment, and if I pay ten dollars a month more at year-end, the furniture is mine, consisting of a Formica table with four chairs, a red Naugahyde sleeper sofa, one occasional chair, a double bed, and a dresser with broken drawers.

I have moved in with only my luggage. Rick borrows his dad's Chevy, blue and white station wagon, and we go to the store; it's like a general store, slash five and dime. I bought four glasses, four plates, a cast iron pan, an aluminum pan, two pillows, and a set of sheets. It's then off to the grocery store. I have never done the grocery shopping on my own; no one in the household I came from did the shopping; it was my mothers' domain, no exceptions.

We are back at the apartment, deciding it's time for lunch. I'll make soup and a sandwich. Then discover I have no spoons; a cup will work just fine for soup. Rick leaves to go home, and tomorrow is the beginning of my new job. Here I am. Am I frightened? I have to admit, just being scared would be nice; there's a whole group of emotions battling each other.

I'm up bright and early, in the white uniform and white shoes, another requirement to get the job. When I arrived, the manager gave me a five-minute tour, a time card, this is where you work, and this is what you do. Get started. The day was long; I wasn't working as fast as they expected; I'll catch on soon if they tell me all the little things expected.

I was there five days a week, on time with a revolving schedule. Rick came over when he could use his dad's car, or a friend would bring him. The first time he didn't go home until the wee hours of the morning. His mother, Jean, was beyond angry. She said he was setting a bad example for his brothers and sisters. If we were going to sleep together, we better get married. I don't know, would we have married if the parents hadn't insisted. I didn't understand the choice was mine. Having spent my formative years accepting what you should and should not do, according to someone else's demands, the thought of being brave and choosing your own lifestyle wasn't a consideration I knew. I always thought I had a mind of my own, but there was so much here I didn't know. The lack of worldly knowledge left me looking to others for direction. We made the necessary doctor appointment for blood type and marriage application.

The Doctor suggested birth control pills, which I readily agreed to, and within a week, we were married at the Los Angeles Courthouse before a justice of the peace with the secretary as a witness. I bought my wedding ring, a basic gold band. No one attended; there was no party.

We could now live in the same apartment. Rick didn't have a job or a car; he would be on active duty in the Navy in a couple of months. I didn't realize that he was more dependent on me than I was on him. Although he could have gone back to his parents, I didn't have that option.

Jean came to the apartment while I was at work and brought us kitchenware, pots and pans, silverware, a mixer, and various little things we didn't have. I guess her heart was in the right place; she just wasn't a friendly person.

About two months into the cafeteria job, the manager told me he had more employees than needed. Since I was the last one hired, he needed to let me go. One of the girls I worked next to said the manager wanted to hire his nephew. His nephew would be taking my place in a week. Time to find another job I can walk to. I started working at the local bowling alley coffee shop; it was union, so another deduction from your check and tips weren't anything to brag about. I wasn't there too long before I found a little Italian restaurant that is a closer walk. It was required I work a split shift, lunch, and dinner. When the owner hired me, he asked if I had ever served liquor, answering no he showed me how to pour beer and wine.

Rick has started active duty, hitchhiking 74 miles to the base at Point Mugu Naval station.

One day during work, the owner turns the radio sound loud and over the speaker I hear. President Kenndy has been shot, everyone stops what they're doing, and the streets are in a frenzy. My boss tells me I can go home; he won't be serving anymore today. I walk the street; women are crying, men are either very quiet or swearing. The next few days were a blur as the nation was putting itself back together. Combined with all the turmoil of the Vietnam War, it was an unsettling event even for someone who paid no attention to politics or what the government was doing.

Jean came over with a friend who was selling her car. A 1956 Buick, in good condition, and she only wanted $200.00. Everyone thought it was a good fit for us. I went into the cupboard where the tip money is and proceeded to count the bills, then I went to the rolls of quarters, onto dimes, now nickels. I have $195.00 with only pennies left, absolutely no other money; it is embarrassing. The lady decides she will accept the $195.00. We now have a schoolhouse green Buick, and Rick will check into the insurance since I don't drive.

I have found myself in a world where all the men in my life, starting with my father, saw no reason for me to drive. Work, yes. How to get there, they didn't concern themselves?

My mother was pregnant when I left home, and now the baby is here; both are well and doing fine. I called at Christmas time from my in-laws ' phone as part of their gift to me. It was more thoughtful than I realized at the time. I spoke with both my parents and Frank, the conversations were short. You could almost hear the wheels turning; there was more to say on everyone's part, but how to say it, and so it goes unsaid.

Rick, previously in the reserves and now on active duty for two years, has been hitchhiking to the base at Point Mugu. I marveled that the plan of arriving on time worked so well.

Rick said, "The white uniform gave the drivers a safe feeling, and they were happy to help a serviceman get to his job."

While home on leave, and we now have a car, a friend of Ricks from high school, party buddy follows him home, stopping at the traffic signal; his buddy rams the back end of our car. No one is hurt, but the Buick is totaled, bent the frame. Poor thing looks like a lowrider. The other vehicle, a Lotus, which the friend just purchased, is in worse shape.

Rick called his Dad; with Chet's help, the insurance money came in faster than expected, and Rick and Chet went to look at cars. After work, I went with them to help choose the vehicle. They found two, one is an overhauled black Chevy with a new engine, and the other is a red and white Ford Fairlane, one year newer. Chet thought the Chevy was the better of the two; Rick liked the Ford. I didn't have an opinion;

my experience with cars was in the minus category. I only needed to help pay for them; it isn't like I'll be driving it anywhere. So we bought the Ford.

We didn't have a honeymoon or a vacation, and Rick had time off, so I arranged to take a week off of work, and we would drive up into northern California. Traveling through the Redwood Forest was awesome. I had never seen trees that would tower over you and one to drive through. It was magnificent. The forest is dark, with fern and pine needles on the earth, and you can hear the breeze blow through the trees as they sway in the wind.

Driving the roads was quite spectacular; we started up a small road into a mountainous area, only the Ford wouldn't go; it just kind of sat there.

I asked, "What seems to be the problem?"

"It doesn't have enough power to go up the mountain." There wasn't anywhere to turn around. Fortunately, he didn't have to back up too far. Instead of mountainous driving, we continued north into Eureka and spent the night.

Eureka was interesting because I had never seen it before. Most of the people looked like life was the hard way. The following day breakfast was at a downtown diner, and we decided to head back home. We were both tired, the sky was grey, and it was damp and cold. We are almost out of town at a traffic signal. The car in front of us stops abruptly for no apparent reason. Our car taps her rusted car in the back, and she coasts into the intersection. There's no damage done to her vehicle; we have a broken headlight, but as we get out of the car, she's claiming her neck is hurting, she's upset, and the list goes on. The police come, file a report, and we exchange insurance information. We all know it's our fault, even though she didn't have her foot on the brake and there was no reason to stop. Again, it's turned over to the insurance, and we are driving south only during daylight hours with one headlight. Rick gets the headlight fixed, and the insurance adjuster worked settling that claim, which took over a year.

I'm at the Italian restaurant working; a guy comes in to order lunch and a beer. I serve him lunch, and he says, you look young to work here. I wasn't sure what he meant, and I didn't pursue it.

"Oh, most people think I'm older."

The customer said, "How old are you?"

"A lady never tells, would you like anything else."

The following day, the restaurant owner says, "Dianah, we need to talk."

"Ok," I think there must be a problem.

He says, "How old are you?"

"I'm eighteen."

The unhappy owner asks, "Why didn't you tell me?"

"You didn't ask."

He said, "You know you can't work here if you're not 21 years of age. Do you realize the amount of trouble you can get me into?"

"I only knew I was supposed to be twenty-one, but I needed a job."

"Well, I have got to let you go," he said.

"Do you want me to leave right now?"

"No, I need you to finish your shift; I don't have anyone else, and the inspector won't be back today," and the owner returns to his work.

The next day, I was pounding the beat, looking for another job. When there wasn't anything within walking distance, Rick drove to some coffee shops he knew of. Within two days, I had another job, morning shift, that's what I wanted. The only catch was getting to work. It was 7 miles, and if you're driving, it's not a big deal. But for me to get to work by 7:30 AM, I needed to be out the door by 5 AM, walk down a deserted street past a factory, not the most reputable part of town, and catch a bus. The bus would take me to a shopping mall; I would then walk across this huge parking lot before sunrise to catch another bus. The following bus arrived at an intersection at the bottom of the hill about a half-mile from the restaurant. If I were lucky, which wasn't every day, I would get to work on time.

Rick's Mom told him, let Dianah have the car or move closer to her work. After a couple of months of the grueling schedule, Rick checked out two apartments while I worked. He didn't like the one directly across the street from the coffee shop; he said the one down the road with the swimming pool, where the rent was about 30 percent more, was better. It was a pleasant unit; we never did use the pool, and a grocery store is closer to the first apartment, but I thought he knew better.

Rick is on base, and I stop at the store on my way home from work, needing milk and other heavy items. I considered myself pretty strong. The plan was only two grocery bags, one in each arm and a purse over my shoulder. The walk was through beach sand, no sidewalk, and I could not hold up the bags any longer at about halfway. What to do? I can't let a whole day's wages just sit while I carry one bag home, hoping that the other bag will still be there when I get back. Since I have already been walking all day at work, I did not want to take another beach walk. Both bags are sitting at my feet, and I pick up one, walk about 200 feet, put it down, and walk back to get the other one. Doing the switchback would take forever; I was berating myself for being so overly confident. Just about then, a red pickup truck stopped, backed up to where I was standing, and asked if I would like some help. Instant reflex, I should say no. He didn't look like a bad guy; I'll take my chance. He put the bags in the pickup bed; I climbed in the truck, directed him to the apartment building. I thanked him for being so kind; he simply said, you needed help. He was gone, and I never saw him again, but he was my angel for the day.

We were residents of the apartment for almost a year, and most of that time, Rick was on base. There was generally a party planned when he was home. Parties consisted of alcohol and some food with hypothecating bits of theory and way too many opinions going nowhere.

Into our second year of marriage, Jean began asking when we were going to start a family. My first thought was, why do we want to create a family? In the beginning, everyone was concerned that we married because of necessity; now that theory is obviously false, and now you need grandchildren?

To begin with, I objected to the thought; however, it became a constant question whenever we were in contact with the inlaws, so I started to give the idea of family more credence. If there were children born in our early 20's by our early 40's the children would be raised, and it wouldn't be a prolonged process. Initially, I gave no thought to children, and my sole concern was not to get pregnant. But I am now married, and asked Rick if he was ready to have a family? The conversation is short, and the arrangement is set. I would stop birth control pills with an expected time frame of a few months after he is out of the service. The plan took effect as predicted. We opted for a less costly apartment; I stopped working about seven months into the pregnancy, and he was out of the Navy two months before the baby was born. According to the doctors, the delivery was to be at the end of November. Jean was ready for me to go to the hospital on Thanksgiving Day. As everyone knows, these were not planned events. Jean said Christmas day will be the day. I had gained so much weight, I felt like a balloon ready to explode. Christopher was born on Dec. 31, and everyone congratulated Rick on the new tax deduction.

Fortunately, they didn't include me in the celebration. I had cared for children from the time they were born, but I had no education on how a mother would physically and emotionally feel after childbirth, and not a nurse or relative was there to assist. As with most everything else to this point of my life, there are several sayings to address the situation, such as-wing it or fake till you make it. It seems whether it's starting school, driving a car, starting a job, or having a baby, it's just thrown at you, and you're expected to figure it out. There are no words of encouragement or advice on what to do or not to do. Somehow most new mothers muddle through with hopefully not too many mistakes.

When I came home from the hospital, Rick's parents came over hypothetically to bring dinner, primarily to hold and see the baby. I have this indelible picture in my mind of that day. Grandma Jean holds Chris, a cigarette in one hand and beer in the other while calling him Chrissy. I knew I couldn't stop the smoking or the drinking, but

Chrissy was taking it too far. So we settled on the nickname of Toph, or Topher.

Rick was working the graveyard shift. Alone in the evening, around 3 AM, I would play with Chris when it was feeding time. A first for me in the world of enjoyment when it came to babies. He was a happy baby, and his requirements were minimal. For about three months, the roller coaster life smoothed, and I could breathe.

A letter from Frank arrived; no mail ever came from home unless something was wrong. I quickly opened the small envelope and started reading. The letter was indeed from Frank, not something Frank wrote with my mother's instructions. He told me he met a girl, liked her very much, and thought she might be pregnant. Frank was worried; he wasn't quite 18 yet and didn't know who he could talk to about it. I knew I couldn't call him; the whole family would be listening. I decided a letter was the best I could do, and I didn't want to put anything extra on the outside of the envelope, such as personal or private, because that would only cause more questions. I explained to him about getting started, the steps, the expenses, and the first person to talk with would be her doctor. I tried to be as supportive as I could be and not leave too much unsaid. As it turned out, Mom opened and read the letter, which put Frank in a world of hurt. Then it was discovered, the girl was not pregnant. It wasn't too long after all that, Frank joined the army, which I believed was at my Dad's insistence. From the comments I heard, Mother never forgave Dad for enforcing that move.

Now Rick and his parents(mostly Jean, I'm sure)decided we should have a house. During this time, Rick came home with a brand new car. A Dodge Dart, it wasn't pretty but was supposed to be dependable. We bought a house in Torrance, a small two-bedroom, one bath with the water heater in the kitchen corner. Chet moved the water heater outside for us by the back steps and put a metal-type shed around it. We didn't need a down payment because Rick was a California Vet, and our monthly payments were no more than rent; the only difference was upkeep and utilities. It was nicer than the apartment, though smaller.

Rick had vacation time and asked would I like to drive to Wisconsin to see family. Of course, Toph was a few months old. It would be just a matter of packing the proper articles; disposable diapers had just become commonplace on the store shelves and a cooler with milk; the rest was easy. I called home and said the plan was to stay about ten days. It was lovely weather in California but cold and rainy in the Midwest. The drive there was easy, and when we arrived, the family had made accommodations for us to stay. By the second day, things were not going well. Rick was uncomfortable, and the house was so overcrowded. I couldn't be myself; the family wasn't sure what to do. On the third day, we left, drove back the northern route. The first night in Minneapolis, the motel toilet backed up, and the motel owner accused me of putting a diaper down the toilet, which I hadn't done. He reminded me of my Grandfather; once he had something set in his mind, there was no changing it. Within three days, we were home; I called home to let everyone know we had arrived home and to apologize once again for the abrupt departure.

Back home and upkeep. The lengthy back yard has a wood fence on both sides, 150 to 200 feet, sloped down to an alley gate. Both front and back yards are St. Augustine grass. If you have never mowed St. Augustine grass with a reel mower, prepare yourself, it is no small feat. This was an older home, and so was the grass, at least 4 inches thick. I was at home with Christopher, so I cut the grass with a reel mower. My plan to mow was to get a running start, go as far and as fast as you could push, and then back up and run again. A beautiful orange hibiscus sat by the front window, and a bougainvillea climbed the trellis by the entry door. I could trim the plants any way I wanted, and they would bloom better than before. The two rose bushes were as happy as could be. I loved the California flowers. Everything grew so wonderful; I decided to try my hand at gardening. Picking an obscure spot by the fence, I planted six tomato plants, and they were huge bushes almost overnight.

I didn't see any blossoms yet, but I thought it might be a bit early, and the chosen spot didn't have enough sun. I did notice an enormous green worm. I am not a bug fan, I didn't want to touch it, but it was eating the tomato leaves. I found a stick, and this worm had eaten so much it was bulging. When I touched it with a stick, it exploded with green slime squirting on me. I screamed; Toph was next to me, just barely walking, and he started to cry. He had no idea what was wrong. I looked at him; he was clean. I took the hose and hosed myself off. Toph and I went into the house. I told Rick he would have to get rid of the tomato plants; I would have nothing to do with those bugs, and when I did a second exam, there were scads of worms.

Rick and I had gone to a party, and Toph was spending the night with the Grandparents. Arriving home, I asked Rick if he wanted anything before bed.

Out of blue, he said," You know I don't love you, but I'm not leaving." I was taken aback by his statement but not surprised. My thought is if I do all the things he asks, shouldn't that work? We have a child, a house, a car payment; we have obligations. If I do everything a wife can do, this marriage can still work. After all, you didn't just call it quits because you changed your mind. I had no concept of the long endeavor I was anticipating or was there someone else. And I didn't know if it was me he didn't like or being married with responsibilities.

Early one morning, just after Rick had left for work, the neighbor's son called and said I couldn't get my mother to answer the phone. This neighbor was an elderly lady I had just met. The son told me where the spare key was and would I please go over and check on her; he could be on his way and arrive in 20 minutes if needed. I hurried over to the house, knocked on the door several times, and there was no movement in the place. Finding the spare key, I opened the door, calling for her. There's no response; I start walking through the rooms one at a time until I come to the bathroom. The door is closed, I call for her, and there's no answer; it's not locked. I open the door; she's on the toilet, slumped over, wedged in the corner between the shower and toilet, unconscious with no clothes. After determining this lady was still alive, I needed to get her out of the corner, which took all my strength and then some. I now have her seated upright, hopefully, steady but still unconscious. I put a robe around her and ran for the phone to call her son. I explained in a few short words, then asked if he wanted me to call the ambulance.

"No, my mother is diabetic; there should be orange juice in the refrigerator. Get her to swallow about half a glass, and I am on my way.

Once she swallowed a little orange juice, the body started to recover, and within minutes, her son arrived. I asked if there was anything else I could do. He said, no thanks; I'm taking her to the doctor. I left and never saw either of them again.

While starting potty training for Toph, Grandma Jean decides Toph should have a cute little black puppy. I tried keeping the dog in the kitchen with newspapers; the whole kitchen would be a newspaper. Thinking the kitchen must be too big, I put it in the bathroom at night. We only have one bathroom, so at 6 AM, before Rick gets home from work, I'm faced with cleaning up after the dog, taking it outside. I washed my hands, changed diapers, washed my hands, and I was always cleaning. Because I was constantly cleaning, my hands were getting redder and now puffy with blisters and itching. I had eczema with all the standard treatments added to the day, such as sleeping with gloves and soaking in cold water, plus the ointment.

After about two months, I said, "Rick, the dog has got to go. You're not here to train it, and I do not have the patience. Changing diapers is enough. I was beginning to doubt my ability to accept family life.

Rick's mother had never gotten her driver's license in California, and now she decided it was time. Not only did she get her license, but she also bought a new car—a little yellow Corvair with the rear engine. Jean worked at Sears and Roebuck selling appliances, and Chet was a postman. On the way home from an evening out, Jean lost control of the vehicle and crashed. There was no one else involved, Chet was a little banged up, but Jean came close to losing a life. She had a neck puncture that came very close to an artery. Taking time for recovery and insurance settlement, she was able to get back on her feet. The insurance adjuster determined the cause of the accident was the original engineering of the auto, and it was a faulty steering design.

I struck up a conversation with our other neighbor on the right side of the house, she always seemed to be gossiping about someone, but all in all, she seemed like a nice enough person. As time went on, the friendship grew, and I explained that I didn't have a driver's license. She thought that was just absurd. About a week goes by, and she and I go to the motor vehicle department. She watches Toph, and I take the written test.

Now I can prepare for the driving part. Rick didn't see why I wanted a license, but he would take me out to practice. One Sunday afternoon, we may have made it around the block; I was so nervous, there was nothing in this episode to say I had made forward progress; I was in tears by the time we were home. That was the end of my lessons. The neighbor asked how things went, I explained, and she said, "Well, we will have to do something about that."

"You make the appointment for your driving test, and I'll take you there."

I told Rick the plan. He said he would take me, but you probably won't pass.

"Then I'll have to wait six months and try again."

I was stubborn, and my theory was, I will do this.

The day came; I took the test, and I don't remember how I got through it; I walked back to the car. Rick was sitting behind the wheel, ready to leave, and he said, "Well, how did it go?"

"I passed; my driver's license will be coming in the mail next week." That was the end of that discussion.

Four to five months later, it's Saturday, and the day's discussions are not going smoothly. I decide, since the car is home, I'll go shopping, getaway. My mind was neither on shopping or driving; I made a right-hand turn and sideswiped a young lady making a left-hand turn. It was my fault; I didn't look before changing lanes. I was devastated; I gave her my info and came home crying. I didn't do much to her car, but our car had big bumper dents on both doors on the driver's side.

Through my sobs, I told Rick I was never going to drive again.

For the first time, he was understanding, "That's why we have insurance and mistakes happen, the car is still drivable, and no one is hurt. I'll take care of it."

I was still as upset as I could be and angry with myself for not being more careful. It took me weeks to put that incident behind me.

Rick had a high school friend Joe, who was studying to be a mortician. His son was about the same age as Toph, and Joe was Toph's Godfather. Ricks' family is Catholic, and his sisters went to Catholic school. Toph is scheduled for Baptism; I needed to have some catholic background, which I didn't. Somehow we worked around it.

When I was in the last few months of pregnancy and living in the apartment close to the beach, I went to the Catholic Church and said I didn't have a denomination, my husband is Catholic, and I would like to be also. I was only permitted even to start becoming a catholic because I didn't have a previous affiliation. The fact we were already married didn't help. What should I do? I could take a class or have a private tutor. I opted for a private tutor, who was a red-headed young Irish Priest. From the beginning, we didn't see eye to eye. I knew it would be an education, that I wouldn't agree with everything, and I would need to adjust the opinions I have gathered from who knows where.

I read all the material, and we would meet on a weekly assignment. About three months into the course, there was no way for me to agree to all the requirements and not lie about what I would be saying, and why would you lie? That makes no sense. The Priest and I went round and round about the Pope being infallible. I was adamant; the Pope bleeds, just like I do. He's human; he makes mistakes, he is not perfect. Besides that, why does the Pope have to be a man? Oh, that was the final blow for this priest. Now, this was only the beginning of our disagreement; in the end, we stopped the indoctrination, and I did not join the church.

Not too long after Toph was born, Rick's brother Tim and a friend of Tim's were taking a drive on a Sunday morning, after a long party on Saturday night. They had just gone to the store. Tim's wife was pregnant with their first child. Tim and Barbara weren't 20 years old yet. As the two guys were driving home on a quiet, sunny day, they decided not to stop for the train. The rest is a blur, the tears, the pain for all the family. Jean was particularly hurt; everyone said this was her favorite child. She quit work, just didn't cope. Barbara carried the baby to term, but it was born with a defective heart and died within days. Her parents provided for another funeral. Jean developed the theory, Toph's birth was a precursor to her sons' death. Some people need to find fault, and the blame game can take a lot of turns.

Now Joe and Rick are good friends, and the four of us spent a lot of time together, with our babies being the same age. Joe's wife didn't think much of me because I didn't talk enough or voice my opinion. After a few visits, she felt I was an uneducated farm girl and then learned I didn't express my opinion because I regarded the discussions useless. From the beginning, I thought you could talk and discuss issues all day long, but unless there's something constructive to be done about the problem, move on, stop wasting time and energy. Joe's wife and I did not become friends.

Joe and his family moved to Huntington Beach. We went to visit them at their new house. It was a pleasant house, more modern and closer to the beach, not as much city. Rick decided we should move to Huntington Beach, not only to the same town but the same neighborhood. The realtor found us a house, three bedrooms, two-bath just two blocks away from his friend. Joe was no longer a mortician; he joined the police force in Huntington Beach. Some of the unsound pranks performed by two friends could have been disasters, but we all lived through it.

Toph is now about three years old; we have moved into the new house and decided to have an open house because most of the friends and family lived 30 to 40 miles away. We wouldn't see them as much. Rick was working in Santa Fe Springs, a long morning drive from Huntington Beach. We decided that having just one child tended to make a child isolated and more self-centered. So it would be good to have a second child. Therefore, at the time of the move and open house, I was close to having the second child.

The day of the open house, which I had worked on tirelessly, cooking, cleaning, and all the unpacking, was a success. All the friends and relatives showed, some I wasn't expecting. The day was long, but Rick had said we would have dinner with Joe and his wife that evening. Getting home about midnight, we both fell into bed. At 2:30 AM, I rose, walked into the bathroom, and my water broke. I was going to have the baby today. Oh my God, not today; I'm too tired.

I called for Rick, "You need to take me to the hospital. Get the stuff for Toph. I'll get dressed, make some coffee, and we'll drop by your parents first."

Rick said, "Are you sure? Can't it wait?"

The contractions weren't too close. Toph is comfortable with the grandparents, and I called the hospital to apprise them of our pending arrival.

This birth was going to be ahead of time. I had labor pains two weeks earlier, and when I couldn't get a hold of anyone, I just waited, and the pains stopped.

It was a long day at the hospital; I was so tired, I'd fall asleep between contractions. Tim was finally born around 6:30 PM.

The Doctor said, "You have a baby boy, all the parts, fingers, toes are here." I didn't hear him cry; the nurse was cleaning him. The Doc picked him up to weigh, gave him a tap on the bottom, and he let out a fierce cry. The nurse laid him on my chest; I could tell both Tim and I were exhausted. The nurse was wheeling me to the room; Rick was there; he said, look at our baby. I am too tired to move. My head is turned toward the wall; I close my eyes; at this moment, someone is watching over Tim with more control than me.

Rick and I now have the American dream. Two healthy adults in their 20's with two children, a three bedroom two bath home, and a fireplace with a two-car garage close to the California beaches. It's the 1960s, and we are by all measurements on top of the world.

Chapter Nine

CALIFORNIA LIVIN

HUNTINGTON BEACH BECAME home. The neighbors were friendly, with various age groups, children, retired, and newly getting started. Jayne and Perry, directly across the street, have two boys, Tony and Patrick, the same ages as Toph and Tim. Their daughter, Shelly, the oldest of the three, is a pretty petite blonde. Jayne and Perry were salts of the earth. Midwest born and bred, with all the hometown values. It's an excellent place to raise a family, surrounded by friendly people. I could walk out the front door, say Hello to whomever I encountered, and I know who they are and where they live, and they know me. Jayne became my all-time best friend. We had coffee together almost every day; she was one of those constant good-natured ladies, always made you feel welcome, and the door would be open. The beach was only a couple of miles away; there were orange groves and stop signs. It was before the multitude of traffic signals and multi story housing.

Tim's first few months of babyhood were difficult; he would have an earache, bronchitis, or just a lot of mucus, sometimes all three. There were evenings I would take him in the bathroom, turn on the hot water in the shower, get it as steamy as possible, and I would sit on the toilet seat and rock him until the coughing would let up and he could rest. There were trips to the doctor and medications; we barely avoided ear surgery, suggested by the physician.

Amid Tim's illness, I ended up with a urinary infection, severe enough to have me admitted to the hospital for internal diagnosis. One of the neighbors watched over the boys while I was there for a day and a half. There was no contact with Rick; I contacted the neighbor to ease my mind that all was well with the kids. We struggled through those first months, and the illness for both Tim and I started to soften.

A nice hot tub of silky water and soak all your cares away, a rare occasion. It's after dinner; I'm lounging in the tub; Rick is watching television, and the boys are in their room. It's a moment of peace until I hear this ear-piercing scream.

Toph comes charging into the bathroom, "Tim fell; he's bleeding."

"Get your father; I'm getting out of the tub."

Before I can even grab a towel, here comes Rick holding Tim out, one hand under each arm like he's on display. Tim has blood running down his face; he's crying; I can't even tell where he's been hurt. Before I'm out of the tub, I wipe Tim's face; the cut is small but close to the eye.

"Rick, we are taking him to the doctor."

"Toph, what did he fall on?"

"A wooden block, Mom. They are all over the floor."

"It's ok, you put some shoes on, and we'll get it taken care of."

Our pediatrician also does plastic surgery; he takes a quick look, decides there should be several stitches, and tells me I need to leave the room.

"I'm his mother; I will stay."

The doctor then says to Rick, "You need to take your wife into the waiting room; she might become hysterical and make this more difficult." I am still objecting while being ushered out of surgery. If I had just a bit more experience, I would have never let them push me around. They didn't put anything on the cut to minimize the pain while stitching; he was a baby, the medical staff said it didn't matter, he would forget, or so they told me. While I'm in the next room, I hear the screams as the nurse holds Tim still. Tim probably came out of it better than I did, his eye healed with barely a mark, but it was the last time we went to that doctor. The insensitivity of that man, and he was a pediatrician. Tim may have forgotten, but I didn't.

This is the same doctor who said Tim needed to wear a foot brace at night to correct his foot turning inward as he walked. Every evening we would put his shoes into this clamp, one for each shoe with an iron bar between, which would angle his feet outward.

As an adult, if anyone of us had to wear that contraption, we would never be able to sleep with this torture devise strapped to your feet. At the same time, we were in the throws of potty training. Tim would wake up early to use the bathroom, but he couldn't get to the toilet because of this iron bar strapped to his feet, and he wouldn't take it off because I had explained to him this was good for him. If I didn't hear Tim, Toph would try to help. Here you have the picture, a two-year-old in this foot brace on his knees trying to get to the bathroom and a five-year-old struggling to help him down the hallway. As I look back, I say to myself, what were you thinking? Was it essential to toilet train right now, or how about a second opinion on the correction of walking? But at that time, I thought the medical profession knew better, and since there was never enough money, a second opinion wasn't even a thought.

As time moved on, the boys were growing, the communication between husband and wife was waning. It occurred to me; maybe I'm boring. My identity is either as someone's mother or someone's wife. All my thoughts belonged to the children or husband—an individual with no time for herself. I decided to try community college, prepare for an alternative education if needed, and meet different people. I could become more worldly, expand my horizons. I took two evening classes and was never so disappointed in the level of education.

Between the instructors and the students, not only were the classes boring, but there was nothing I hadn't heard a hundred times before. There was no upside to this waste of time and effort. I couldn't take anything advanced; I had no former college credits. The high school I had previously attended was superior to this college. It was a waste of time; I didn't bother to complete the courses.

I started acrylic painting at home, which was enjoyable but again a solitary pursuit and no interest to my husband.

The saving grace was my best friend across the street and my two lovable, adorable children that could try my patience. Tim was an active baby; from the time he could walk, he was on his way to explore the neighborhood. If the door were open, Tim would run as fast as his little bare feet would go.

I would get a call from one of the neighbors, Dianah, "Tim's on his way around the block again." Barefoot, in his diaper, and as happy as a lark.

I would run out after him, calling, "Tim, stop." I could hear him giggle, and he would run faster. He thought it was a game. I just had to hope he didn't stub his toe and fall on the sidewalk before I caught up to him. As I picked him up, he would squirm and let me know he didn't want to go home.

Toph's friends on the street liked to play baseball at the end of the court. The older lady would complain about the boys playing ball in the street. She was concerned for their safety, it was a quiet street, and the boys were considerate of a vehicle that might want to get by, but cars didn't like to stop while the boys got out of the way. Jayne and I never made a fuss about it, the kids didn't want to play in the backyard, and I didn't blame them. I always thought there were too many rules and restrictions.

Toph and Tony were climbing a tall tree hanging over the block fence in Tony's backyard; Tony's house is across the street from us. Toph fell out of the tree and landed in the neighbor's yard behind Tony's house, on his nose. He's now in a stranger's backyard over a block away around the corner.

Jayne called me; she said, "I can hear Toph crying, but I don't know where he is." She and I started hurriedly walking in opposite directions, listening and watching for an unexplained happening. Before I could get around the corner, here he came; Toph's face was covered in dirt. There is soil in his mouth, embedded in his nose, and he can hardly see. I quickly usher Toph to the house and proceed with the clean-up. There was so much soil in his nose; he had difficulty breathing; we just kept flushing and blowing. The poor kid ended up with two black eyes. I thought he would be ok, but Jayne was so concerned that I took him to the doctor the next day. Nope, he'll be ok; take a week or so for the swelling to go down and black eyes to heal. She wouldn't let the kids climb the tree anymore; I thought it was a shame; she may have been too concerned about liability. Kids have always climbed trees and sometimes fall.

There was a need for a second car; grocery shopping was considered a wifely duty, but taking the only car on a Saturday wasn't the plan. Without asking my opinion on what kind of car I would like, Rick and his German friend from work went car shopping for me. They came home with this Buick Electra, the longest and biggest car Buick made at that time. I would have been happier with a truck. But if it ran, I wouldn't complain. Unfortunately, it didn't run very well; at one point, there was a hole in the block, there's this gaping hole about the size of a quarter in the top of the engine. I had never seen anything like it. Rick consulted his friend at work; the agreed-upon fix was a wood peg; he hammered the wood in the hole. I'm not sure what that fixed, but the hole is plugged. Frequently, if the car didn't start, I would get out a hammer, which I carried under the front seat and beat on the engine next to the electrical. I would often get it running and only panic if we were at the store. The car didn't have dents, but that was about all you could say for it. I took the kids and the neighbor kids to the beach on a nice summer day. On the way home, we were stopped at a California safety check.

The checklist went like this: "Step on the brakes,"
" I am."
"Honk the horn,"
" I am."
"Right and left directionals,"
" I did."
"Headlights,"
" I pulled the knob."
"Your tires are bald,"
" Yes, sir."

The officer came to the window, "Mam, you have so many things wrong with this vehicle; I don't have room on the form to write it all down. I'm going to make this a warning citation and suggest taking this car to the junkyard."

"Yes, Sir, I will tell my husband."

Within the week, the car was at the junkyard. They gave us $10 and a receipt for the DMV. Approximately 15 years later, I received a letter from the DMV; they had impounded the car from the side of the road, there were drugs in the trunk, and what was I going to do about it. I wasn't even in California at the time. I called, explained and sent a letter. The DMV didn't contact me again, but I had to presume the car had been on the road all that time.

After this jewel of a vehicle, I still needed wheels. Rick found another car; his Dad's friend was selling his car. You'll never guess, another Buick. Oh my Lord, I'm cursed!

Around this time was when the multiple auto accidents started happening. The neighborhood kids would gather at our garage on Saturday morning to see what damage occurred to the car in our garage on Friday night. There was a whole string of events from a rod through the engine to a sneeze in Monday morning traffic while following to close, and auto problems seemed to go on for months.

Rick was laid off from his job but found another in a short while. The income would be less, and as it was, we couldn't afford less.

He said," Dianah, you need to go back to work until we work this out."

I stated, "When I go back to work for extra income, I will never be able to stay home again with the kids. You know that as well as I do."

Rick said, "No, it's a temporary setback."

"Uh-huh."

I put off going back to work as long as possible, but the necessity was very plain. I took a graveyard shift, 11 PM to 7 AM. Brutal hours for me, since I have never been a night person. About six months into the job, I'm on my way home and woke up just before hitting a block wall fence. I made it home, too shaky to want to talk about it.

The next evening, I talked with the manager, "I can't work this shift; I almost hit a block wall fence on my way home this morning."

He said, "Can you continue for a week. We have decided to discontinue this shift."

"Yes, I can. Do you have anything else for me?"

"What would you like?"

"I would like a morning shift."

"Done deal."

I arranged with Jayne to have Toph and Tim stay at her house. Toph would go to school, with the same classes as her son Tony and Tim was out of diapers. She was already watching them from my graveyard shift job when I needed to sleep during the day. What a fiasco. I didn't pay Jayne enough to make it worthwhile, but she was a good friend and didn't say anything.

Starting the day shift, I needed to be there at 5:30 AM. Therefore, rise at 4 AM, ready for work. Put the kid's clothes out and their breakfast on the counter, coffee made, and I'm off. There were some desperate times when no one else was home, and at 5:30 AM, I would call Jayne to find out if I could bring the kids over to her house so I could go to work. Those I worked with generally asked why I was late, this wasn't the first time, but it was always the same answer. There is no one home to get the boys to school. I prided myself being punctual. The crew I worked with were good people and helped out when needed.

These days were frantic and oh so tiring.

They hired a new girl shortly after I started the morning shift; nice person, not too fast; I tried to help her. When I first started in California, everyone said you have to work quicker. Speed was the name of the game.

After a week, the manager stopped by my station, "Dianah, I'm going to let the new girl go."

I pleaded, "She's doing the best she can, maybe a little more time.

The manager stated, "She's a nice girl, but her best isn't good enough."

What an eye-opener for me; I was always taught, work hard, be on time, and you'll succeed. And, No, life does not work that way. Doing your best may not be enough.

Rick had been talking to a real estate agent; she was convincing him it was an excellent time to sell. But where to move to, his thought was farther out, Corona or Riverside; it's not a pretty area. But if I can take care of the kids and house and not have to juggle kids and work every day. Bigger house, more land, and Rick would be driving even farther to work. Considering time and vehicle, it was not a good plan.

Our Huntington Beach house has a sales contract; we are taking our second trip to Corona. It's dry and brown, with no trees. The place we have an agreement on is nothing too extraordinary, and then we discover the view from the front porch will be a new freeway scheduled to start construction in 6 months. Finally, we agree on something; this property is not what we want. The deposit is gone, and we have 30 days to find another house. Rick drives us to Tustin, says it's a good neighborhood, and there's a house we can afford that's vacant. Huntington Beach was more likable, but this one had a pool. I don't swim and didn't want to try. But maybe everyone else can enjoy the pool.

The move to the new house is completed; there's a family across the street with a boy about Toph's age, but no one for Tim. I had quit my job because of the plan to move to Corona. I could see this house will never be a home for us, some things you just know. It didn't feel right. The days of wedded bliss have been gone for a long time, and it is now a time of mere toleration, and even patience is losing ground.

We have this pool; it's Sunday, and it's warm; there's a friend of Rick's over. We are all out by the pool, swimming suits and setting up for a bar-b-que.

An old-line theory from the navy; if you throw someone in the water, they will learn to swim. Cousins had tried that with me at the lake and now my husband. I can tell you that theory may work for some; when I was underwater in the deep end of the pool, and wasn't surfacing, and walking to the shallow end didn't seem to be happening, it occurred to me, this may not be such a bad way to go. Unequivocally, I do not swim.

It didn't take me long to decide, I would go back to work on weekends, and Rick could spend time with the boys.

This plan was also short-lived. The slippery slope of fate had taken its toll. I finally concluded that life could not and would not continue in this fashion of deceit and falsehoods. After all the years and months of agony, trying to make things better, to recoup, reroute, do something to bring this marriage up from the depths of despair, I just gave up. My decision is made, he can move to wherever he likes, just not here.

I did find it unique the decision could be so laborious, but once made, putting the plan into effect was elating.

When he came home, I simply said, "You need to pack whatever you want and leave."

He was not surprised; I think he was just waiting for me to say it; within an hour, he was gone. As I look back, I wondered how strange. Was I supposed to be in charge all along?

The house went up for sale; the realtor told me, you'll never get that much. I told him I could get another realtor. He concluded my price wasn't so bad.

Rick said, " You'll never make it on your own. I didn't reply. I had to make it on my own and take care of two boys; sometimes, there are no choices. I will do this.

The sale contracts came in on the house within about two weeks, three contracts in one day and one for full price. And they told me it wouldn't happen, I was expecting too much. Then Rick wasn't sure he wanted to sell when it came right down to the final signature. I explained, the realtor has fulfilled his duty; he expects to get paid whether you sign this contract or not. The sale is happening.

To Rick's credit, he decides one-third of the proceeds should go to him and two-thirds to me for the boys. There was all the other stuff to sort out, like an attorney's fee and bar tabs on credit cards. This was when I moved to a motel for the house to be tented for termites.

It all came to fruition, and shortly after, I met Daniel. Life now became more than just a challenge; I could look forward to the next day. The boys were distressed about the move, and I didn't want to alienate them to their father. He was, after all, their father, and some things do not change. I didn't explain why we divorced, maybe I should have, but I didn't know how to tell the kids without making someone a villain. Would it have been better for the kids and family if they knew?

I'll never know.

Chapter Ten

BACK TO CALIFORNIA

WE ARE BACK at the present time, having made it through a divorce, a whirlwind relationship, and an Oklahoma catastrophe.

Daniel, I, Toph, and Tim are in the condo in Tustin, California. Daniel can visit his children and try to help with the teenage occurrences in progress. It is good to be back in California. We have enough furniture to get us off the floor, a fridge; Daniel found us a charming dining room set, and we went back to civilized living. The neighbors could relax, the boys had an actual television, and life was almost routine. At least for the time being.

The time in Tustin is to be short-lived. We only moved there to get the boys in the school they attended before Oklahoma; there was no reason to stay when that didn't work. Daniel was able to sell the gunite company, and we started looking. Where were we moving next?

We did visit Jayne a couple of times, but it was different now. We have both grown a little older, and lifestyles have changed from only a short time ago. Jayne and her family now attend church every Sunday. She stopped smoking, not as many neighbors stop by, and the kids are growing up. We are still friends, just not as close as when we lived across street.

I went back to work in Garden Grove for the same Century 21 Company. I struggled with becoming a salesperson; my straightforward approach is to suttle for most people. All this small talk seems like a waste of time. I found most people don't consider the bottom line first and then work out how to get there. I made some sales, enough to keep me in the plus category. My internal compass isn't working any better than it ever did; finding my way around the city, with only the Thomas Guide to get me to any location, was a whole new learning experience, one that I never truly mastered. The buyers often knew better than I how to get to a place; they would give me directions, and they didn't seem to mind.

We began by recuperating from the Oklahoma move. Once that was under control, the desire to move continued.

Daniel's parents live in Pismo Beach, so we would have lunch and look around as we visited.

Daniel say's, "What do you think?"

"I like it, Daniel. It's a small town, great beaches, and the ocean is wonderful."

"Ok, we'll move here."

Daniel found us an apartment in Arroyo Grande, just at the edge of Halcyon, a quaint little village with unique buildings and the cutest little old Post Office, painted red and white, surrounded by trees, just up the hill from the beach. There was an aura of another time and place; I quite liked the area. The sun always shined, the ocean breezes were incredible, and people were easy to talk with. This could be home for a long time.

I went to work for another real estate company, an all-female office, an independent firm owned by a lady broker in the image of Farah Fawcett. She did lots of zany things but was pretty sharp. The other gals in the office were easy to work with, and commuting to the small towns did not become the ultimate challenge for me like the vast cities.

The boys were happy with the school; Tim joined the baseball team; he looked; great in his uniform. Tim has new glasses, but it's a whole different atmosphere; he has friends and does his best at school. Tim, though not a book person; seems to be doing okay. He's a lovable kid.

Toph got a paper route. The paper route wasn't his plan, but as he got older, he needed spending money. Academics didn't challenge Toph. He was an exceptional student without working too hard at any of the classes, and with no chosen after-school activities, there was too much time without purpose. The paper route became another form of education, dealing with places and people. It worked for a short while, even though this was more of a challenge for Toph than school. Throwing the papers close to the doorstep, making sure you didn't miss anyone, and because it's a small town, it's spread out, meaning a longer bike ride. We helped Toph a couple of times with collections and rain.

Daniel and I had now been together for about two years.

One evening I said, "We need to have a serious talk. You know I have been taking birth control pills, you are also aware it's not the healthiest thing for the long term. We haven't talked about having children, but I think you know my intentions for children have been fulfilled. Do you want more children?"

Daniel plainly stated, "No, I have four children, I'm forty-four, and you have two. More children we do not need."

"I want to quit taking the pill, and I can get a hysterectomy which is a rather large operation, but I'm willing, or you can get a vasectomy, simpler and less costly. Do you want to think about it?" I hesitate, then say, " I am certainly not going to be looking for another partner, are you?"

Daniel's replies were generally lengthy; this was too the point. I didn't know if that was good or bad.

"No, I'll make the arrangements."

Within the week, Daniel had taken care of the operation, came home that afternoon a little worse for the wear, but within a few days, he was as good as new, and I didn't need to be concerned.

Daniel was still with his apartments in Santa Ana, his manager was retiring, and the son was taking over. The son was not an inferior manager but didn't do the same job his father did. Collecting rents became more complex, and the buildings always needed something. Daniel set a plan in motion; he would tear down the four units, the best of the two buildings, but producing less income. Once the building was down, he had plans to build a commercial strip center with two apartments on the second floor. The financing is in place, the plans approved, and a friend of his comes in with his backhoe and demolishes the building, has the debris carried away, and now construction can begin.

Oops! The city said, "We missed something; upstairs apartments must have 20% more square footage than the commercial downstairs. The building is on the property line to accommodate the required parking, and the retail tenants are ready to start their businesses with approval from the city. So within a few days, the plan is to have the apartment increase in size with a top floor overhang, creating a commercial porch type effect. Great, the city didn't have a problem, but we need new plans because this is not the same as the plans submitted.

Daniel rushes to the designer, busy with other projects, and urges him to redraw quickly within the week. This whole process is taking two weeks, but the banking at this juncture is volatile; by the time Daniel gets the plans to the city for their stamp of approval, the loan acceptance has expired. Now there is a new set of requirements from the lender. The interest rate goes up, the loan fees have increased, and the building doesn't qualify with the anticipated income. The search goes out for another lender. Interest rates are running anywhere from 14% to 18% plus this being a mixed commercial/residential loan narrows the number of lenders that will even look at it. Plus, most commercial lenders aren't interested because it's not a large enough loan. Daniel owns the lot; he only needs construction financing to flip it to a permanent one at completion.

Daniel now has a vacant lot with property taxes and weed abatement fees.

We had only been in Arroyo Grande for a short while when my Grandmother passed away. I received a call from Frank; he told me the funeral would be in two days. I asked why so soon, I don't think I can get back. Frank said it was what Agnes decided.

Daniel and I tried to get me a flight; even if I got a plane in time, I still would have a distance to drive; the timing just wouldn't work. I was sorry not to be there; she had been part of my life since I could remember. I had to say goodbye from where I was and hope that she knew.

Summertime is here, Chris and Lisa are staying for a visit. We take them to the beach in Daniel's father's new baby blue Toyota. They allow driving on the beach, so we go right down to the water and let kids run. They are having a good time, and we are both exhausted.

Daniel said, "Open the doors and let the ocean breeze blow through; we'll rest while the kids play."

He put his hand on mine; we closed our eyes, and hours later, the kids came running up. They are shaking us to wake up, my first thought - something has happened. All four of them are talking about the waters coming; it's going to get in the car. We look down at the sand; sure enough, the ocean is splashing at the tires. Not only do we need to move quickly, but if we ruin his dad's car, we will never hear the end of it. Daniel tells the kids to run up ahead, for they are full of sand and need to get cleaned off. Daniel starts the car to move forward, but because there's more water, there's now a small river we must cross without splashing it in the car or getting stuck, which people do all the time. A tow truck sits at the beach entrance for the tourists who get stuck on the beach. We slowly pick our way through the water and hope it's as shallow as we think. Success, we navigate to the pavement, the kids have brushed off as much sand as they can, and we head straight to the car wash. There has never been a car so clean; we made sure no speck of sand or saltwater was anywhere on, under, or in that

ME AND DANIEL

car. Daniel even cleaned the engine compartment, checked the trunk, dried, and polished it. One would have thought we were a couple of teenagers who had taken out the parents' car without their permission. Daniel's father was a stickler for detail, and although he had a great sense of humor, he could come down on you like a ton of bricks.

His father, Daniel A., is having heart issues; he would be in the hospital with another dose of medications every so often. One of those times, Daniel had to be in Orange County on business and asked if I would pick his Dad up at the hospital. Of course, I'll just plan for it. The following day he was to be discharged at about 11 AM. My office was just down the street, and knowing how prompt hospitals are, I arrived at about 11:05 AM. Daniel A. was sitting at the front door on a bench getting ready to walk home.

While he was in the hospital, we went to visit. I was smoking at the time, and he asked me for a cigarette.

I said, ``No, you can't have one in the hospital."

Daniel said, "Dad, you're on oxygen; you'll blow the place up."

Daniel A. was cantankerous, adamantly he proclaimed, "Then get out."

And we left. Now I'm late picking up Dad DiSandro; I get out of the car, open the door for him. Try to help him get in the car, which he will have no part of, and I drive him home. When we get there, Anna helps him in the house; I apologize. Anna says it's all right, don't worry about it. That evening when Daniel came home, I explained the circumstances.

He said, ``Ya, that's Dad."

Daniel's Mom and Dad decided to get a new television; they gave the old one and some other items to Goodwill, who would come by with a truck to pick up everything. I asked Daniel if his parents would give the television to the boys since they were just giving it away. His Dad said, "No, he told Goodwill to pick it up, and that was that."

Daniel liked cars; if it had wheels, it was worth looking at and maybe buying. On February 7, 1978, he purchased a 1968 Dodge Charger, super auto, that looked like it was speeding down the road even when standing still. Toph thought it was the cat's meow. He also bought an Oldsmobile in February and traded it for a truck in March. In June, he bought a Honda motorcycle and sold it in July.

Daniel always had a good reason for vehicle movements; most of the time, he made a few dollars, even after registrations and minor improvements, and as he said, "There's another one right around the corner."

His Mom and Dad were having an Anniversary; Daniel wanted to do something nice for them. So we were taking them to The San Luis Bay Club overlooking the ocean for Sunday Brunch. We had used their car because it was more comfortable for his Dad. Dad wanted to drive. The vehicle was a monsterous1968 Chrysler New Yorker with a 440 engine, lots of power. Dad was short, so Daniel had to put a wood block on the foot feed for his dad to reach it. Dad was not a slow driver; everyone was in his way. But we made it to the restaurant, with Daniel asking his Dad to slow down a bit. It didn't make any difference.

When Dad visited the apartment, Daniel asked him to pull out friendly and easy, don't disturb the neighbors. The kids watched from the balcony as he spun the tires with the rocks flying and screeched out onto the street while the kids were yelling, Go Grandpa Go!

We got to the restaurant; the maitre'd seated us. It was all very posh with linens and silver and piano playing. With the sun shining through the windows and views of the ocean, it was a beautiful morning. The coffee is served, and Daniel A. says, I'm not sitting next to those, and he used a term I had never heard before. Daniel and I looked at the people at the following table, who we knew were insulted but didn't say anything. I don't think either one of us realized the degree of discrimination his Dad could portray.

Daniel said, "Dad, stop it, be quiet; they have a right to be here just as much as anyone else."

His Dad was not going to sit at that table. So Daniel called over to the Maitre'd, who moved us to the other side of the room. I think

Daniel bought their breakfast. What started to be an enjoyable morning ended on a rather sour note.

Daniel always did as much as he could for his folks when he was in town. The doctors, the dentist, register the car, and his mother to the grocery store(Mom didn't drive), and anything they might need.

Sometime later, his Dad was saying the heater in his Chrysler wasn't working. Daniel went over, spent a whole afternoon replacing the heating coil. He comes home for dinner, just washed up, and the phone rings; it's his Dad.

"Daniel, the heater still doesn't work."

After dinner, Daniel goes to the auto parts store, buys a hotter thermostat, returns to his Dad's, and puts the new thermostat in the car. He tells his Dad, it's done and should be warmer than you need.

His Dad gets in the car, starts it up, and calls out to Daniel, "I don't know what you did, but it still doesn't work."

Daniel walks over to the car, gets in on the passenger side. Look at the dash.

He says, "Dad, you have got to move the lever to turn it on." Daniel turned it on, and there was more heat than anyone needed.

His Dad didn't say anything, and Daniel came home at about 8:30 PM and said, "I need a shower. I'm tired."

Daniel has been making multiple trips back to Orange County; it's a four-hour drive. His apartments needed attention, and whenever the kids had something going on, he did his best to be present. Lisa needed significant dental work, and Daniel left plenty of time to make her appointment, but there was an accident with a milk truck and another truck blocking the whole freeway. His four-hour drive turned into six, and he always drove back the same day and missed Lisa's appointment.

On one of his drives home in his blue and white ford truck, fuel is getting low. The standing joke for this truck was ten mpg standing; still, it was doing well if it got ten. It's the era of the fuel crisis when people are shooting each other at the gas pumps. He's almost home, only 5 miles to go; it's 2 AM, and the only station open is the one he's just about to. The fuel gauge has been essential for the last half hour.

He stops at the station; the attendant comes out, a scruffy-looking character in a dirty station shirt and greasy jeans.

He says, "The sign right there says trucks only."

Daniel points to his vehicle, "It's a truck."

The attendant replies, "Commercial vehicles only."

Daniel says, "Come on, man, it's 2 in the morning, there's nothing else open, and I don't have enough fuel to get into Arroyo Grande.

The attendant just walks away and says over his shoulder only commercial vehicles. Daniel gets in the truck and gets maybe a mile; it's not going any farther. He coasts off to the side of the highway and hoofs it home. I hear him open the door; I get up and can tell right off that something isn't right. We take the car and a siphoning hose back to the truck. Daniel works to get fuel out of the car into the truck, and he accidentally swallows a bit. I thought he wasn't going to make it; he coughed and spit and smelled like fuel for the rest of the night. After all that, either the truck didn't get enough gasoline, or who knows, but it wouldn't start. He took a rope out of the trunk of the car, the Ford LTD, tied it to the bumper, and tied the other end to the front of the truck.

Daniel said, "Now you are going to drive the car, don't drive too fast and don't stop, I don't have power steering or power brakes, so it's much harder to handle."

"Ok, I'll be careful and get us home." I got onto the freeway, down the off-ramp, and we are in town, almost home. The traffic light turns red, I need to make a left turn, but Daniel says not to stop. I look both ways; there's no one coming; it's like 3 AM, so slowly, I keep going, Daniels tapping his brakes. If I stop suddenly, I don't think that's a good thing to do. Too late now, I'm almost in the intersection, and oh my, we are through it, past the light, no oncoming traffic, and no officials with flashers. I get us to the apartment parking lot and get the truck positioned as best I know-how.

We get out of the vehicles, Daniel says, "What were you doing?"

"You told me not to stop."

He hugged me, and I wanted to give him a welcome home kiss, but he still smelled like gasoline, quite unbearable. After washing up and brushing his teeth, it didn't dampen the odor.

"Daniel, how much fuel did you swallow?"

"Too much."

The next day he went to a metal fabricator and had a 50-gallon tank made and installed in the back of the truck. He was taking care of business. It took a week to get the 50-gallon tank and have it installed. Then within a day after installation, we discovered it was leaking. Both for finances and safety it's unsound. He went to where the tank was installed to get the leak repaired. They wouldn't stand behind their work. After much to do, Daniel decided to take them to small claims court. Oh well, they guessed they could fix it after all. It seems to be a lot of poker playing and who has the best bluff. My education keeps growing.

We were always taking trips back to Orange County for one reason or another. There was Dean's graduation, the oldest son, Chris's confirmation, Chris and Lisa's school conference, then Lisa's confirmation, plus several business meetings in between. We took the four kids to Knotts Berry Farm; they took the rides; the usual junk food and chicken dinners were supposed to be the best, so we gave it a try.

This trip had been overnight, it's a holiday weekend, and we are on our way home. Daniel's asleep, I'm driving, the kids are in the back seat, we are north of LA, and I say to the kids, "We always take that road, it says this road will take us there too, what do you think?" So we take the alternate route.

About 20 minutes later, Daniel wakes up; he looks around and says, "Where are we?"

"We took the other turn off; it said it would take us home."

"Dianah, we are on the way to Bakersfield, about 100 miles out of the way."

"You never told me that."

"You know that there are no fuel stations open today. Pullover and let me drive; if we are lucky, we'll make it into town to an open station."

So now we are on a country road, driving at about 45 mph. It's not your typical sunny California weather; the sky is gray, there's no rain, just very dreary, and nobody is talking. I see a station up ahead and think, oh, see, that wasn't so bad. He just keeps driving; I look at him and think, what are you doing?

Daniel says, "If you're wondering why I didn't stop, the station was closed."

"Oh."

As the drive continues, I watch the fuel gauge getting closer to empty all the time. We finally get into Santa Maria, 2 hours later, the red fuel light has been on for a while, and any station will do. We coast into the pump. I breathe a sigh of relief.

As we pulled back out onto the highway, I said, "I'm sorry, I didn't know I would make it such a tough day."

"Daniel said, "I know you didn't do it on purpose, but please don't ever do that again. If you want to take a different road, wake me up, believe me when I say, that would have been so much easier."

"Ok, is there anything I can do for you when we get home?"

"Let's have dinner and go to bed early, I don't mean to grouch at you, but I'm exhausted."

So that's what we did. I screwed up big time. I always seem to get lost and go in the wrong direction. I thought it would be nice to give the boys a treat; we could go to the drive-in theatre. We get ready, we even know what movie is playing, I get on the right road but guess what, I turn the wrong way. We end up on the other side of town and barely make it to the movie in time. Toph even told me I was going the wrong way, but I said, I'm on the right road. Some parts of my life don't flow no matter how much I try.

The month is March; Daniel has found a piece of property in Oregon he wants to see. He'll call his Aunt and Uncle to let them know we are coming and we can stay for a couple of nights. Toph and Tim will go with us; if we leave on Friday, they will only miss one school day. We drive to the Grants Pass area, stop at the relatives, have dinner with them and retire for the evening; it's been a long day.

Early this morning, I said, "Daniel, it's cold."

He looked out the window; there had been a snowstorm during the night. The electricity was out, the snow was deep, and this is a mobile home, all-electric. I hear, don't flush the toilet because the pump won't work. Uncle Charlie wants to go to the store, find out what's going on because the phones aren't working either. Well, Charlie can't get the door open for the snow. Daniel goes out the other door and around the house, shovels the snow, and now Charlie can get to his car. Charlie's car is in the carport; when he backs out too fast, he centers the car over the snow, and now the back wheels aren't touching the ground. Daniel comes back with the shovel, and he takes over driving for Charlie to get out of the driveway. In the meantime, a snowplow comes by so they can get to the highway. Later that day, the electricity was back, and we could relax. We called the fellow with the property, a house on a few acres, and decided it wasn't what we had in mind anyway. They had water issues, so we took a pass. That evening, we went to dinner at an all-you-can-eat place; it was super busy. The following day we had breakfast with the family and drove home. The drive home was no small feat. The weather was still poor, and the mountain road to go down was iced. It's now late at night; we can see the truck in front of us skidding from one side to another, at 20 miles per hour. You can't go too fast or too slow, or you'll start sliding. No, we didn't have chains. It was so scary; I couldn't bear to watch the road. Once down the mountain road, it was still a long way home.

It's a sunny morning after coffee, the boys are in school, and neither Daniel nor I have any appointments for the day. He says, let's take a drive to Pozo. Pozo is a tiny country town, where you can pass right by and not even know it's there. We, however, are going to take the back road, over the hills. The road is neither paved nor maintained, so Daniel says this should be fun.

We are off the highway and starting up the country road. There are lots of ruts, and the higher we go, the deeper the crevasses. Daniel says I got this. We'll walk the wheels one at a time until we get to the top. The mountain road with a steep downward cliff on one side, the mountain on the other, and with each wheel movement, he needs to check just where the wheels are on high ground. By this point of the drive, I am no longer in the car. I'll stand behind and watch.

I said, "You know, if you get stuck, it's a long walk back."

Daniel is a very determined soul.

"After about a half-hour and he's progressed maybe a 100 feet, I hear, guess we can go back and have lunch in town.

"What do ya think?"

"Now you're going to have to back down; there's no place to turn around."

"It's okay, much easier than going up."

I didn't understand, so whatever he wanted to do, I'd go along with it. Generally, he works it all out, and everything is fine. As it ends up, we have a nice lunch in town, the area has excellent restaurants, and we get home before the boys return from school.

My guy, so much I don't understand, and yet he is so loveable.

The year is still 1978; nothing has slowed down. Life is as complete as we can make it. Tim just got a new pair of glasses; he is just the cutest thing. Baseball uniform, long hair, and an award-winning smile. We are all busy doing individual tasks and trying to be aware.

I have a real estate transaction connected with a business in Orange County. Daniel knows the owner, and my broker has a pilot's license. We have decided it would be advantageous to fly into Fullerton Airport; the client would pick us up, then fly back. The whole trip shouldn't take more than 4 hours. Daniel, I, and Merrilee meet at San Luis Obispo airport. She has rented a four-seater Cessna; Daniel sits in front with Merrilee since he has experience flying, I sit in the back. Our pilot seems to be a little stressed, maybe just tired. We take off without a problem and follow the coast south, but she's unsure where to head for Fullerton.

ME AND DANIEL

As we approach LA, Daniel says, "Did you file a flight plan?"
"No."

As we fly over LAX and watch for jets and commercial airlines, I particularly do not want to be in their way. We make it past LAX and head for Fullerton; the smog is getting thicker. Once there, the airport isn't visible until we have passed it. You can see diagonally through the pollution, but not directly under you or above. The tower had given us the ok to land, but we missed it, so they sent us 5 miles out, and now we are seventh in line. It takes a good 20 minutes to get back to the landing position. I hear Daniel saying, now is the time to touch down, don't overshoot the runway. We land; I can tell Merrilee is exhausted; maybe after lunch, she will feel better.

As we deplane, a Rolls Royce pulls up, and the driver, a big guy with a chauffeur's hat, walks over, ushers us to the car, opens the door, and welcomes us to Orange County. The people on the sidelines are saying, is that someone famous; who are they? The chauffeur is our client, and the Rolls Royce is one of his collections. The auto once belonged to the Pope and was stored at the Vatican; Bob showed us the emblem in the glove compartment. Then Bob took us to lunch and his antique business. Lovely Spanish hacienda on a corner in Fullerton, filled with some novel antique furniture. He wanted to sell, and as realtors, we wanted to list. Bob was a wheeler-dealer; as it ended in negotiating, Bob sold the property himself. But introduced us to another seller, the largest auctioneer in California, and Daniel sold the business to a couple of Jewish business people from New York. It was the strangest sale ever. The auctions were held in an old warehouse leased from the property owner; there was no inventory, a couple of old desks in the office, and a window air conditioner that got stolen just before closing. However, the business made money, and the buyers paid dearly for nothing more than the name.

About 3 PM, we are back in the air, on our way home. The San Luis Obispo Airport is directly in front of us; it's a clear sunny day, wide-open farmland, nothing in your way; we are the only ones in the air going to land. The plane is directly over the runway; Daniel says Merilee, put the nose down; you need to be on the runway in the first third; we are now at the second third and heading towards the end. Daniels says the farmer will be mad if we tear up his cabbage patch on the other side of the fence that we are about to run into. Merrilee hits the nose wheel on the pavement; the plane bounces 20 feet in the air. I see the people running out of the airport; I hear the fire engine. We are the only plane in motion; all this commotion is for us. I'm thinking it doesn't look like this is a small matter. In the meantime, Daniel has taken the copilot's stick and pulled the plane back in the air. He turns the control back over to the pilot, and the tower says, make a long sweep, go out as far as you need to be comfortable, which we do. As she was preparing to land, again not getting down soon enough on the runway and bouncing, but we were able to stop, and some men from the airport came out to greet her. We went to our car and home. The day had been exhausting.

One would think we were always doing exciting, challenging things. But every once in a while, there are the usual daily living things that happen. Such as, the refrigerator stopped working; well, it didn't stop but close enough. So we went to the local Sears appliance store, and there, sitting on a display the correct size at the expected sales price with a sign on the top, says ice maker is included. We let the salesperson know this is what we would like to purchase, just as we see it. No problem, the delivery will be in two days. The fridge arrives on time; the servicemen bring it up the stairs; our apartment is on the second floor-13 steps. They get it in the kitchen, plug it in, and the delivery guys start to leave.

I said, "Don't you have to hook up the ice maker?"

"Mam, you don't have an ice maker."

"But that's what we ordered."

"Sorry, you'll have to talk to the store about that."

Daniel calls and gets the run-around. He says, "Grab your purse and the polaroid camera; we are going to Sears."

Arriving at the store, we ask for the manager, who promptly comes out.

After explaining what we ordered and what was received, he says, "Oh no, that sales price is without the ice maker."

I said," But the sign sitting right there on top of the fridge with the sale sign says you'll get an ice maker, as Daniel is taking a picture of the poster and fridge."

"Mam,"

Again with the Mam!

The Manager says, "The sign was accidentally put there; the ice maker has never been included."

Daniel says, "That's false advertising; I'm sure the local paper would like to hear about it and, if necessary, small claims court."

The manager decided we were more trouble than we were worth, so we came home with an ice maker, and Daniel installed it.

Daniel's Dad is in the hospital again, lots of medication that doesn't seem to be agreeing with him. So every day, Daniel makes a trip to the hospital and then takes his Mom to whatever she might need. Dad's been there for over a week, it's a heart condition, but he's supposed to come home tomorrow.

I'm still just getting started in the real estate industry when Daniel tells me there's a mobile home in a park in Oceano where the lady that owns it wants to sell.

"Daniel, I can't sell a mobile home unless it's on land." He says, well, let's just talk with her and her boyfriend, see what the scoop is. So we talk, look at the house, and discover they would make a trade for Daniels' 10-acre parcel that he bought in Nevada, sight unseen. In the meantime, I had a buyer who couldn't afford to buy a house or anything I could find him, but I told him about the mobile home. He was thrilled, a place close to the beach. Within three weeks, it was all put together; the one couple had ten acres in Nevada, the guy who couldn't buy anything had a house by the beach, and Daniel had cash in hand. I was just a person getting an education on the possibilities of business and thinking outside the box. There were no listings, no real estate sales agreements; they all went to the title company and said this is what we want to do.

Autumn has arrived, the plans for Thanksgiving this year will be different. Daniel's daughter, Denise, and her boyfriend will be driving their dune buggy and staying in Oceano by the dunes; some of their friends are coming along with dirt bikes and camping gear. Chris and Lisa will be here, and so it will be busy and fun eating out on the beach. Toph has a school friend who has a small dirt bike. His friend said he wouldn't be using it on Thanksgiving Day, and it's alright with his parents if Toph just borrows it for the day. When Toph talked with us, we said it was fine, but you must make sure you don't break it. He's a friend and is very generous. We have bought all kinds of food, roasted a turkey, pies, all the things you would expect for the day.

As morning arrives, we take the kids to the beach with their gear and Toph with his friend's bike. The rest of the group was already there; they had been tenting overnight. After spending about an hour watching everyone race the dunes, we said, "We are going back to get the food, and we'll meet you at your campsite. Daniel said, "Toph, you haven't ridden the dunes before, don't go too fast over the top. The wind blows the sand from the west; the drop-off can be a sheer cliff if you are going east.

We left to get dinner, and we are now on our way back, a couple of miles away, when we hear an ambulance and fire engine. I look at Daniel, he looks at me, and all I can say is, "I hope it's not one of ours." As we pull onto the beach, we see one of the kids racing toward us way too fast in the dune buggy.

We meet up in seconds; he's so exasperated he can hardly talk. "Tophs, laying in the sand on the other side of that dune."

We rush to the dune, run over the top, and there he is, flat on his back, the bike a few yards away.

As I run down, I can't tell what has happened, and I say, "Toph, where does it hurt? It's his leg." He can't move.

Daniel said, "Don't move; the ambulance will be here in a minute."

The first thing Toph said was, "The guy who found me, I had him check the bike; the bike is ok, nothing happened to it."

The ambulance guys put him on a gurney and off to the hospital. The other kids made sure the bike was taken care of, and we rushed to the hospital as fast as possible. When we arrived, they tried to get him comfortable while the doctor on call was being summoned. Small town, a small hospital, and the only doctor was having Thanksgiving Dinner. When he arrived and checked Toph's leg, he came out and gave us his spiel about how parents shouldn't let kids ride dirt bikes, how they shouldn't be on the dunes, and how we had interrupted his dinner.

My only question is, "Are you going to fix his leg?"

He didn't smile, "They are taking x-rays now, and he will be staying overnight."

I waited at the hospital, and Daniel took the food to the kids and the bike back to the friend's house.

The hospital wanted insurance or a retainer. I gave them Rick's card as part of the divorce settlement. I didn't have insurance; I was self-employed, just getting started and working at making ends meet. Rick had let the insurance lapse, so neither doctor, hospital, or ambulance was covered. I don't know how, but he took care of it. The ambulance even charged for sweeping the sand out.

Toph had a severe break, and the Doctor set it about two degrees off, but of course, we didn't know that until they took the cast off, and then it was too late. Fixing would mean an operation. When he came home, there were 13 steps to climb to the apartment; Daniel helped him up, using crutches. The first week was uncomfortable, but he was good about being on either the bed or the couch. If I wasn't home, Daniel was, we picked up his schoolwork, and we all worked it out. Toph said, "The worst part of the whole thing was when it started itching under the cast. The cast went up to his knee, down and around his foot. There was nothing narrow enough and long to fit down into the cast.

The friend with the dirt bike stopped being a friend. His parents thought we were going to sue them. We didn't blame them; we were concerned the bike was returned in the condition it had been lent. There were no winners in that scenario.

December and Christmas are upon us. Life and work continue as always. Daniel and I are working on a real estate transaction, which is closing the auction business. The buyers have put up all their money, signed the papers, and the seller has taken off on vacation. His contract has to have an original signature, be notarized and close before December 31st. The closing agent needs a couple of days to record it, or it won't meet the tax guideline, nullifying the sale. On December 27th, Daniel and I are at the LA airport waiting for our flight with contracts in hand. There are no expedited shipping or electronic signatures; it didn't count in 1978; the mail is out of the question, no one can be trusted.

We continue to wait for the flight; I ask one of the attendants when we leave.

She says, "Oh, that flight already took off; they changed gates, didn't you hear the call?"

We scramble to the ticket counter to get another flight to Yakima, which won't be until later this evening. If we arrive in Yakima at about 8 AM, with no sleep, no shower, and everybody better show up on time, we still have a chance of saving this transaction. The seller has this friend, a good ole boy real estate broker from Oregon, who will advise him on California contract law. Daniel and I are in Yakima the following day, tired and sweaty, and need a toothbrush. Our bags were on the first flight. We get to the broker's office by 10 AM. The seller hasn't arrived; he shows up about 11 AM. We got his signature after too much conversation and hemming and hawing about what was legal and what wasn't. After all, it was the sellers' attorney who drew up the contract. We have to be on the plane by 1 PM, back to LA by 3 PM, and get it recorded no later than 5:30 PM, Friday, New Years Weekend. The next business day is January 2nd. The sale must be recorded before year-end, or the seller does not get his tax break, and the sale is canceled. As we arrive in LA, I'm checking us out of the airport, and Daniel is on the phone making sure everyone knows exactly what they need to do. It was rushed from one hand to another and recorded at 5:26 PM. Did we feel we had accomplished something? No, and yes, it was a fair commission check, but the frustration and tension went way beyond the paycheck.

New Year's Eve came and went; we lay in bed in each other's arms and wished the world away for a day. If we could do nothing for a week, how wonderful that would be. However, that was not our life, a whole week of doing nothing, it would be madness. Eventually, it's New Year's morning with a bit of coffee and a walk down by the beach, the waves are reaching for our toes, the smell of the salt air, arm in arm with the sensation of the good life. The boys come with us, and we will check on Daniel's parents before the day is over.

Chapter Eleven

WHAT NOW 1979

DANIEL, I, AND the two boys have taken up residence in Arroyo Grande, California. We have a small balcony overlooking the neighborhood to the ocean. The sun is always shining with an ocean breeze. We planted a few cherry tomatoes behind the garage, and they are flourishing, with more tomatoes than we know what to do with; we made salsa and gazpacho, plus anything else that comes to mind. This area has so many fresh foods in the fields and is almost next door.

Dad DiSandro went to the crating sheds, where the trucks are loaded, and a worker gave him a whole crate of veggies and said, share this with your neighbors.

Daniel's father invites us for dinner. Compliments were over the top, the best fava beans I have ever tasted, and I have never duplicated his recipe. I'm sure it wasn't anything complicated, but the planted homegrown fava beans were fresh and oh so good. It was delicious.

The restaurants here are fabulous; the city restaurants can't compare. The food in this little town is the best, with the restaurant competition for the tourist and available newly picked produce, the shops here have outdone themselves.

We are making multiple trips to Orange County, a four-hour one-way drive, and we never stay overnight; it's demanding and time-consuming. The kids in Anaheim have events to attend, the apartments need attention, and there seems to be some unfinished business to tend continuously. How much can be accomplished in one day?

One late evening, I was the tired driver, coming through Ventura on Highway 101; the bright lights of oncoming traffic in the southbound lanes shining in my eyes didn't stop me from nodding off at the wheel. Daniel was asleep in the seat next to me, and the boys were sleeping in the back. One of us bolted just before I started swerving over the division line into the oncoming traffic.

Daniel spoke firmly, "Pull off to the side of the road. Neither one of us is fit to drive."

I pulled off the highway, getting over as far as safely possible. I brought the car to a stop; stomped on the emergency brake; I was shaking, my hands were sweating, my heart was pounding, I felt like I had just had the beating of my life. That was too close. We rested for an hour, and then Daniel drove home. He always seemed to have a reserve of more stamina and strength than I do. I considered myself tough, but if I admitted needing help, Daniel would be there. Don't mistake this; I didn't like saying I needed help. Pride and ego made it difficult to admit my faults. It's one thing to let yourself know of your shortcomings, but it's challenging to ask for help when you think you should be capable.

When I'm at work, I feel guilty because I'm not home taking care of my family; I think about everything unfinished at work when I'm at home. Neither Daniel nor the boys are getting on my good side right now, and they haven't done anything wrong. Try as I might, I want some me-time. One evening I did just that, time for myself, I went out with girls. It was my birthday; I deserved it. Right? When I got home, which was late, Daniel told me Toph had made a cake, and he and Tim had prepared dinner and a gift. Because I was so late, the boys were already in bed. Daniel only said he was disappointed. I thought, oh, how could I screw up so badly. Why was I so selfish? Now I feel worse. Once you do some of these stupid things, there is no undoing. Could I be nicer to everyone? I was already doing everything I knew how to do. I could only promise not to repeat the same blunder over again. Life will go on, and this, too, I will put behind me. The trick is not to fill the trailer you are dragging behind you, and don't open the box of unwanted memories. Close the door on regrets.

Daniel listed the 8 unit apartment building with me as the selling agent. This building he has owned forever it's small studio apartments, and it is old. A Spanish-style stucco painted schoolhouse green with a flat roof. But as an investment, it produces a better than average income. Numerous calls are coming in asking about the property; most of the calls are of no future use. As a real estate agent, the plan was to switch and bait for other listings since the property was far away. Not all plans are fruitful. The sales force in the office are not pleased, it's too far away for them to see, and they are unfamiliar with the location—consequently, all the calls are for me. When you have an office full of commission-paid people, no one wants to turn over any potential sales to anyone else.

One retired lady in Santa Ana became interested in the units. I suggested she take a drive-by. If she liked what she saw, I would make an appointment with the owner to show one unit. I did caution her not to disturb any of the tenants. Nice enough, gal, but she doesn't listen too well. She called me back a day later and informed me the lady in unit four was raising chickens on her kitchen table and had more than one chicken. The stacked cages are on top of each other, and the tenant is selling eggs.

I said I would let the seller know.

"And by the way, how did you know there were chickens in the apartment?"

"Oh well, I was standing outside looking at the building, and Mrs. Wong came out to ask what I needed. I told her I was only looking at the building, and she invited me in."

I am holding the phone and shaking my head, "If you remember, I asked you only to drive by, not inspect the building, and specifically not to talk with the tenants."

She said, "I thought you would want to know about the chickens."

I said, "Thank you, is there anything else you would like to know when I call the seller?"

"Let me think about it, and I will call you back."

The next day she did call back and talked for a long while without saying anything specific. Every time I tried to pin her down to make a commitment, she would evade me. As it worked out, she never bought anything.

While I was pursuing real estate, Daniel was challenging himself with taxes and the IRS. They contended he made unallowable deductions, such as coffee and donuts for his crews, including chargeable phone calls and many little things amounting to approximately Three Thousand dollars. Daniels detailed information on any file is unique, every receipt, notes on every phone conversation with dates and time of day or night. Daniel had multiple files of calls and sending information to the IRS for a year, and they were still hounding him. So his plan is, go to court.

One could say Daniel is a fighter. He is not afraid to step out of the norm and take on a business battle. Daniel is sure he is right, and just because they are the IRS, that did not give them the right to run roughshod over him. However, I never knew anyone who prepared for things with as much detail as Daniel. So, he has his two boxes of files categorized, memorized, and ready for the scheduled court date.

The week before the court date, the IRS Agent calls, "Mr. DiSandro, do you suppose we could meet and try to work this out."

"I have been trying to set an appointment with you for at least a year, and no, this week will not work for me. I have Tuesday free next week if that works for you?"

If Daniel is anything, he's assertive. That was also a new word in my vocabulary. I didn't want or need to be aggressive, but I found that assertiveness would need to be one of my dominant traits to get anything accomplished in business—a whole new category of behavior.

Tuesday it is, Daniel is on his way to Orange County again. He takes his files, dressed in a suit and tie. The look is quite dapper. A no-nonsense trip to Daniel, all business and authoritative as he walks into the agent's office. There's the usual greetings, coffee, and then it's down to the reason for the appointment. Eliminate the tax bill.

After the agent has gone through the first three months, he says I don't know why you're here. We can drop the case right now.

Daniel sternly proclaims, "You have been annoying me for the better part of a year; I have taken my valuable time and put all these files together for your benefit. You are getting paid to be here, and for all of this, I have not received anything but harassment; you cost me and my accountant time and dollars. Will that be refunded to me?"

The agent mumbles, "No."

Daniel says, " I didn't think so. Let's continue with the rest of the year. "

Daniel took off his suit coat, loosened his tie, and took out the April file.

By 4:30 PM that afternoon, the tax year in question is resolved. The IRS agent determined an amount of $300 and change due.

Daniel said, "You can send me a statement of the breakdown and amount due, and I will send you a check."

He packed up his files and put his coat on. Said goodbye to the agent and proceeded out the door.

Before driving home, Daniel stopped by his kid's house to say hello, changed clothes, and by 8 PM, he was on his way to do the four-hour drive back.

Gene Fults, Daniels concrete man and construction buddy with Gene's girlfriend Pam, drove up from Norwalk in the Los Angeles area to visit us. Gene was on the short side, muscular and good-looking in a rough kind of way, and Pam was sweet and cute, with dark hair and just a couple pounds too much, maybe one dress size. But, Pam always had a smile, even with all the shenanigans Gene put her through. Gene is divorced, he says. His ex-wife has remarried, she says, but sometimes it would sound as if they were still married. Gene had three or four kids; all are hell on wheels. More than just minor teenage stuff.

The four of us jumped in Genes trans van and drove to the Madonna Inn. The property is ornate, Cinderella-style, set back into a large rock formation with a winding drive past the white rail fence containing the purebred cattle. The old-fashioned light standards are painted pink with white globe lights. The two-story building is Swiss Chalet style painted white. It has a shake roof and sculpted rails with a circular staircase. Inside, the restaurant there are copper tables, ornate silverware, colored goblets, carved wood everywhere you could imagine, and the bathrooms were magnificent. The men's room had a waterfall urinal, and the flowers in the women's restroom were of all beautiful colors, with tiles and marble everywhere. The setting is just before San Luis Obispo, a rather fashionable town.

We had breakfast, always tasty, and after breakfast, like we didn't have enough to eat, Daniel and Gene stopped by the bakery counter to buy apple strudels for the drive. Madonna's is noted for having the best apple strudels within 100 miles, and they sell out early.

We are at the counter, and Gene says, "I want eight apple strudels."

Daniels speaks to the gal at the counter, "How many do you have?"

She says she has 18; Daniel, without hesitation, says," We will take them all."

Gene turns to Daniel, "There won't be any for other people waiting in line behind us."

"They have all kinds of other pastries, Gene. It will be okay, you'll see."

We left the Inn with 18 apple strudels at five dollars each and drove north as far as San Simeon to visit Hearst Castle. I think we ate most of the strudels before arriving at the castle. The property was breathtaking with the gardens and pools, the luxurious rooms, and a mansion on the hilltop overlooking the ocean, a glorious day.

Pam and Gene spend that night at our apartment. Morning coffee has started, Pam and I are on our first cup, and Daniel joins us while Gene is in the shower. Daniel says, watch this; he goes into the hallway at the water heater closet, and we hear Gene grumbling.

"DiSandro, you don't have any hot water."

Two seconds later, we heard him swearing; there was too much hot water, then it was cold.

He comes out of the bathroom, "DiSandro, you SOB, that was you messing with the hot water."

We all laughed and gave Gene some coffee to get his day started.

We had gone with Gene and Pam one time to Las Vegas. Gene didn't drink anymore, but he liked to gamble. We weren't there more than a couple of hours, and Gene had gone through all his cash, borrowed two or three thousand from Daniel; when that was gone, Gene asked Daniel to get money from a credit card.

Daniel said, "No, it's late, let's go home."

After a bite at the coffee shop, we started home. The Trans Van was not in the best of conditions. Gene had used a piece of PVC pipe to hold up an overhead cabinet. On our way to Vegas, Daniel pointed at the dashboard to say, what's this? But his finger went through the dash before he could finish the question.

We were in the Trans van late at night, and the lights on the vehicle began dimming. Gene pulled over and switched to the RV battery. It didn't have a much better charge than other batteries. The two guys thought it must be the alternator. By the time we got to Los Angeles, there were no headlights. It's not safe on the LA freeways traveling at night with no headlights. The amber running lights were lit with the house battery, but we didn't even have dash lights nor flashlights. Gene says I can't tell how fast I'm going. We needed to get to Norwalk, just north of LA. There would be no stopping at traffic signals or stop signs; we had to keep the beast moving. It ran just long enough to pull into his driveway, and no mishaps with other drivers or the police. Gene got the cash he owed Daniel. He and Daniel were alike, always had a hidden cash box. We wished them well and did our 4-hour drive to Arroyo Grande.

Daniel's father is back in the hospital again; we didn't talk about it, just tried to do whatever we could to help. Daniel had some thoughts about the doctors and the medication, but none of us had enough knowledge to do anything different than was already being done. When it was time for his Dad to come home, we would be there to keep him as comfortable as possible.

Life continued, we worked, and Daniel knew how to have fun. I was a worrier, but with help, I was learning to let my hair down. We found a haunt in San Luis Obispo that met our fancy. Tortilla Flats, the restaurant, had chips and salsa in a trough. The trough is about 10 feet long, with baskets and dishes at the end. Serve yourself to all you want, you could sit at the bar or the high-top tables, and they served margaritas by the pitcher. The drinks were good, and the place was always busy. Weekends had a Mariachi Band. The menu was extensive, but we mainly went for happy hour. We didn't go too often, but Tortilla Flats is a favorite place. We have passed by other restaurants with the same name, but none came close to the original.

One Friday evening after a particularly tough week, Daniel said, "We need some entertainment."

It's about 4:30 PM when we arrive and choose our table, Daniel orders the Margaritas, and I get the chips and salsa. We were on our first glass at about half full, and a couple we knew asked to join us; the place was getting packed, and they ordered another pitcher. No more than a half-hour later, another couple asked to join, and they ordered another pitcher. By this point, I lost track of how many pitchers, how many glasses, and about 8 o'clock, the one couple says, let's go to our place and use the hot tub.

I turned to the gal next to me and said, "I don't have a swimsuit with me."

The guy says, 'We don't need suites.'

I looked to Daniel; he said, 'I think we need to head home.'

Stepping up to the truck, Daniel said, "How do you feel about driving?"

I didn't think it was the safest thing for me to do.

He said, "Ok, I'll take the back road and stay off the freeway." We helped each other stay on the road and slowly made it home. Uber didn't exist, and people then just didn't think about taxis, nor were they available in the country. We didn't go back for a long time; too much alcohol was just not our thing.

Daniel's life is going into a whirlwind, and I am feeling the repercussions. Denise is getting married. Daniel listens to all the plans the bride and the groom and their mothers want. Daniel doesn't care for what they're planning. He suggests it would be nice to rent a hall and have it catered. Since the bride's parents, as per custom, were the ones to provide the event, he thought if it were ok with Denise and Lillian, he would like to do that. I heard Lillian preferred to have the reception in her backyard, but Denise's mother-in-law wanted it in their backyard. So, after much to do, the wedding would occur in the groom's parent's backyard. The emotions of the event had surpassed the red zone. On the ceremony day, I happened to step into the bedroom where all the girls were getting ready, and Denise was in tears; something wasn't right. I just told her it's a small thing and all would be fine. Daniel had asked for some cake to take to his parents since they couldn't attend, but there was none to be found. It was indeed the strangest family gathering I had ever been to. The midwest families of my relatives were always; please eat some more food, take some with you, can I get you anything else? So I was like a duck out of the water, and I wasn't a relative; therefore, Mum's the word.

Bride and groom did say their vows, a somewhat chaotic reception took place, and they went on their honeymoon. The aftermath was a time of silence, and it was apparent the families would always have some discord, whether acknowledged or not. Daniel and I didn't discuss the events afterward. It was over and not to be repeated.

ME AND DANIEL

Daniel came home on Saturday afternoon; I had been at work, and behind the truck was this kind of funky-looking travel trailer. It was gray metal, 17 feet long; the curtains inside were falling apart. It had light wood paneling, a mustard color stove, and orange vinyl on the seats. The bathroom consisted of a toilet and a small sink. There's a small refrigerator, a dinette, and a sofa made into a bed. It wasn't beautiful, but it was functional.

Daniel said, "We haven't had a trip in a while; summer is coming, the kids will be out of school." "What do you say?"

"Ok, I say, "Where do you plan on going?"

"Haven't decided yet; there's work to do on the trailer first."

Daniel did all the things he wanted to make it road-worthy. He greased the hubs, checked the axles, and added an anti-sway bar to the hitch. Then he had to put electric brakes on the truck and wire it to the trailer. Electrical was not his forte, so always a frustrational challenge. The truck needed a new engine, brakes, and so on. My only job was to clean, make sure the refrigerator worked, the toilet was ok and made some curtains, plus pack for the trip—my first experience with RVing. Because the plan was for all four of the kids to travel with us, we needed a place for them to sit. Unfortunately, it's illegal for them to ride in the travel trailer, so he found a camper shell and put two bunks for seating and sleeping areas in the pick-up bed for the kids. If we are not working on this project, there's still the property search, and every time we find something with the possibility of working for us, we make an offer.

The number of contracts was numerous. Daniel would be the buyer, and the proposals were always to his specs. Daniel didn't like the real estate forms, and we would cross out line after line of rhetoric. When I would present the offer, the listing broker would, without fail, give me this lecture about all of this vocabulary being drafted by an attorney and that it needed to be there. After doing this so often, my rehearsed answer is that a legal contract is a written agreement between buyer and seller. If the seller doesn't like the buyer's proposal, they can counter the offer or reject it. What I have brought to you is what the buyer wants to offer. I even had some agents tell me I didn't have any control over the buyer; although that may have been true, I wasn't about to tell them. I would say it is your obligation legally to present this offer whether you like it or not. The decision is up to the seller.

Consequently, a good percentage of the offers didn't go anywhere. But if you didn't put it in writing, they wouldn't take it as a serious proposal to buy. I got to know many of the agents in town and which ones I should not contact.

Daniel drew up a living together agreement; I thought it was amusing. It said that we would treat each other well and financially take care of our individual responsibilities. Now I know things can change, but there wasn't anything I wanted to get from Daniel other than love and caring. If there was financially something he wanted, there simply were no assets. I might be a deficit anyway, but I think he likes me, so we signed the agreement. Years later, I found it in a drawer and threw it away. When Daniel and I had been together just a few months, he asked me if I wanted to get married or would like to be married.

My answer was. "No."

He didn't say would you marry me? Which put me off a little. But I wasn't looking for marriage; I had been so disappointed in what they called this institution of marital bliss and had worked far too hard at it for far too long.

I told Daniel, "I was neither ready, and it was far too early in our relationship to make that decision."

Daniel said, "If you are sure that's your decision, you need to know I won't ask you again."

"That's okay, if and when, somewhere down the line, I decide I want to be married, I will ask you. If you don't answer me, I'll ask you again."

I stated, "If we love each other, trust one another, and care, what is that piece of paper and the government going to do for us?"

We didn't discuss it again. At the time, I didn't know what Daniel was thinking. Was he disappointed or relieved? I couldn't tell, nor did it matter. I did know how I felt; there was no question here I had been pondering.

The real estate office where I was working was growing weary. I didn't seem to be making progress and had chosen another office I thought had a better reputation and a solid foundation. A young Broker in his mid 30's, nice looking, divorced, running an office of seemingly better protocol. I started making inquiries and shortly changed offices.

I had only been at the office a couple of weeks when one evening Daniel said, "We need to talk."

As he started talking, I could not believe what I was hearing. Daniel was accusing me of getting together emotionally and sexually with the new broker. I asked him where these thoughts were coming from, and there was no clear answer. After way too much rhetoric and both of us upset, sleep finally set in. The next night it was the same scenario. After attempting to reason this out and in tears, I told Daniel, I love you and want to be with you, but not like this. I watched my parents do this very thing for years, and it never got better; if anything, it grew, with no love to be found. If you can't get past it, we have nothing and need to go our separate ways. It's not what I want, but I will not try to defend myself every night over something that has never happened. I grabbed a pillow, went to the living room to sleep on the sofa, and cried on my pillow.

Later in the wee hours, Daniel came to my side; he said, "Dianah, I'm sorry, I didn't want to make you cry. I don't want to be angry with each other. There is no reason why I should think those things; maybe it's male menopause. I promise you; I won't ever do this again. Please come back to bed with me and let me love you."

I picked up my pillow; he followed me into the bedroom, held me while I cried some more, and kept telling me I won't make you cry again. The evening slowly quieted, we went back to being caring individuals, but for the entire time I worked at that office, Daniel watched. When I was invited for a plane ride with the broker, Daniel asked me to please not go, and I didn't.

Daniel senior feels a tad bit better and wanted us to go fishing with him off the pier. If you were fishing from the dock, there was no license needed. Daniel got his fishing gear, and his dad had some extra poles, so all four of us went to join his dad fishing. I don't think I have ever been fishing before. As a child, only the men went fishing.

When we get to the pier, Daniel shows the boys and me how to bait the hook. Everyone is instructed that if you want to fish, you have to bait your hooks. It took me a bit to get over picking up the worms and squishing them on the snares. We were fishing for little red snappers. There are six hooks on a line. Everybody gets set up, baits their lines, has buckets for the fish we will catch as we sit on our stools and wait. I think Toph and Tim were more patient than I. I'm looking around, take a walk up and back on the pier. A few fish are caught, but nothing exciting.

I pick up my pole and start jiggling it, softly saying, here fishy, fishy. Here fishy, fishy. Low and behold, there's a tug on the line. I pull up the pole; there's four fish. Everybody is impressed, mostly me. I do the bait thing, repeat the process, and who would have guessed more fish. So the boys thought they would try it, but it didn't work. They moved up and down the pier, thinking it might be the spot. Still not successful. Even Daniel started moving his pole, but he didn't call for the fish. I had filled a pail full of fish, just getting ready to say that's enough when the fish and game department comes by. He says, you know, ten fish is the limit for each person.

I said, "Yes, sir, but we are all together, the family you know, and we are sharing the bucket."

He gave me the evil eye; it looks like you still have your limit. We packed up and headed home. Unfortunately, Daniel's Dad was none too happy, he didn't catch more than one or two, and the only female in the group captured the most fish. I did tell everyone, I don't clean fish. You can throw them back or clean them, but don't look to me for cleaning. I'll cook if you want.

It's time for a vacation; Daniel has an elaborate plan. Because of summer school, Chris and Lisa won't be available for two weeks. Toph and Tim are out of school now, but we still have work to finish up.

The two boys never had the opportunity to spend time with their grandparents and aunts and uncles in Wisconsin. I talked with my mother about the boys' staying with them and becoming acquainted with their grandparents for a week before we would arrive.

Arrangements with an airline for the boys flying to Milwaukee nonstop have been set. A stewardess escorts them off the plane and to a station where my brothers can pick them up. We'll drive out with Daniels two children, and everyone could get a little one-on-one time. I didn't find out until much later there hadn't been an escort for my two guys flying into Milwaukee, we didn't have cell phones, my brothers were running late, the boys were worried. They didn't know where they should be waiting and wouldn't recognize their uncles if they saw them.

What determines an overprotective parent or one who is putting the child in harm's way? And how do you estimate age and knowledge of the ability of a young person to handle things? I suppose because of the expectation for myself to be a capable adult by age 10, I thought of my children as more grown-up than some parents would have?

The Uncles and the boys met within a half-hour and headed to the Grandparent's house.

When memories fail us, the picture in our minds' eyes becomes distorted from reality. I believed that my parents would be happy to have time with their only grandchildren, and aunts and uncles would appreciate meeting their nephews. I had a misconception; though it was not hostile, it was not a fun warm household for that week. Tim, in particular being the youngest, was an odd man out. So he spent much of the time by himself. Mistaken identities happen, even when it's family.

In California, Chris and Lisa are getting ready to fly to Denver as soon as summer school is out, and we will pick them up at the airport.

Because the length of the trip was extensive, we needed a head start. The plan is, arrive in Denver on the way to Wisconsin and pick up the DiSandro kids.

The whole logistics of this trip seem somewhat convoluted.

Daniel and I have packed the RV and truck with everything imaginable. We set out on our journey. Our first stop is Boulder City, Nevada, where Daniel has a friend from long ago. It's a brief, unannounced stop to say, "Hi, we were in town," and we are then on our way. We stop at Hoover Dam to marvel at the structure. Daniel's background in construction and concrete gave him a much larger appreciation of the design and magnitude of the entire process.

We went into Las Vegas for an exciting theater performance at The Riviera Hotel starring Bob Newhart and Bernadette Peters. The next day Daniel and I viewed Circus Circus, the Stardust, the Flamingo, Caesars Palace, and the Barbary Coast. Breakfast was exceptional at the last hotel, and we are on our way east.

The day is hot; the windows are rolled down. I can't turn on the air conditioning because the engine is new; it needs to be broken in yet. We are driving into St. George, Utah; the red soil and mountain backdrop is breathtaking, with the town and the Mormon Tabernacle in the background. We didn't stop, it was early in the day, and we had a long-distance journey before nighttime. By late afternoon, we are both feeling weary. Zion national park, a desert park is just ahead, it wasn't hard to find a spot to park, and we set up in no time. I rushed over to a bit of stream and sat in it, and Daniel joined me; we didn't bother changing. There were trees with shade; the water rippled over our bodies; it wasn't very deep, just enough to get wet. The need to cool off was more significant than anything else. Daniel told me that our clothes would dry in about a half-hour once you get out, which they did. The park was relaxing, with a few trees, not too many people, and the rocky mountains in the backdrop. We found a restaurant, sat next to the window, and they brought us homemade brambleberry pie, and as always, with a cup of coffee.

Daniel put his hand on mine; "Sweets, are you having a good time?"

We had been pushing hard and ahead of schedule. Come early-morning, we hiked to the Emerald Pools, about 3 miles, and now it was time to keep moving. Drove through Sinbad Canyon and on to Breckenridge, Colorado. The drive is peaceful; we are in the mountainous terrain, it's green, the sun is bright, and the only thing today on the agenda is finding a place to spend the night. It's a two-lane paved road and directly in front of us is an RV park. I never did figure out if Daniel knew about these places or just had a better insight for travel. I guessed it was both. The gal at the office said we could have our pick here at the front of the campground or up the mountainside to the campsites to the side of the mountain road. Daniel asked me what my preference would be. Naturally, I said up the mountainside. I had forgotten about the engine in the truck being new and didn't give a lot of consideration to parking on a mountainside. My first try at rving; every part is a unique learning venture.

I wasn't driving, and I just thought there wasn't much Daniel couldn't do. About halfway up, the truck was not going to pull this trailer any farther. Turning around was not an option until we got to a campsite for space to turn. He backed down, around a curve, and a camp used by four guys with motorcycles is blocking part of the road. They are having a good time, drinking beer and barbecuing. Daniel asks one of them out front if he could move his bike a little so we might turn around. The camper just ignored us and walked away. They didn't look like they would be hard to get along with, but not one of the guys was accommodating. Daniel tried to do the turn; there just wasn't enough room without coming too close to the bikes. I asked Daniel if I should talk to one of the guys.

Daniel said, "Stay in the truck."

So I was of no help. By the time we were at the bottom of the hill, his exasperation had gone beyond the boiling point. The word was, we will continue until there's another place, and I'm not driving up to another mountainside for camping. Daniel parked the RV and truck at a Holiday Inn parking lot where we spent the night.

We went on a goldmine tour the next day, not all that interesting, and then walked into the Buffalo Bill's cemetery. As we looked over the Denver skyline, there was the brown haze of smog. It took away the feelings of wide-open spaces and the wild west, just another big city. The evening took us to the Windmill Restaurant where Daniel had been 20 years ago. We were collecting menus, and Daniel convinced the hostess that since we come back every 20 years, they should donate one to our cause. The hostess smiled, handed us a menu, and said I'm not planning to be here when you come back. We thanked her and were on our way back to the parking lot.

The rig is ready for travel and off to Stapleton Airport to pick up Chris and Lisa from Orange County. Lunch was on the schedule, and then we rode into the prairies and flatlands and cornfields. Lisa said she didn't care if she never saw another corn stalk. We camped at a truck stop in Des Moines, Iowa, had breakfast at the truck stop, and continued the drive. Somewhere in Iowa, there was a campground we could see from the highway, with a sign saying fishing was available. We all decided it was time for a break. I pulled into a spot for the night, and Daniel found the fishing gear. Fishing was a little pond in front of the campground; that was your fishing hole. Chris and Lisa put their poles in the water and waited. Chris decided to walk into the pond, so Lisa followed. Something bit her, so Daniel walked over to the RV, took out a lawn chair, and put it in the pond. Lisa sat in the chair with her feet up while holding the fishing pole. Half an hour later, everyone is bored, so we pick up all our paraphernalia, and it's back to the truck.

On our way to Mom and Dad's house, we were in the vicinity of Amana and the Amana stores. We thought we might have a tour of the Amana factory, that wasn't possible, but the store had items besides appliances. As we always did, we did the bargain hunt. Daniel found two ceramic crocks on sale because the lids were missing. I found a wool hat, not a summer item, at a reasonable price. It was a fun stop, and now back on the road to Omro. Arriving in Omro, we parked in the driveway, and everyone was there. I, of course, hugged Mom and Dad, but Toph and Tim were the hugs I needed. As expected, Mom had lots of food prepared, and everyone was jubilant. The next day the guys all went fishing on the Fox River in town. Tim showed me the pet shop he walked to about two miles out of town. Daniel wanted to look at a couple of farms that were for sale. We drove and looked; none of it made good economic sense for the time being. After visiting for a couple more days, it was time to head out. The kids had to rearrange how all six of us would travel and sleep in a predetermined space. It was to be a work in progress. The Rv would sleep four, and the two carpeted runners in the truck bed slept the other two. It was not like staying at the Hilton.

Driving south from Omro, Daniel wanted to take all the kids to the Capitol building in Madison. We arrived in Madison on Friday at about mid-day. The Capitol is a beautiful structure and in the center of the dome is a magnificent brass pendulum that swings down from the crown to the marble tiled floor. It's not only attractive but majestic in size and precision. We toured what we could of the building, and then it was time to leave.

At around 5 PM, the traffic is horrendous, and you know who is driving. Lisa is sitting upfront with me, and Daniel is in the truck camper with the boys. Madison being a circular city, all roads circle the Capitol building; if you're not paying attention, a person could be driving in a circle for hours. I'm negotiating traffic, trying to stay on the proper highway, and pull the camper. Daniel is pounding on the window that goes from the truck to the trailer.

"Lisa, what is your Dad trying to tell us?"

"He says there's an ice cream shop over there on the right."

"Lisa, does he know I'm in the left lane and have four lanes to move over into?"

Lisa doesn't know what to say, I am more than a little frustrated, but I put on the blinker and slowly start moving to the right. Everybody out there can see this woman does not know what she's doing. By the time I get in the correct lane, I have passed the ice cream shop. Daniel is saying no big deal.

No big deal! Do you know what you just put me through? I pulled onto a side street, and there was nowhere to turn around. So I drove to the end, a dead-end road on a hill. I stopped, pulled the emergency brake, stomped out of the truck, handed Daniel the keys, and said, it's all yours.

He said, " There's nowhere to turn around."

"And who's fault is that," I snarled back. I hadn't been that angry in a long while.

Daniel backed the truck down the street and found our way out of Madison.

We stopped in Duluth at the St. Regis paper mill and took the tour they arranged especially for us. Someone from their offices took us through the plant as there was no planned sightseeing. It was interesting; we could ask questions without a whole group of tourists surrounding us. We followed through the log milling process, onto the pulping vats, and over to the enormous paper rolls. One had become dislodged and rolled out on the floor by the mile.

After leaving the mill, Daniel found a state campground where we spent the night and roasted hot dogs for dinner. Come morning; we made pancakes over the campfire. This is another first for the boys and me, an area of scenic space with trees, the campfire ring, and a picnic table, with virtually no one else around. The campground was everything you would expect and more.

Driving north over the bridge from the USA into Canada, we came across the Boise Cascade paper mill. They didn't have a tour either, and there were a few windows to look through, so we moved on.

We are now at Rainy Lake in Canada. Beautiful spot, the lake was crystal clear with a snow-covered mountain in the backdrop; the sky was sunny, temperature about 70 degrees. God's place on earth. The water is crystal clear, the snow-covered mountain reflection in the lake is a photographic dream; it is perfect. The boys went back to get their fishing gear and waded into the water, which was cold. A short while later, a game warden came by. He smiled, asked if we had fishing licenses. We told him we didn't know a permit was needed.

He said, "Well, that's okay, you're not going to catch any fish in that lake. It's glacier water, and there's no fish of any kind in there."

Well, it was a gorgeous spot, but we'll move on. We happened upon an Indian Village and drove slowly through. There was no reason to stop.

On the outskirts of Winnipeg, as I was looking out the window, I said, "Daniel, did you see that?"

"What? I've been watching the road."

"We just passed a tavern, and this Indian guy was dragging a woman out by her hair; she was on the ground and had this long black hair, and he was dragging her along like she was a sack of potatoes." I was astonished. I thought maybe we should go back and help her.

Daniel said, "No, we are in Canada, we're not citizens, and this is Indian country. It's none of our business; how they choose to live their lives is up to them. Getting involved would cause us nothing but problems, and chances are she would be on his side and with him anyway.

"Okay, enough said, I'll let it go."

Once we were in Winnipeg by the river, Daniel found the docks, and there was a paddle boat with tours. He asked if I had ever been on a ship like this?

"No, and yes, I would love to take a ride."

I know I am blessed. I have my own personal tour guide. I would have never found all these places on my own.

All six of us got our tickets and walked onto the vessel, it wasn't huge as we think of cruisers, but it was two stories with the big paddle-wheel and the pilothouse. We took our seats, and it was to be a three-hour tour. A few minutes into the tour, there was music. Part of the group on the boat were Ukrainian dancers touring in Canada, and they were taking a sightseeing excursion also. One of them asked us if we minded the music and them practicing their dance. We were thrilled, at least I was. I didn't bother to ask anyone else; I got a free Ukrainian folk dance show, which was beautiful. They are truly talented, so limber, kicking their feet out from a squat, and the music is joyous. The musicians are as capable as the dancers; everyone is still in costume, just coming from a show. They entertained us for at least a half-hour and danced in the aisle. The group smiled, they drank, everyone was having a good time. I didn't see too much of the scenery down the river, but I can say it was better than being on a big cruise liner. The only thing I regret, I didn't take any pictures. It's a memory I will always have. The kids are watching the dancers. Daniel is sitting by my side, his arm around my waist; I could not have been happier.

The Royal Canadian Police academy is in our pathway of travel. So, of course, a stop there was necessary. They were most courteous, gave us a small tour and the history of the Royal Canadian Police.

Daniel asked the Mountie if he would recommend a good place for dinner. We were hungry and too tired to build a dinner. The Mountie advised us of the Pizza Inn at Moose Jaw, and we spent the evening camped near there.

We have driven past hundreds of acres of sunflowers, haystacks as prominent as skyscrapers. We've seen deer, elk, moose, and eagles.

Along the way at a roadside stop, no towns within miles, Daniel says," I think it's time for a break."

We all climb out to stretch our legs; all four kids are off on the run heading in different directions.

Daniel hollers, "Don't go beyond the site of the Rv; there are wild animals, bears, and you never know what might happen."

Another family drove in; as a large black bear came strolling in to check the garbage bins about the same time.

Daniel calls, "Everyone, get into a vehicle."

Lisa and I scrambled for the Rv, and all the guys ran for the truck. The other family was trying to feed the bear; then, her two cubs entered the scene. The cubs are at the truck windowpane and the Rv, while the other tourist family remained standing out there watching.

Lisa and I could feel the Rv rocking; I locked the door, hoping it would hold and they wouldn't break a window. Eventually, the bears got bored and decided to wander off. Fortunately, the bears weren't hungry because the other family watched the bears offering them food, but the bears just moved on. We had enough excitement at that stop; we each went to our riding places and left.

We are on the CanAm Highway, and it did multiple switchbacks over and under the railway. Daniel started slowing down after moving for a long while, and I heard a thump, thump, thump. He pulled over by the railroad; sure enough, it was a flat tire with the tread coming off.

I had the leisure of looking around while the guys had everything under control. I found a railroad spike that was left beside the rails. It became a souvenir and stayed with us wherever we happened to move. Twenty minutes later, we are back on the road, with only minor damage to the undercarriage of the RV from the tire tread hitting it.

In Calgary, we viewed the Palliser Hotel, circa the 1900s, with the lobby portraying the image of a movie set. Ornate, polished, wood moldings, marble floors, high ceilings with lovely light fixture displays. I could have stayed much longer; however, we did have four children that were not quite in tune with the refinements of life, so we tried for the gardens. We stopped on the outskirts of Minnewanka at a campsite while the kids took off on the run for the clubhouse that had pinball machines. We stopped to make dinner at this location because the campground had grills for a barbeque. Dinner is ready, and the kids are still playing with the machines. I round up the four of them, and both Daniel and I give the spiel of what are you thinking with all this beautiful countryside, and you're in there playing pinball machines? They didn't get it, and neither did we. The following morning we are off to Banff and Lake Louise.

The patios, the flowers, a waterfall, and the Banff hotel were stunningly modeled after European design. Again, more time would have been delightful if there were more hours in a day. We had lunch on the patio and drove on to Lake Louise.

Lake Louise is grand; as we drove up the road, there sat this multi-story hotel in the backdrop of a shimmering lake with tree-covered mountains surrounding the entire picture. Dali would have called it surreal. But there was more to it; opening the entrance doors to the waiting area took one back to the early 1900s, even the furniture, and it wasn't new furniture made to look old; this place was original. It had an unmistakable aura. The lobby wasn't all shiny and new, a little dusty and worn. People from decades past had been here. I was more intrigued than anyone else; I could almost feel the people who had been here before. But it was time to join the family; we all went outside after giving me a few minutes.

Daniel said," Should we canoe across the lake?"

I replied, "You are aware I don't swim."

"Dianah, the reason for renting the canoes is to stay out of the water."

"Oh, he thinks he's cute."

Reluctantly, I succumbed to renting the canoes. Chris and Toph are in one canoe with life jackets, and Daniel, Lisa, Tim, and I are in the second one. Daniel is expecting me to paddle. I don't know how, but how hard can it be?

The fellow renting the boats says, "The lake never gets above 40 degrees; the water comes down from the glaciers. If someone falls in, they have about 5 minutes to get rescued before hypothermia takes a set. That was just enough to bolster my lack of confidence.

About halfway across the lake, Daniel and the two boys in the other canoe decide racing to the other side could be fun. I was not a good oarsman; Lisa was older and taller than Tim, so Lisa would be Daniels' partner across the lake. Midway we changed positions in the canoe. The canoe rocks and tips and the cold water spills in. I did not consider this a good time. Everyone is seated with wet feet, and the race is on. The boys won to the shoreline, and now we had to come back. Not my finest hour, but everyone else had a good time.

After leaving the lake, we drove to the gondolas that took the skiers up the mountain. We all looked around and sat in the gondola, and nothing was happening; the ski season wasn't for another three to four months; it was time to leave.

Camping in Kamloops, we made breakfast over the outside grill of pancakes and side pork with coffee. Next, we were driving to Jasper, where the Glacier ice fields are, but everyone was getting tired of traveling, so we turned around and came back about halfway to the ice fields. There's so much country; it's hard to see it all. The following day we crossed the border and drove to Bellingham. We did a tad of sightseeing; it's a pretty little town, had breakfast, and scurried around the area. Dinner is at the Black Angus Restaurant; it was a generous tasty meal. I think we all slept well that evening. The plan was for everyone to relax, including the drivers. It's a fascinating trip, but after a month of travel, the kids are getting road-weary. They need days to unwind.

The weather has been in our favor all the way, sunshine, no rain or storms, and the only scorching weather was just as Daniel and I came into the area of Zion National Park, where we sat in the stream to cool off.

Today we are on our way to Olympia, WA. The drive through Seattle is busy and fast, but after this many miles, I have gotten the hang of it and have found most people don't push as hard on an RV, or maybe it's our RV that looks a little ancient.

We took the tour at the Olympia Brewery, a clean, friendly establishment. The copper brewing kettles were spectacular; everything was polished and shining. Even the walls were tiled and bright. After the tour, Daniel and I had a beer sample, the kids had soda, and we marveled at the manicured grounds with a steep slope the gardener is mowing. Then, it's time to move on.

Daniel said he wanted to visit Don Pedal and Madeline in Gig Harbor before leaving the area. He found a rustic campground with a grill and a pleasant wooded area to set up for a couple of evenings. The following day we found the Pedals' house and visited with Don and Madeline. Daniel and Don had gone fishing and camping together, and even though he was a former brother in law they were friends; Madeline not so much. I tried to help the kids from being overly bored, so we picked blackberries by the roadside. On the way back to the campground, we stopped at the fish market and bought this massive filet of salmon to grill for dinner. Some corn on the cob, and it was grand. Daniel fixed the fish, and we grilled the corn. I set up the table and drinks—what a wonderful dinner.

The following day the guys tried their hand at fishing but had no luck, and we then went to tour Vashon Island. Islands are fascinating, scenic wonderlands, with all the waterways, different living styles, especially compared to living in the desert areas of California. There has been an eye out for real estate everywhere stateside, just in case we come across a real find that says this is it.

We are now back on the highway, stopped for a break in Chehalis, and looked for more real estate. Drove on to Longview and rested with pizza and a leg stretch. The drive through Portland was tough with the traffic at peak travel time, but moving on to Salem; we found a wayside stop for the night; more pizza was the vote. The days are getting longer, all of us are feeling the need to be home. Breakfast is at the local Truck Stop; we're too worn to play camping and cooking over a campfire. We take a break at the Rogue River to fish and then drive to visit Uncle Charlie and Aunt Jeannette, a pleasant stay and visit. They live in the country on a hill and have always made us feel welcome. Jeannette makes us all a massive breakfast in the morning. She had it all working before we even were up. Coffee, eggs, bacon, pancakes, pastries, juice, and anything else desired. Their home is a small mobile, and there's a place for everyone. All of us ate beyond our capacity, and Jeannette asked if we wanted more. I think they enjoyed the food and our company. By noon the food had digested, and we were back on the highway. It's overly warm; all the kids are in the camper bed of the truck. The sounds from the back are getting louder, and in the front cab, we can feel the truck bed rocking. Daniel stopped, went to the back, and impatiently said, "Ok, everyone out!"

The kids got out on the side of the road, Daniel climbed back in the truck, and we left. Then, about 10 minutes later, he turned around and went back.

CM said, "See, I told you he wouldn't leave us."

Daniel sternly stated, "I don't want to hear anything from anyone."

It was late when we reached Salinas, California; we pulled the truck and trailer over, had a snack, and slept.

Breakfast is in King City, and we pull into Arroyo Grande and the apartment before the day is over. It was good to unpack, take a genuine shower and sleep in our own bed. We all agreed the trip should have been two, maybe three weeks, not over four weeks.

CM and Lisa took the greyhound back to Anaheim. They had about a week to get ready for school. I don't know where the summer went. Daniel called his folks, and they stopped by for a short visit. Dad was having trouble getting up the steps to the apartment. Toph and Tim took the greyhound to San Jose to spend a week with their Dad. I was back to work, and Daniel needed to check on the apartments. No downtime, but we didn't get bored. I don't think I ever heard, what is there to do? We were always going somewhere.

All the children were becoming teenagers, having thoughts of their own. Things were changing, and no one had prepared us for our kids growing into adulthood. We knew our parents hadn't had the answers, and neither did we. The trips between the different households started when one or both of my boys stayed with their father periodically. On Daniel's side, he worked at helping with a college for his eldest son, a daughter married, a son who would soon want a car. The challenges were emotional for both children and parents. So many times, if a problem arises, the first response is to fix it. But, sometimes, there doesn't seem to be a fix, no matter how many different recipes you try. So you do what you think is the best for the situation at hand and pray that it works.

Daniel thought buying property in Wisconsin would be a good thing to do. We took a quick trip, flew into Chicago, and drove to

Omro. It's winter, snowy, and cold. We started to look at the properties with information previously obtained. Unfortunately, I believe there was a lack of honesty in the presentations. The properties all had significant flaws, such as sitting in a swamp. A local realtor showed us several places, but none of them fit the bill. There needed to be an income for dollars spent.

As she was driving, Daniel said, "There's a mobile home park back there in the trees."

The realtor replied that it was for sale last year, but he decided to keep it when it didn't sell. Daniel convinced her just to drive through. We liked what we saw and asked our agent to contact the owner. There was the usual negotiation. But we didn't get a complete agreement, and it was time for us to be home, so we said our goodbyes to family and acquaintances.

The property search continued in California; days turned into months, each as hectic as before.

Daniel found a property in Atascadero about 15 miles north of where we are living. The drive up over the mountain pass is not one I relished twice a day, but I had no intention of changing offices. The boys are still visiting their father, and Toph is staying with his father for a while.

This property was going to take more creativity than usual. It ran alongside Hwy 101 and had an oversized garage to block a lot of the sound. The mobile home was old and abused, but the financing was perfect. Daniel had a small down payment, assumed the first loan, and created a second loan which the seller held. The deal was in the bag. Daniel wasn't concerned about the mobile; he could sell or have it hauled off and put a newer, larger one on. I thought it all sounded somewhat iffy, but the price was right. We needed to start somewhere, we had both given up homes when the divorces happened, and time was slipping by. Tim came back to start school and was not at all happy with the move. He liked Arroyo Grande and his friends. A couple of weeks later, we went down to Arroyo on the weekend but couldn't find his best friend, and life just kept moving.

Daniel did find a newer, larger mobile home to put on the property and sell the old one to a rancher as housing for his workers. We started some finished work in the garage.

There is an unfinished building, just framing, and a roof covering a floor in the back of the lot. The wood was gray from sitting for a long time, and we didn't know how long it had been left unfinished. But the building project included bricks stacked in one corner of the property; more lumber piled in the yard, and the inside of the garage needed drywall. Daniel wanted to make a room in the garage, maybe even a bathroom, as separate living quarters. Gene, Daniels' concrete man, said he would come up and help move the building. They cut it in half, using one half for a covered porch along the front of the mobile and the other half for a porch to the garage. My job was to clean the mobile home we just moved in. I had just finished cleaning the old one, so we could sell it. I told the guys I was tired of cleaning everyone else's dirt.

While Gene and Daniel were working on the decking, Toph came home, and Gene showed Toph how to twirl a hammer. I said, "Guys, this young man has just recovered from a broken leg; I do not want to rush to the hospital because he was hit in the head with a hammer. Gene agreed to put the twirling hammer lesson on hold.

I was making breakfast, and I heard this pounding. I thought Daniel and Gene, with the kids' help, had finished the deck. Gene was pounding one post that was not as straight as he wanted by the front door, and he was beating it into submission.

So I said, "Gene, when all else fails, it's the hammer that will make it right?"

"Yup, the best tool ever made; we got coffee?"

It's Sunday; Gene had to start for home and work on Monday. We continued to clean up. The next part of the plan is to paint and color coordinate the garage, porches, and mobile home. Color choices for the construction-minded guys consisted of brown and tan, maybe a little white, but you didn't want to get carried away. Sometimes the guys were overly practical. Yes, brown and tan wouldn't offend a buyer at resale and it would weather well, but isn't there a little more color we can put into life.

Daniel said, "By the time we lay the bricks for the walkway and put a gate at the fence; you will see how much better the look will be."

Both Daniel and I were feeling guilty about the boys having to change schools again, it wasn't fair to them, but how else in life were we ever going to get ahead? Daniel thought a dog would be an excellent addition, giving Tim a comfort zone. We came home with the cutest puppy, all of us were so pleased. Nightfall came; about the time we were all ready to sleep, the dog started howling. It howled and cried all night long.

Daniel exclaimed, "You know it's a hound dog?"

The dog had some fancy name, but the animal was still a hound when it came right down to it. I wistfully tried; let's give it one more night; maybe it just needs time to settle in. The second night was worse, and the baying became louder. We are now into night number two with no sleep. From the other side of the bed, I hear the dog has got to go tomorrow. And so we took the dog back. Tim was disappointed but understood. He hadn't been able to sleep either. There was no trying for another dog, not now anyway.

I am still working in Arroyo Grande and found it more challenging to show property within the hour. Commuting has never been for me; I consider it a waste of time. Even though Daniel was a big help, working, and housekeeping while trying my best with family left me mentally frazzled. Daniel is still talking with the seller of the mobile home park in Wisconsin. The longer the talks go on, the less convinced I am that the purchase should happen.

We have moved onto the year of 1980, every day there seems to be a new project. Daniel is always thinking about investments. I am always drumming up new business. Playtime and family life have to fit in between as time and energy allows.

Daniel attended his eldest son's 21st birthday in Las Vegas. My boys were in school, and I didn't want to be in Las Vegas or attend the party. It all worked out. But never have I seen him so tired and stressed, from a picture I saw of Daniel at the party. His report was, everyone had a good time. The desire to be at the party would have left Daniel apprehensive if he hadn't attended. He was trying to help this son through college, which wasn't falling into place, a burden with no control over the outcome.

I was happy to have him back home, we hardly ever slept in, but the following day I crept out of bed, made the coffee, and set it by his nightstand. On rare occasions, not only was their coffee in bed but a small breakfast served by the one who was up first.

When Daniel and I first started sharing the same household, he said, ``Dianah, when we get up in the morning, it's only right to say, Good Morning. Get the day off to a good start and acknowledge the other person."

"Daniel, I don't have a problem with that; I just didn't grow up that way. We just didn't talk to each other."

Each day has a "Good Morning and a Good Night," with very few exceptions. Plus, both times of the day required a kiss and a hug. It was a closeness of unaccustomed pleasure.

During the 1970s, in our San Luis Obispo County residence, the culture included Afro hairstyles, bell-bottom trousers, and tie-dye shirts. Daniel and I didn't do the tie-dye shirts, but bell-bottom pants were a must; there were no other choices, and we gave the perm afro look a try. Daniel's skin burnt from the perm solution. We wore Vans tennis shoes and knew about all the latest health food.

The mobile home project in Wisconsin is a work in progress, with the appearance of actually happening. If we move to Wisconsin, then getting a California Brokers license won't do much for me. New plan. I'll contact the real estate commissioner in Wisconsin and get the requirements for that state. Much to my surprise, the commissioners' office sent a timely letter asking for my existing qualifications. I sat down at the typewriter and methodically went through each class I had completed and included all the information of the California license. As I waited for a reply, the Atascadero property is going up for sale, and preparations are in the works to move once again. I advised Daniel to list it with a local agent to get the best deal for this property. I was still working in Arroyo Grande and didn't have the knowledge I thought was needed to get the best job done.

An agent chosen with a local company had a contract in hand within 30 days. The push is for a 30-day move and Wisconsin property purchase, packing our belongings, and picking up Toph after middle school graduation in San Francisco. Tim and Toph are moving to Wisconsin with us. I needed to wrap up any loose ends of ongoing real estate in Arroyo Grande, plus put my California real estate license on-hold status.

The Wisconsin property is 36 wooded acres with 15 mobile home spaces set back in the woods with no visibility from the road and a lot across the street on a pretty little lake with a unique Dinner Club just down the road from it.

Meanwhile, Daniel is setting up all the moving vehicles. He has the ford pickup, a full-size Chrysler, an extended dual axle trailer, a collectors car, and we will need to rent a moving truck. Oh yes, I have the ford LTD, and there is a boat.

Daniel gets the okay to park the collectors' car in his Dad's carport. The boat is pulled with the Ford pickup truck and loaded with everything we can fit in without breaking the axles. The Ryder rental truck is as heavy as we can get it. The Chrysler is supposed to haul the trailer enclosed with sheets of 4x 8 plywood, and we painted the whole thing black. Daniel said we needed to look presentable driving down the road. We would attract less attention—No-load for the Ford Ltd, except to fill the trunk and back seat. I had to look through the steering wheel; the rear end was like a lowrider. We were loaded and just needed to test each vehicle for road readiness. The iffiest was the Chrysler; the bumper hit the pavement when Daniel hooked the black trailer to that car. He went through days of hassle getting a hitch put on the vehicle;

no one wanted to, saying the vehicle is not designed to pull. Picture this long low brown Chrysler with a black vinyl top and a monstrous black dual axle trailer topped with a blue tarp stuck at the bottom of the driveway because the hitch is stuck in the pavement.

Daniel said, "Dianah, not all plans work. We just need a few alterations."

I think this is totally insane, but I didn't say a word.

Plus we have too many vehicles for the number of drivers. The move is to Wisconsin, and no one in California can help us drive. Daniel and I talk it over and decided from all my brothers; Dan is probably the best choice as a driver. Dan agrees to help drive and takes a Greyhound bus from Omro to Atascadero. New plan. Sell the Chrysler. Get a hitch put on the rental truck to pull the trailer.

Glitch number one, the Chrysler, doesn't sell. Dad DiSandro says there's room in the carport. Glitch number two, the rental company says no hitch, not legal. Finally, Daniel finds a welder who agrees to put the hitch on; we're not going to worry about legal. We are loaded, hooked up with all towing apparatus; the boys are riding with my brother Dan in the truck, towing the boat, also with a blue tarp, we're color-coordinated. Daniel leads the way; my brother is in the middle of the caravan because he has never driven cross-country, and I am pulling up the rear. Did we look respectable? I don't think so!

It's the morning of another move; this time, it's one driver for each vehicle. And off we go to Wisconsin. First, we went south to Orange County on October 31st, 1980; we stopped in Pismo Beach to say goodbye to Daniel's parents along the way. We spent the evening in Anaheim, with goodbye's to everyone there. The next day's consumption was checking the loads, re-enforcing the hitch for the black trailer, and Daniel needed to collect rent from the apartments and talk with the new manager. We have dinner with CM and Lisa, and the following morning, November 2nd, the long trek has started.

My brother Dan has never pulled anything long distance on the major highways, so we all try to watch closely to avoid mishaps. There are numerous trucking firms with big rigs at one long stretch of road, and it's necessary to change lanes. Dan gets close to nipping the trucker's bumper as he pulls back in. Fortunately, the trucker was calm and didn't get excited. I guess the driver could tell we were caravanning and moving long distances. Daniel is pushing the rental truck; even though I'm two vehicles back, I can tell he is working the load for all it's worth.

Late on a windy afternoon, we arrive in Moriarity, New Mexico. Daniel is watching for a motel on the eastern outskirts of town for a fast morning start and a big parking lot for all our towing vehicles. As I run into the motel, the icy wind nearly blows me away. I get two rooms, one for Daniel and me, and one for Dan, Toph, and Tim. After finding a quick nondescript bite to eat, it's back to the motel and crash for the night.

The motel service is notified for a wake-up call, and the alarm is set; the motel doesn't call. It's frigid; I turn on the shower; we're in a hurry.

Daniel says, "Have you taken your shower?"

"I don't think there's any hot water; "I'm waiting."

"Try the boy's room."

Two minutes later, "They don't have hot water either."

Daniel takes a cold shower; I wash my face. The room is freezing, the water's even colder, we haven't had coffee, and we're tired before even getting started. Dan is outside motioning to us; the hitch on the rental truck is holding by a thread. Meanwhile, Daniel is voicing his complaint with the motel manager, who happens to be the owner, about no heat, no hot water, and no wake-up call. Daniel says he wants a refund on the motel bill.

The Manager says, "My wife takes care of the bills, and she's sleeping; I don't want to wake her. She usually gets up in an off mood."

Daniel didn't have time to stand and argue; he needed to find a place to fix the hitch.

My brother is listening to all of this, and he says, "I'll get my pistol out; that guy will give us a refund."

Daniel and I look at each other, we say at the same time, "Do not get any kind of a gun out."

"Dianah, did you know he had a gun?"

"No, did you?"

"Well, let's make sure it stays put away."

Daniel unhitches the trailer, jumps in the truck, and is on his way to find a welder. The drive has taken us to ranch country, cattle, and sheep with miles of nothing else. He finally finds a country coffee house at a four-way stop, filled with cowboys, and it's more than mud on their boots. They tell him there's no garage or welding shop within 50 miles.

Then one of the guys says, "The ranch down the road, about 10 miles away, has a welder in his barn; he'd probably do it for you. Just take the road out front until you come to Michael's Corner, turn left, and it's about 3 miles more."

Daniel finds the ranch without any road signs. It's a prominent place with an enormous workshop in the back; there doesn't seem to be anyone around. He hurries to the shop, opens the door and fortunately, the owner is there. Daniel explains the circumstances, and the fellow has no problem. He puts a better weld on than the original.

Daniel asked, "How much for the service?"

The rancher didn't want anything; Daniel gave him $50 and said, thank you, you saved me more than that. On the way back, Daniel stops by the little restaurant, gets us all coffee, hot chocolate, and donuts as a holdover for the next stop.

We arrived in Wautoma, Wisconsin, on November 6th with everything in tow. Drove back to my parents' house to drop Dan off, and they made accommodations for us until we could get set up in the mobile home park. The next day we signed papers to complete the purchase and went directly to buy a mobile for a vacant space in the park. The mobile will be set in three days and become home. We hurry to the electric company. We need the power on for the mobile and the park. The gal behind the counter said, I have all your info; you are all set and will receive a bill shortly; that was before we could even give her our name.

We looked at each other and said, "She probably knows more about us than we do."

November 10th, we are in the mobile home and unpacked.

November 16th Daniel drives to the Oshkosh airport to fly to Orange County, California, to sell his eight-unit apartment building.

November 18th, my brothers picked up Toph and took him to get his deer hunting license. Family deer hunting from the 21st thru the 23rd out at the old farm, where we all lived with the Grandparents, is a tradition.

I sent in the application and payment for my Wisconsin real estate Brokers license, and my mother is preparing for Thanksgiving Dinner.

On November 20th, Daniel came strolling into the house, very pleased; I could tell by the smile on his face. With a warm kiss and strong hug at the door, I asked how his trip was, did everything get finished as it should have.

I said, "Daniel, Now, you don't have to worry about the apartments anymore, and what's in the brown paper bag on the table?"

Daniel is smiling, "Just hang on a second, let me get settled, and I'll show you. I'll tell you all about it."

I make us fresh coffee; the boys are outside as I patiently wait at the table.

He sits down to enjoy coffee, "It's good to be back."

Daniel picks up the brown paper lunch bag and dumps all these little plastic bags with notes on them scattered about the table. I read ruby, emerald, topaz, and the list continues. Each certificate says how many carats, with the registered value.

"Daniel, you carried this, like that, on the plane?"

"Now, who would think I'd have a half-million bucks in my lunch sack."

"This is what you took for the sale of the apartments?"

"Yes."

"Did you get any money?"

"No, but the buyer paid all the costs, and the Broker took gems for his commission."

"So now what are you going to do with them?"

"Dianah, come here; you worry too much." He holds me tightly, "Which gem would you like?"

"Oh Daniel, I'm not looking for a gem, only concerned about what you have done."

"The seller of the mobile home park has already said he will take $30K against the mortgage, and My Dear; I took twice the certified value in gems as the sale value of the property."

It still didn't sound good to me, but then it wasn't my investment; I was only concerned for all his hard work, and all he had to show for it was a few tiny stones. But if the Mobile home park seller took 30K, it was 15K Daniel was giving him.

A couple of days later, the closing agent called; there wasn't enough money held out to pay the property taxes. Also, are you aware of the tax consequences of exchanging real income property for personal use?

Daniel says, "I'll call you back; I'm in the middle of something."

Daniel calls Tony, the accountant, and relays the scenario.

Tony scans the file, "You have enough depreciation and write-off to take care of the exchange liability. Don't worry, Daniel. The property taxes are the title company's responsibility; they made a mistake, that's why you purchased title insurance. Have a Happy Thanksgiving."

While Daniel was gone, Toph asked if he and a friend could go out for the evening. I asked him all the usual parameters, time, place: where, and reason. The evening came; I met the boy, saw his car and Tim, and I watched television. I said it was time for bed. Tim knew Toph was supposed to be home, but he wasn't going to say anything. At 12:30 AM, the whole house gets a jolt. I knew immediately; the car hit the house. I jumped out of bed; there was snow on the ground, and Toph came into the house. The first thing out of his mouth, the car skidded into the corner.

"You better hope it's not bad; you're in enough trouble just for being so late. Have you had anything to drink?"

The answer was, "No."

I checked the house the following morning, and yes, you could tell something hit the home, but it wasn't structural. I'll leave it alone for now; there seems to be enough friction in the household.

Thanksgiving is at Mom and Dad's. Mom and my sister Linda have been cooking for a week, and Dad tells us he got this great buy on a black market ham. At first, I thought, I've never heard of that brand of ham. Oh, Dad wasn't talking about a brand. Someone stole a truckload of hams, and a buddy of his told him where he could buy one.

Mom baked the ham with cranberry sauce, sweet potatoes, corn, mash potatoes, salad, rolls, and after dinner, the dessert was pumpkin pie, apple pie, or lemon meringue with ice cream. Daniel raved about this meal for years to come. It was a splendid dinner which everyone enjoyed. One of the better family days; everyone was there, and no bickering. Every once in a while, things work.

Christmas will soon be here, but shopping for clothes right now, preparation for the cold weather or the snow is necessary. We all need boots, and the boys need extra clothes for school. Daniel has to make another trip back to Orange County, and while he's gone, it snows. Fortunately, the plow service for the park completed its early morning run, but that doesn't take care of getting the car out of the garage and down the driveway. The ford truck is fine, but the LTD is temperamental. It doesn't want to start in the cold weather. It is now put in the garage and plugged into a heating tape, and you still can't count on it to start. The boys missed the school bus; I got the car started, but the road was icy, and it took me four times to get up the slight incline at the stop sign. I know no other route, so we just kept trying until I must have softened the ice. Fortunately, no one was behind me.

"Hey, guy's Christmas will soon be here; let's get us a tree and have it all set up before Daniel gets back."

Toph says, "What store are we going to?"

"We will go out to the back in the woods and choose one that's not too big. We'll take a saw and an ax. If it needs some trimming, we'll do it here at home."

"Tim, you'll help us choose, right?"

Walking back into the trees with the deep snow, and you could see your breath from the chill in the air, I didn't want this to be an all-day adventure. The days are short, and dusk starts around 4 PM. Tim would say, what about that tree or that one. Some were too little, too tall, too skinny, and we kept walking.

"There's one; what do you guys think?"

Toph looks around, "Mom, I don't think we are on our land anymore."

"It's okay, just a little tree out here in the middle of nothing. No one will miss it, and we won't leave a mess."

The boys carry the tree while I take the tools, and we are back at the house in no time. A little trimming, set it up inside, and before the day is over, we have all the ornaments for Christmas on the tree.

"What do you boys think? I would say we did a pretty good job."

The school atmosphere is a challenge for Toph and Tim. If you were not born and raised here, the attitude was stifling, but I thought the prejudice would fade with a bit of time. Tim couldn't make friends, and the teacher was unhappy with his performance. Toph had some fights. Tim generally struggled with school but managed to get along. I spent some time with Tim's schoolwork but didn't understand the continuous effort needed. Toph never got in fights; was it because he is a teenager or the kids, the school? I only knew it wasn't working, and neither one of the boys would confide in me.

One of the tenants just a few houses from us has a huge german shepherd, and one of the other tenants said the dog almost bit her. I reassured her, Daniel would soon be home and address the dog.

I went to pick Daniel up at the Oshkosh Airport. Boy, am I glad he's back; I feel like a fish out of water. I made a new soft blue pantsuit for a special look and put on my leather high-top boots, laced up the front, my brown leather full-length coat, and the wool plaid Amana cap Daniel had purchased for me. I thought I looked stunning. It is late in the evening at this almost empty airport. I could see three young people dressed in farm boots and oversized heavy parkas, above me, on the walkway, two gals and a guy pointing at me and snickering. I guessed they thought I must be a hooker; why else would I be by myself all dressed up in the airport. I couldn't wait for Daniel to arrive.

It was a long 45-minute wait, and he walked through the door. I can see the tiredness, but Daniel smiles, sets down the briefcase, and opens his arms as I run in for the warmth of his love. As his arms wrap around me, all the fears and loneliness disappear.

"Oh, Daniel, welcome home."

A brief kiss, and we will be on our way. I glance up at the three in their parkas, and the stance indicates I wasn't all that entertaining after all.

The following day at coffee, I explained to Daniel, the tenant with the dog, and what the other tenant said. Breakfast is over; Daniel puts on his boots and coat and walks over to address the upset with the dog. Daniel simply stated, "If the dog is outside, it will be on a leash, or you will need to move."

While washing clothes at the laundromat later that week, we over-heard, "That's the guy that came to Marci's house and threatened her with a gun about her dog."

Daniel was livid. He went to revisit the tenant, "I see that dog out just once without a leash; eviction will be immediate."

Sure enough, it only took a few days, and there's the dog, no leash. Daniel drew up the notice; I served it, she had two weeks to vacate.

I informed her, " If the house is still here, the rent is still due."

I could feel the stares and whispers from the town folk, "Those are the people from California."

I knew having tenants was not easy, but I wasn't prepared for this. Daniel didn't say much on the subject, but we were all feeling the strain of uncertainty.

ME AND DANIEL

Daniel had been outside working, checking everything like he always did no matter where we lived.

I called out, "Would you like a cup of coffee?"

When Daniel walked in the door, he said, "I would like to know what happened to the corner of the house?"

So I explained the evening Toph went out with a friend and when they came back, it was icy.

"Why didn't you tell me?"

"You already had so many things going on, I checked it, not too bad, and I wanted to give you some downtime and also not have another reason for being upset."

I knew he wouldn't be happy. The following days are filled with too many events.

Daniel said, "We need to find the local junkyard."

"Whatever for?"

"I'm going to buy a television antenna; the reception is terrible with all the trees around the house."

"You think you'll find an antenna at the junkyard."

I always love his smile, especially when he's just gone way beyond my comprehension of the moment.

"No, love. I want four lengths of black iron pipe to stabilize the antenna from the ground. We can't put it on the house; there's nothing up there I can nail."

We are off to the junkyard. Driving into the front gate next to the office are bins filled with pipes. Eventually, someone comes out, I roll down the window, and Daniel says, we would like four lengths of your black iron pipe.

The guy says, "Can't sell you that pipe."

I said, "Is it already sold to someone?"

"No."

I ask again, "We only want four lengths, and you have more than that."

He says, "Can't sell it."

Now I'm exasperated, "Why can't you sell it?"

"If I sold it, I wouldn't have any inventory."

Okay, I give up on the iron pipe. "We are looking for a wheelbarrow also; how much for one of those over there?"

"Those are not for sale; I use them for moving my stuff around."

I think to myself, does this episode have anything to do with us being from California?

Daniel shakes his head, "Let's get our antenna and go home."

As we drive to the highway, I ask, "How are we going to put it up?"

"We will buy extra cable and affix it to the garage; it might work even better."

The antenna is purchased. The TV cable runs over the existing junk pile, yet to be removed, and onto the garage. The boys just came home from school and want to help. Toph and Daniel are on the roof and have affixed the antenna. Now, all we have to do is point it in the direction of a good signal. I go in the house, turn on the television; Tim stands about halfway to relay the message on which way to turn the antenna. After a frustrating half-hour, we get maybe one channel. Daniel has another plan. They remove the antenna from its mounting; Daniel gets the pickup and puts an extension ladder on top of the camper shell. He climbs the ladder which is leaning against this round oak tree. The ladder is wider than the tree; there is no stability. I get up on the camper shell to hold the ladder, and Toph works at handing him the antenna with a hammer and strapping. Daniel almost has it up, and the ladder slips; I can't hold it steady. Daniel grabs on the tree with both arms and gets his feet back on the ladder.

He smiles down at me, "Are you ok?"

"Daniel, let's get this finished so that you can get down from there."

The television is working, and we get three channels, with everyone still in one piece.

Meanwhile, we are planning to thin out some of the trees—an oak tree of a two-foot diameter in the way of the driveway and snowplow, and the tenant is upset because of our plan to take it down. My brothers come out with chain saws and axes to start logging. That particular oak tree was hollow inside, and with that knowledge, we called the Ag Department, who sent out a representative for a botanical survey. He informed us of a root rot running through the park, affecting many of the oak trees.

The next plan is to take down sickly oaks and thin out the pines. My brothers are cutting away, and the piles of firewood are growing. One stack is oak, and the other is pine. The plan is my brothers cut the wood, and half of whatever they cut is theirs, and we will sell our half. Daniel and I also helped with the stacking and moving of the wood into piles.

One of the tenants with a newer mobile home decided he wasn't happy with the $15.00 rent raise or that we were bringing in natural gas to save everyone the expensive electric bills and propane. There was no cost to them for the gas line; they just needed to convert any appliances on propane to natural gas. Daniel volunteered to convert the tenant's appliances at cost, and they still complained, even though the savings would be anywhere from $50 to $100 a month. Daniel wasn't complaining, but the attitude was starting to wear on him also. The fellow with the newer mobile decided he was moving, and he was taking the power pole and the meter with him. Daniel informed him he couldn't do that; it was the property of the park. The guy called the sheriff, who came out and told Daniel this fellow bought the pole and meter; it is his. Daniel parked his truck in the driveway, locked the doors, and no one was leaving. He told the sheriff one more time; the tenant can take his mobile, the power pole is in the ground with the meter attached, and it will stay. I'm not moving my truck, and the truck to haul the mobile can sit on the highway as long as it wants. And to the Sheriff, your vehicle is on my property, so best you decide what you're going to do if you want to use this driveway.

The sheriff and the tenant decided they would leave the power pole and meter so that the mobile could get moved. The following week we are served a notice for small claims court, the date of which Daniel would be in California taking care of the apartments. My job is to go to court. The following week I went to the courthouse and waited for my case. The judge identified the parties, and the tenant stated his case.

When it was my turn to speak, the judge said, "I don't need to hear from you. This shouldn't even be on the docket; the case is closed in favor of the defendant."

I wasn't even sure that was me, but I guessed if it wasn't, someone would let me know.

The Christmas celebration at Mom and Dad's house is on Christmas Eve. Farmers didn't have time in the morning for Santa Claus and opening presents. Santa and presents happened in the evening after milking the cows and all the other animal chores. Although everyone gets a gift, ours was a time to get together with family, food, and smiles. Though the family is no longer on the farm, the traditional time continues.

We have two vacant spaces, and there are already possible tenants with newer mobile homes. Daniel plans to expand the park, and to do that, we must have another septic system. We contact the county health department, they tell us we need to have a hole dug, no less than 6 feet deep, and this is who you call. Daniel makes the call, gets the price, and the guy says he will be out early Thursday morning to dig the hole. Thursday morning Daniel and I are up bright and early, I make extra coffee, and we wait. The guy doesn't show; Daniel calls, and there's no answer.

We have other things going on. The previous owner had disassembled a bowling alley, with the pin-setting equipment directly behind the tenant and between us and the garage. We have a large trailer and load all the ironwork, which the junkyard stated they would buy. He wouldn't sell us anything, but he will buy almost any metal we come across. It's a good week's worth of work, and my brothers are still sawing and moving timber.

Once the trash has been removed, and the timber is in two relatively neat huge piles, I take it upon myself to start cleaning up the place.

Daniel has put a new roof on the garage, and I painted it dark brown with white trim and an orange accent. Daniel built a pump house, I painted, and we ordered a new entrance sign in all the same colors. Now another point of contention with the road department. The sign was too big, too close to the road, and we didn't apply for a permit. The previous owner had his name as the park identifier. We were changing the name to Silver Lake Village. For the next month, we made concessions with the county. We moved the sign farther off the road, cut it smaller, and eventually, after we sent them a check, the sign was now visible from the roadway.

It's a Thursday morning; Daniel jumps out of bed, "What's that noise?"

The digger for the septic test site is here and digging a hole.

Daniel said, "We didn't tell him where we wanted it."

We ran to the site, and he already dug a pit.

Daniel says, "This is not where I intended to put the next system."

The contractor says, "This is the best spot on the whole property."

Daniel says, "What about back there just beyond the last mobiles?"

"Oh no, the soil back there has too much clay; it wouldn't work."

We pay him and say to each other; he probably knows better than we do, as the place for a septic.

I call the county to let them know the pit is ready; they can come out as soon as possible.

The morning of the inspection, here comes these two kids. Barely made their 21st birthday, and they say, "We need a ladder to get down in the pit."

I think this is what they do for a living, and they don't have a ladder, but Daniel gets them a ladder. They both climb down in the pit, and the chippier one says to me, "You need to step aside; you're blocking the light. I can't see the soils."

I step back while he takes his penknife, scrapes a little dirt in his hand, and says, "This won't work; the soils aren't right."

I said, "What do you mean the soil isn't right?"

"Well, Mam, (again, do I look like a Mam), as he says, you can see right here, there's some clay, and it just isn't good for a perk."

As his sidekick says, "So we are done here."

I said, "Not so fast, we have been waiting for two months, and this is the report you give us. I don't think so. If I pull this ladder up, you are in the pit, and I quite frankly don't care."

Daniel put his hand on my shoulder, "I think we need to let them out."

"I don't know why, they're supposed to be working for us, we pay taxes, and it pays their salary, and that was a piss poor inspection if I have ever seen one. Anyone can come out, scrape a little sand off the side and say it's no good. What kind of credentials do they have? We don't know."

Needless to say, we didn't get our septic permit.

Chapter Twelve

1981 What's Next

JANUARY 1981, THIS won't be like other years.

The boys are off to school, and Daniel and I will go to the Kountry Court Coffee Shop for breakfast. The coffee isn't terrific, but the food is good. One of the local gals, while in college, married a fellow from India. They are the owners working the restaurant in rural Wisconsin. Her brother is the cook; he makes luscious pies, and down in the basement, he grinds and spices their tasty breakfast sausage. Another brother who's a sheep farmer comes in and helps with serving coffee and cleaning tables; he's a lively sort with a sense of humor. This brother keeps the restaurant friendly and people coming in. He's the only one who doesn't have a problem talking with us.

After being gone for 20 years, I now understand why I left. I can't find my comfort zone. We smile and say hello. Once in a while, there's a person who's not intimidated by someone new. Joel, the dairy farmer, is one of those people. We happened to be sitting at the counter next to him, and Daniel has never had a problem striking up a conversation with anyone.

During the greeting, we discover Joel went to Ag. College and is now farming his father's land and his own.

Daniel said, "Do you always plant the same way, in the same direction?"

"Yup, every year."

"Have you ever tried planting diagonally or east to west instead of north to south?"

"No, that won't work."

And it was time for Joel to leave and go back to the farm.

We have checked out other properties now from Waupaca to Stevens Point to Appleton and south to FonduLac, and so far, there is nothing that meets our requirements. Our property needs have always been so varied that it confuses any real estate agent, so we just keep looking on our own.

Most of our drives take us through Omro. The alternative roads, particularly for shopping, are 10 to 20 miles out of the way. On one of the drives, we made the mistake of not stopping at Mom's house. I wanted to be home when the boys got back from school, and we didn't want to have a meal with the family; there are times when you're just not hungry. Someone in the family saw us drive through town, and now Mom wanted to know why we didn't stop. We couldn't say we just didn't want to stop that day, so instead, we excused ourselves by saying there was an appointment waiting for us. From then on, we either stopped or drove the long way.

I still need to take the real estate test for my Wisconsin license. A certain amount of study is necessary; various items are much different from California laws and customs. Taking these real estate tests is an unwanted necessity, and one per state is more than enough.

The more time that passes, the more difficult it's becoming for Toph. The controversies at school are growing; he's found a girlfriend down the street within walking distance, and I don't know if that's a good thing or not. Tim seems to be an annoyance to Toph, and Tim gets a kick out of tormenting his brother. There's no one around for

Tim to spend time with. I'm at a loss; I can't be in the school to see what's going on and can't watch their every move, nor would that work. What do I do to make their life better?

I don't feel equipped to be raising two teenage sons, and I don't expect Daniel to be their disciplinarian, nor does he want to be. There are few alternatives. The boy's father always said he could do a better job than me; here's his chance. My lifestyle isn't working for the kids. I don't think Toph wanted to be with his father, but being in Wisconsin wasn't working either, and at this juncture, there was no planned move anywhere. My Mom and Dad said Toph could stay there. That was a no; I didn't want the same tactics for raising children as I had grown up, nor did my mother need another body in an already burdened household.

Later in January, I made arrangements with Toph's father, and we drove him to Milwaukee for the plane to San Francisco. On the way there on the freeway with heavy traffic, a young girl clips my back bumper. I find a place to pull over, exchange information, and explain we are on the way to the airport with no time to be wasted, back on the road and to the airport. We get Toph to the gate, check to make sure he has everything. Oh, it's so hard to say Goodbye. I felt I was saying goodbye to a part of life I still wanted and didn't know how to keep. The tears didn't come until after he left and the plane was gone.

No one ever explains the amount of fortitude needed to keep going and the decisions; you can only hope when there are choices you don't want to make, that you chose the lesser of the evils.

Daniel has been having days of not feeling well; he can't say precisely what's wrong and doesn't take a day to rest.

Tims back at school, I take him to a basketball game, thinking maybe sports will lighten his mood.

Daniel says there's been some wood stolen; I call the sheriff's office. Of course, nothing happens.

Daniel gets a call, and his father is back in the hospital; he needs to make arrangements for someone to get his mother back and forth;

she doesn't drive. Fortunately, a kindly neighbor, owner of an ice cream shop where his Mom and Dad would treat themselves to a Sunday afternoon indulgence, was there to rescue the predicament at hand.

In the meantime, Daniel has made arrangements to trade some gems for a cabin cruiser. We meet the owners at the attorney's office, where they have the opportunity to select which jewel they want for the cruiser—a 29-foot wooden boat in good condition with a cradle and all the running equipment. The wife chooses the gem she likes best, the blue heart-shaped sapphire I had decided on when Daniel asked me which one I wanted. Daniel looked at me, I looked at him, and neither one of us said anything. He should have taken it out of the package but forgot.

The transaction is completed, and we are on our way home. Daniel says, "I'm sorry, I didn't mean to give that one away."

"It's ok; there are others; I don't wear much jewelry anyway."

We needed to get the boat from the FonduLac area to the Oshkosh marina, and everyone assured us it was easy. It's about 10 miles on the river to the marina; the seller volunteers his help. My brothers Dan and Joe, and Daniel and I all meet the seller at the marina. The boat cradle can go in Daniel's truck; he and Dan will drive to Oshkosh while Joe, I, and the boat seller will power up the river. We are not off to a good start. He has a hard time getting the engine started; after much to do, he and Daniel get it running, it seems the carburetor is the issue and not considered a monumental drawback as carburetors are known for faulty ways. We are underway, and it's a beautiful sunny day. The river has abundant trees and vegetation on either side; the water sparkles, almost perfect. About halfway to our destination, the engine quits, just plain stopping in the middle of the river.

Mr. Seller checks it out; turns to Joe and me, "Yup, we are out of fuel; I guess I should have checked it before we left."

You think! We have no extra fuel onboard and no alternative power, not even a paddle.

As we are debating how to get out of this predicament, I notice a

ME AND DANIEL

group of excitable people onshore, and they are waving their arms and yelling at us, "There are pylons in the river; you'll damage your boat. Stay in the center of the marked waterway."

But with no power, we are floating, drifting toward shore, and the posts put in for docks long ago are now underwater, not visible, but just waiting for an unsuspecting boat to blunder into the area with a predictable hole to be punched in the hull. So Mr. Seller throws out the anchor, and at least we won't drift far.

We are now stationary, the day is moving on, and we cannot contact Daniel. And so we wait. Eventually, a generous good samaritan boater stops by to ask what the problem is; after the explanation, he speeds off and is back in a half-hour with fuel. The seller asked; for money; I told him I didn't bring my purse, and of course, Joe didn't have any money, so the seller reluctantly paid our rescuer.

I think we are on our way; the boat starts but isn't going anywhere. Aha, no one pulled up the anchor. What kind of boater is this fellow? He tries to get the anchor up, and it won't budge; by putting the boat in gear, it secured it snuggly to whatever was holding us in place. Joe tries to loosen the anchor one way, then another. They try backing the boat a little, no help. The decision is made to cut the anchor rope; not only is it a good rope, now shorter, but there's a very expensive anchor at the end of the rope. Gone! We are only running 2 hours behind schedule, and Daniel has to be concerned about our delay.

We finally arrive with the seller expecting payment for the fuel, Daniel pays him, but there is no credit for the anchor and rope. Daniel's not pleased about rope and anchor, but he has a cabin cruiser with arrangements to place the boat in the cradle for all the work he intends to do. Another project.

During this time, we investigated planting an apple orchard and put that plan away. It was just too long-term. From there, we went to making sausage and sausage links. We gathered a lot of information, but in the end, dealing with the food and drug administration and probably the agriculture department was far too taxing. Real estate seems to be our know-how. Putting all the other possibilities aside, we keep wanting to trade the mobile home park and keep looking.

Daniel has a small boat with an inboard engine, also wood of about 19 feet and again heavy. We haven't had time to work on the cabin cruiser, and the weather is getting better for a bit of R, and R. Tim didn't favor going boating, but I insisted it would be fun out on the river. You can bring a fishing pole if you want. We had heard about Lake Butte de More, much larger than our little lake across the street.

It's Sunday, the sun is shining, and off we go. We got out on the lake and thought it might be best to follow some of the other boats, as the water seems to be shallow, and with this heavy of a craft, we don't want to bottom out. We've been on the lake for a half hour or so. Tim didn't want to fish, he had a line in, and the boat surged. The line flew up, and the hook almost caught his eye. Fortunately, Tim wasn't hurt, but the fun of fishing has left. We follow a large cabin cruiser that sits low in the water when suddenly there's this scraping sound; the prop is floundering beneath the water and then stops. The engine is quiet; we are not moving. As Daniel and I start investigating, we are sitting on top of a rock; the water is shallow, maybe waist high, and the prop is bent and ripped. Now what?

Watching for other boats, one comes by and says he would help if he could, but he doesn't even have enough power to get us off the rock. He told us if he sees anyone capable of helping, he will send them our way. We try rocking the craft to get it off the rock as we wait, but we're also afraid the bottom will get torn and could sink the boat. Now it shouldn't be a big deal, the water is shallow, but I'm worrying in the back of my mind. The water may be slight here, but what about over there. I don't swim; I could probably drown in two feet of water. Do not panic; Daniel has enough concern, and I don't need to worry, Tim. Eventually, a couple of guys come in a small fiberglass boat; they say they can tow us into the nearest dock about 2 miles away. It was a long two miles; when they first hooked us, I was sure we would have a hole in the bottom to get us off the rock. The boat scraped along the entire midsection; the prop was hardly turning, even though the engine was running. Daniel said the shaft was possibly bent. Silently, I say, why do we have boats?" And not just one!

The two fishermen and their little boat did an admiral job of getting us to the marina; Daniel gave them something for their time and fuel. Daniel then could get the boat onto the trailer; after that, we would examine the damage at home.

The bottom did get damaged; Daniel smoothed and sanded the hull, put a layer of fiberglass on the damaged area, more sanding, and then layers of paint. The shaft was bent and needed replacing, also the prop. The prop looked like someone chewed on it. These items are stainless steel and always, without fail, cost more than you think they should.

It was then, I was informed, "There are two days when you enjoy having a boat, the day you buy it and the day you sell it. All the other times, you just pour money into it."

It is now in usable condition, but many other projects need tending.

Most of the metal trash had been cleared off the property. Things are pretty well aligned; we brought in gravel for the road. One very proper lady who lives at the edge of the park likes to take an alternative driveway to her home, but it's through a low-lying part of the property and generally muddy. Her words were, I want to take the scenic route; it's easier to park close to my house. She drove a new baby blue Ford Thunderbird with white walls and did not like to get her car dirty. It was imperative that she have the scenic route graveled. I explained we could only gravel the main roads at this time. If you want to gravel that portion on your own, I won't object, but there will be no credits or compensation. She was pretty insulted and would alternate roads depending on the weather. But she was cute with her perfectly coiffed hair and color-coordinated immaculately pressed suit. It didn't make any difference where she was going; it could be the butcher shop or the ladies auxiliary; perfection was what she expected.

I did want the front of the park cleaned up of brush and bushes, which consisted of about two treed acres. I started cleaning, convinced an unwilling Tim he could help. Daniel came out and started pitching in. Once all the big major brush was cleared away from the road front, Daniel said, this is way too much for raking; why don't we do a slow burn. We started the burn in a small section; the leaves and pine needles were moldy and wet underneath, so lots of smoke. It was going reasonably well, so we expanded a bit. Then a breeze came up; the smoldering started moving faster than we were keeping up with it. Now there was a lot of smoke filtering up through the trees and out to the road. Soon I heard a helicopter overhead and shortly after a fire engine. Daniel went up to the front of the road and told the fire department we had it under control.

Daniel hooked up a hose that would reach some of it, and we worked at smothering the rest with dirt and wet leaves. It was now about 5 in the afternoon when a car drove by. A fellow gets out and asks for the park owner; I tell him we are it. Daniel, Tim, and I are black with smoke and ashes; you can barely see our eyes. We are NOT the epitome of ownership. This person wants information to rent a space and move to the park. Daniel needed to tell him that now is not the best time; we have space available for you; please return another day. He never came back.

Once the smoke settles down, an elderly tenant in the back told me he had emphysema, and even with his windows closed, the smoke would seep in. I apologized, told him I didn't know about his health.

Then he said, "You know, come spring, the poison oak will come back thicker than ever, and we always wanted all the brush-up front to keep the road noise down.

I was at a loss for words, apologized again, and went home to clean up. We did a little more clean-up and put tools away the following day, but there would be no more burning.

Daniel's oldest son has his master's degree and applied at universities to get his doctorate. There didn't seem to be any California colleges he could get into, so Daniel started looking and using any contacts he might have. The young man came to visit us at the mobile home park, and he and Daniel went to Bowling Green University, Kentucky, and the Indie Speedway in Kentucky, plus a couple of other colleges. Daniel also set him up with an interview in New Orleans with a recommendation from an alumni friend. After all of the interviews, Daniel, his son, Tim, and I went to Chicago to the John Hancock Building, The Sears Tower, The Futures Market, and the Chicago Zoo. We had breakfast at a lively cafe in the central Chicago Financial District with the Mater,d' giving us milk dud's for the out of towners. We had a good time, but it was a one-day venture, and it was hard to take it all in.

The month of May is here; notification to test for my Wisconsin Brokers License arrived. It means a trip to Madison, the closest testing site. Daniel and I are up early; it's about a three-hour drive. I took the law test, as I had already prequalified for all the other parts. In an hour, the exam is completed, we find lunch and drive home. A long day, but now I have the license and can go to work if needed. Daniel's help makes these tasks so much easier; I would have been a nervous wreck with my lack of direction and always being queasy about testing. With the two of us working together, we are just tired but relaxed.

There doesn't seem to be a month without a significant event. Daniel's eldest is having a graduation party, the state of California said I could know to take my final brokers exam, and we need to check on Daniel's Mom. I ask my Mom if Tim can stay with her while we get all these chores done. I confide in Tim; it will be a lot of driving with minimal downtime. Tim said he was ok with that. Tim had been on enough trips with us to know how hectic it could get. Daniel thought it might be nice if my sister, Anna, came along as a third driver, but she needed to be financially responsible.

Within a few days, we are ready to leave. The Ford LTD is towing the boat for repair at Aki's mechanic shop in Anaheim. The second night, we arrived at Grand Junction, Colorado. Day number three, we are driving west out of Colorado, and I smell something hot.

"Daniel, is the car overheating?"

He checks the gauge; everything is fine.

"Well, maybe it's just the pavement that smells hot."

Daniel looks out the rearview mirror and pulls over as soon as he can. The wheel has frozen on the boat trailer, the hub stopped turning, and we are in the middle of prairie land. We have a gallon jug of water with us which Daniel pours on the hub and tire as the steam from the heat sizzles up. The nearest town is about 10 miles. Daniel tells me the plan is to let the wheel and tire cool, drive slowly, and pull off the road every few miles until we get to a garage that can unfreeze the wheel. Car, boat, and passengers arrived at a garage still in one piece, and the hub was so hot that the mechanic had to cool it down before working on it.

Mr. Mechanic is a nice guy; he stops everything else he's working on, finds the parts at another garage in town, does our repair with the boat still on the trailer hooked up to the car. We are back on the road with a bill of about $75.00. Not too bad. I think our angels are working overtime.

I take my turn at driving as we arrive in Las Vegas. Daniel is tired, getting blurred vision. The plan for Anna to help drive isn't working. Her one time behind the wheel, she forgets to fuel. We spend the night on the outskirts of Vegas, but driving down the strip is not an option with the boat, and both Daniel and I are too tired, plus perturbed at Anna for not keeping up her end of the bargain.

The following day we arrive in Anaheim, immediately take the boat to Aki's, so we don't have to drag it around town. We set up overnight accommodations at our friend Pams' place. Pam has a one-bedroom apartment. So Anna is sleeping in Pam's bed, and Daniel and I are on the floor. Daniel has always slept all-natural, it's sweltering, and Pam gets up in the middle of the night for water. Oops! A bit of embarrassment from both parties, a laugh, and Pam says, well, you're not the first man I've seen. We all go back to sleep.

Trying to catch up with as many friends as possible, we stop by Jayne Liens' house, and thankfully we catch her at home. It was good to see her; we hugged and how are you and did our best to catch up with the years in between since we used to live across the street from each other. Now our little kids are six feet and taller, no more babies. Jayne and I both had to acknowledge we were not young anymore.

A graduation party is going on for Daniel's oldest son, and we drive over. The kids are glad to see Daniel, but the other part of the family asks him to leave. Daniel talked with his kids for a few minutes, and we left. Anna had stayed with Pam, and the next day, the two of them were going to Disneyland with the benevolence of Pam. They were then driving to Pismo Beach and stayed with Daniels folks until we could get there.

We were on our way to Sacramento after picking up the boat from Aki. I had three days of school and a test for California real estate.

It's then back to Pismo Beach, visit Daniels folks, thank Pam, and we will be off to Oregon. I didn't find out till later that my sister also asked Daniel's parents for money to go shopping. I found out much later; Daniel sent his folks some money. Talk about being embarrassed.

We headed to Oregon, Grants Pass area, to see Daniels' Uncle Charlie and Aunt Jeanette. We spent two nights; Uncle Charlie drove us to Crater Lake. We had dinner with them, breakfast in the morning, and went north to Seattle, WA, to visit Daniel's daughter, husband, and Daniel's new grandchild. While visiting the kids, we take the boat for a spin on Lake Union. It is typical for Seattle to be overcast and a little chilly; we are in the middle of Lake Union, and we ladies say it's time to find a bathroom. The men look at us like we are from another planet, and then I hear, try over the side of the boat, there's no one out here in the lake.

My reply, "I don't think so."

The closest place the kids knew of was a government marine facility. We pulled up close to shore; the gals jumped out of the boat and ran for the restrooms. We are walking back to where the guys are waiting for us when a security guard sees us.

He comes charging over, yelling; "You can't be here; you can't use anything on this premises. I'm going to report you; I want your drivers' license, I'm going to give you a ticket. I'm going to report your boat, you'll see".

We leave and try not to harass him, and he doesn't know the boat is registered in Wisconsin.

We do a little more touring on the lake and then home. The following morning, we are going to Bellingham and, as always, gazing at the property as we drive. It's time to get back to home base, a three-day drive with no mishaps, and we are home.

My sister does not attempt to reimburse anyone of the people she has borrowed from, including us. I regretted agreeing to have her join us; Daniel was considerate, working to give something memorable and appreciative. Now the family pride is tarnished once again.

I started looking for employment; I'm unsure if I want to start another pursuit in real estate. It always takes time to get established before there's any actual income, or do I just want to work at a restaurant until we know that we are staying or leaving.

The experimental airshow is taking place in Oshkosh, and Daniel suggests we attend. I tell Tim this will be fun. The attendance was astounding; there are acres and acres of aircraft of all kinds, shapes, and sizes. People use the plane wings as a part of their tent because there are no rooms or houses. Every spare place is reserved a year in advance.

We walked through the field looking at all the sights; I said, "Daniel, are we allowed to be in this section of the show."

"Dianah, you worry too much about what we can not do. Think positive; why not be here? It is interesting."

Later we just walked over and sat in the grass to watch the show. We both knew we were supposed to go through the gates and pay to see the show, maybe next time. What a wonderful experience; fabulous. The historic collector planes did their demonstration. The experimental craft is fascinating. The Navy did an air show with spectacular showmanship, and Qantas Airlines, with its massive aircraft, was also part of the show.

However, the coup de gras is the show's end, and all the craft takes off to go home. The controllers are in the center of the field, directing air traffic. We are sitting as close as possible with our eyes focused on the clear blue sky. The air controllers are waving their wands like they are at a heavy auto traffic four-way stop intersection. Each plane takes off as directed, one right after the other; it's magical. The sky is littered with experimental planes, like a flock of birds. Every plane or gyrocopter is different. I have never seen anything like it. After half an hour of watching this spectacle, we decided it was time to go because the take-off flight pattern would continue for hours. We make our way home.

Tim is back in school, and the parents are invited to attend the cafeteria lunch program. As I went in line with Tim, it wasn't the kind of food I remembered when I worked the cafeteria in High School. I thought the food was substandard in this school, something they took out of the freezer and put in the microwave. Only one other parent attended the lunch, and she was sitting several tables over. I thanked Tim for letting me have lunch with him, and I told him if he wanted to bring his lunch, I would pack his lunch instead of eating the school food.

I have been job hunting, but not diligently. My heart isn't in finding a job in this town. I don't like the town, coming back to this area is the last thing I needed.

There's friction, no work, definitely no fighting, just uneasiness-no happiness, not too much loving. Toph is gone, Tim's unhappy, the mobile home park is a constant annoyance, the towns are not friendly, and I'm tired of having dinner every week with my parents. How do I say to Daniel, what have we done? I don't understand how it could have gone so wrong. We have discussed moving, but at this time, I am packing his and her boxes, not planned for the same direction. I don't want to go without him, but he's not talking about it.

It's September 3rd, late evening, and the phone rings. Daniel's cousin is on the phone; Daniel's father passed away while on his way to the hospital in the ambulance. I listen; I know whatever it is, there's a significant problem. Once Daniel hangs up the phone, he tells me it was his father, and they couldn't revive him. His mother did everything she knew how to do and then called 911.

I went to Daniel's side, "Oh, I'm so sorry, Babe."

I put my arms out to him; Daniel came to me with his head next to mine; we held each other, and he wept.

Daniel cared. He loved his father even though they weren't close and disagreements were constant. Once he regained his composure, it was time to make flight arrangements and get to his mother's side. She had never lived on her own, didn't drive, didn't write checks, and she had been with her husband for over 50 years. He needed to be there for her. It was his obligation as the only son to take care of things.

Daniel made all the arrangements. I packed his bags and asked if there was anything he would like me to take care of from this end. Nothing he could think of, and he would call if there were things to be addressed.

"Dianah, I don't know how long I'll be gone. I know Dad wanted to be cremated. You know Mom's situation, there are so many things I need to take care of."

Daniel is ready to leave for the Milwaukee Airport at 4 AM the following day. It's cold for September; the morning is dark as I walk with him to the truck. I kissed him goodbye, drive safe, and I wish I could go with you, but you know it's not possible. Another kiss, another hug, and my love is on his way.

Daniel has been busy notifying people, taking care of arrangements for his Dad, and trying to do for his mother what he can. He has always been a person of many talents, and while he was doing all these items for the family, he was also making arrangements to rent a house in Tacoma, WA, for the two of us, plus have room for children.

On September 8th, Daniel Senior's services are held, and his ashes are to be spread over the Pacific Ocean by the pier where he loved to fish. The plane was scheduled for 10 AM, and the family was all there waiting. Ten o'clock came and went, by 10:30 AM Daniel was calling, where is the plane?

By 11:00 AM, Daniel is on his way to the Oceano Airport, "What in the world is going on? This is my father's funeral. Do you have his ashes?"

The pilot stammers, "Yes, we have been ready, but the plane had a flat tire, so it needed to be fixed before takeoff."

Daniel says, "Ok, I'm on my way back to the pier, and I expect to see you in the sky in no less than 20 minutes. My family has been waiting long enough. Are we in agreement?"

"Yes, Sir."

As promised, the Pilot is over the pier area; the family says their prayers and goodbyes and retreat to the house for lunch and coffee.

On September 8th, Daniel gets a phone call from his son-in-law in Washington. Daniel is now a grandfather; his first grandchild is a girl, strong and healthy. The mother is fine, and the father is trying to make sure everything is ready for her when she comes home.

Daniel gets on a bus to Seattle from his mother's area on September 25th to see his daughter and his new grandchild. While he's there, he also checks out the house to buy. It's not too far from where the family lives. I keep things under wraps in Wisconsin and packing boxes, with no apparent thought about the future plans. While Daniel is away, he doesn't tell me that he's not feeling well again.

September 30th, Daniel is flying into Milwaukee, his truck has been in the parking garage, and he's making the 2 to 3 hours drive home. He walks in the door, puts his suitcase down, holds out his arms as I rush to greet him at the door.

He wraps his arms around me, "Oh Daniel, I missed you." The kiss is warm and genuine.

"It's so good to have you home."

Daniel goes to hug Tim. Tim's not into hugs right now, so it's more like a nudge. Daniel picks up his briefcase and suitcase to take to the bedroom while I make coffee and dinner for the weary traveler. Whether we are making the right choices or not, one thing is obvious. We want to be together, there's no convenience to it, and it's not one-sided; I can feel that from my innermost feminine intuition. Even though it's not often said, he loves me and make no mistake, Daniel likes to talk, but some things are difficult to express. So what will be the next plan?

It's football season; Tim mentioned the game, I suggest we give it a try. I used to like the games as a student. And it is different watching a game when you don't know any of the players. The game was fine, and Tim spent time with other kids, but it was cold. And it is different watching a game when you don't know any of the players. We stayed to the end; it was Tim's night out.

I told Daniel, I just can't live here. I left for a reason, and I have discovered many of those reasons still exist. We are now making arrangements to move. Daniel has made management plans for the mobile home park, and I have explained to my parents, we are moving.

November 10, 1981, we loaded the car, and truck pulling the boat with as much as we could shove into every nook and cranny. All the preventive items of winterizing the house and arrangements with the manager to sell it. Daniel fueled the vehicles and had them winterized for a cold, snowy trip.

I had a heart-to-heart talk with Tim previously.

"Tim, I know how much you dislike moving; I also know you don't like the school here, and friends have been hard to come by. The move we are making I consider necessary. When we arrive in Washington, we will be renting a house, which means the home is temporary. Then, there will be another move in an unknown time, and we still have Daniel's mother to consider. I don't know how long she can stay there by herself."

Tim is thirteen; he doesn't do well with a lot of changes. His life has been one upheaval after another, and his likes are always taking a back seat. He cherishes his friends and loves animals. After examining the entire picture, if I had made the other choice, I can't say his life would have been better had Tim gone with us to Washington.

"Tim, would you like to try living with your Dad? If it doesn't work, you are welcome back at any time. Tim, you are always loved no matter where we are. Your Dad has been married for a few years now; he has a house in a neighborhood, something like Huntington Beach was, and it doesn't appear he will be moving. You can have a bike, go to the same school and make friends you can keep."

The look is one of confusion, he doesn't want to keep moving, and he doesn't want to leave what he knows. He doesn't seem fond of living with his Dad, but he and Daniel aren't necessarily getting along. It was more than I wanted to have him face. There were choices to be made, and unfortunately, I could only give so many options.

My heart was breaking, but I wanted to give Tim the best life I could. I couldn't give him a better life by myself. I wouldn't ask Daniel to change how he lived. Life was not mine to dictate. I am intelligent, hard-working, and resourceful, but I don't have a college degree or a background in executive employment. There's not even anyone I could borrow money from if I were in dire straits. All of these thoughts are too much to relay to Tim, so I keep my shortcomings to myself.

On the other side of the equation, I liked moving; it's exciting, challenging. Seeing new places, meeting new people, staying at one job in one house for a lifetime makes me a boring person. Then I think of my obligation to children. I've known people who gave up everything for their children. In some cases, it worked as they planned, and in other cases, it was a wasted effort for both parents and children. When it worked, the children were loving, educated, and caring for their parents. When it didn't work, the parent was always dissatisfied, and the child generally was selfish and lazy. Real-life is far from the TV Brady Bunch.

So as the imperfect being that I am, I do the best I can with what I have. There's a trust in the Lord that has always been with me. I can't say life to this point is easy, but when there's a problem I don't know how to handle, I ask for help. When I ask, the answer is there, and it might not be the expected answer, but it seems to be the solution that works after looking back. If I could put aside pride and stubbornness and ask more often for a helping hand, things might be more manageable.

Daniel, Tim, and I drive to Minneapolis. We spend the night at a motel, and early the next morning, we take the car to the airport for Tim's flight. As I give Tim hugs and too many instructions, Daniel gets a hug this time. Tim gets on the plane, I do my best to keep tears to a minimum as Daniel and I stay to watch the plane leave. During the last two days up to this point, I was in a fog; everything was in slow motion. The comprehension of what life was throwing at me was leaving me numb. In the back of my mind, I kept questioning the choices I was making. Deep down, I knew of the options I had; the decision would still be the same one. Mind searching is a strange game.

There is no turning back now, we drive directly back to the motel, get the truck and boat, and I follow in the car. Daniel and I don't stop until it's about a time when Tim should have arrived at his father's house. I call from a payphone, yes Tim has made it there safe. His Dad is none too happy with me, but then he never was, and the unhappiness is with me, not Tim.

For those who delve into astrology or number sequences for meanings in life, Tim's flight was dated 11/11/1981 at 11 AM. One of the meanings is love, protection, and guidance. I've read numerous times that there are no coincidences. Did I make the better choice? I'll never know.

By November 13th, we are just outside of Bozeman, Montana, the road is plowed, and the snowbanks are high. It's bright, sunny, and cold. Daniel pulls off the road at a way stop, with me always following. As he turns off the engine and departs the truck, the truck and trailer start to slide sideways. There's a steep ravine at the edge of the pavement, I honk the horn, and about that time, it hits the curb and stops.

Daniel looks my way as I'm getting out of the car; he smiles and says, "Were you worried?"

"Oh, no. I was just testing the horn; I wanted to make sure it worked."

He gives me his great big hug and says, "Are you ok?"

ME AND DANIEL

"I'm ok; you parked there on purpose, right?"

A little laughter and "Let's stretch our legs a bit, then we better get back on the road. It's icy, and we'll be driving slower; make sure you stay far enough back in case we start sliding."

"Gotcha, I need another hug."

On November 15th, we are driving into the Seattle area. It's raining heavily, with sleet and mud. The traffic is moving fast; I'm not used to the curvy roads; both Daniel and I are working hard in this weather and the maze of streets in bumper-to-bumper cars. It takes a couple of hours to get to the other side of the city and his daughter's house. Exhaustion is setting in, it's late afternoon and getting dark, but we arrive in one piece, have an evening meal, and sleep.

We must find a house, and we scramble. The kids give us newspapers to check for rentals and sales. Because the area is large and we don't know the neighborhoods, we give up the search and choose a rental close to family. Daniel can see his granddaughter.

On the 22nd of November, Daniel and I drove to Ferndale, Washington, to visit Toph. He seems to be happy living with his Aunt Jill; it wasn't working with his father. It's so good to spend time with him, and it has been a long time since I had seen Jill. She was a teenager the last time we visited, and she now has a family. Toph came walking up the dirt driveway smiling, in good spirits, and looked like a young man that lived in a logging community. He keeps growing tall, he's thin with a plaid shirt, blue jeans with red suspenders, and the hair has gotten longer. I had such mixed emotions, was proud of him, and missed him terribly at the same time. Hugs and kisses are mandatory, and Daniel gives him the manly Hug-hand shake. We visit for a couple of hours; Toph shows us his room, we walk outside, and then it's time to leave. Ferndale is just north of Bellingham and has several farms, but also logging. If we could buy in Bellingham, we would, but to date haven't found anything. We drove back, and by the 2nd of December, we had moved into the rental house. Furnishings were what would fit in the truck and on top, plus the boat, so there's necessary shopping, which gets accomplished at Goodwill in downtown Seattle. I was amazed at how big and how much stuff they had.

The following week, I called schools for the boys regarding health records and legal directions for emergency purposes. Daniel's mother decided she would like to visit her sister Jeanette in Oregon, and Daniel was able to make arrangements for her to fly to Oregon. The plan was for her to stay two weeks.

But the sisters never did get along very well; within a week, his Mother called, "Daniel, I want to go home."

Daniel and I drove to Uncle Charlie's, and Aunt Jeanette in Oregon spent the evening and proceeded south. We made arrangements for Tim to spend some time with us over the weekend, so we picked him up along the way and then on to Pismo Beach. The weekend passed quickly, and we needed to get Tim back for school. Tim has a new motorized car his dad gave him, which he shared with us. We drove the four hours north for Tim and Daniels; mother came with us to spend Christmas in Washington until she was ready to go back. She would get to see her Great Grandchild and not be alone on Christmas.

Daniel would drive her home when she was ready, and then he would make time to see his other kids.

We have spent a considerable amount of time on the road; Toph spends some time with us at Christmas and is smiling. Daniel's mother, who's never lived alone and is in her 70's is coping with widowhood. Tim is in school, developing friendships, and his Dad's new wife has a son close to Tim's age. They may not be the best of friends, but there is company and companionship. The Mobile Home Park is doing fine with the chosen manager. We'll need to go back; there's a garage full of household belongings and a cabin cruiser at the marina.

Life is moving on, not exactly as planned, but we are onto our next adventure in the Northwest. You are pioneers, stated a friend.

Two individuals are strong and confident to carry on, holding each other in a warm embrace. Morning coffee, with a kiss and a hug, and our love is as strong as ever. We'll plan our next day. I'll get another real estate license. It's just a matter of doing it or getting a temporary job until we find a spot on the map, even if it's temporary.

Daniel is a dreamer and a wanderer, and I am willing to follow. Home is nothing more than a house filled with love. It's not the dwelling, the feelings inside these walls, whatever the structure may be, create the warmth of life, wherever it is.

Once again, Daniel takes my hand, he takes my hand, "Dianah, I will do for you whatever I can."

I put my hand on his cheek, and we kissed tenderly.

"Daniel, we will live one day at a time."

At this moment in time, we hold each other in the warmth of love as the world continues to turn and we move into our next adventure.

CPSIA information can be obtained
at www.ICGtesting.com
Printed in the USA
BVHW030625291121
622746BV00001BA/38

9 781977 241078